Ancient Christian Texts

Commentaries on Genesis 1-3

Homilies on Creation and Fall
Severian of Gabala

TRANSLATED WITH AN
INTRODUCTION AND NOTES BY

Robert C. Hill

Commentary on Genesis: Book I
Bede the Venerable

TRANSLATED WITH AN
INTRODUCTION AND NOTES BY

Carmen S. Hardin

EDITED BY
Michael Glerup

SERIES EDITORS
Thomas C. Oden and Gerald L. Bray

IVP Academic

An imprint of InterVarsity Press
Downers Grove, Illinois

InterVarsity Press
P.O. Box 1400, Downers Grove, IL 60515-1426
World Wide Web: www.ivpress.com
E-mail: email@ivpress.com

InterVarsity Press® is the book-publishing division of InterVarsity Christian Fellowship/USA®, a movement of students and faculty active on campus at hundreds of universities, colleges and schools of nursing in the United States of America, and a member movement of the International Fellowship of Evangelical Students. For information about local and regional activities, write Public Relations Dept., InterVarsity Christian Fellowship/USA, 6400 Schroeder Rd., P.O. Box 7895, Madison, WI 53707-7895, or visit the IVCF website at <www.intervarsity.org>.

The Scripture quotations quoted herein are from the Revised Standard Version of the Bible, copyright 1946, 1952, 1971 by the Division of Christian Education of the National Council of the Churches of Christ in the U.S.A. Used by permission. All rights reserved.

Design: Cindy Kiple

Images: Saints Peter and Paul by Carlo Crivelli at Accademia, Venice/Art Resource, NY

> *Monogrammatic cross: Early Christian monogrammatic cross from Monastero, at Kunsthistorisches Museum, Vienna, Austria. Erich Lessing/ Art Resource, NY*

ISBN 978-0-8308-2907-1

Printed in the United States of America ∞

Library of Congress Cataloging-in-Publication Data

Commentaries on Genesis 1-3: Bede the Venerable and Severian of Gabala/edited by Michael Glerup; translated by Robert C. Hill and Carmen S. Hardin.

    p. cm.—(Ancient Christian texts)
   Includes bibliographical references and index.
   ISBN 978-0-8308-2907-1 (hardcover: alk. paper)
   1. Bible. O.T. Genesis I-III—Commentaries. 2. Bible. O.T. Genesis I-III—Sermons. I. Glerup, Michael. II. Bede, the Venerable, Saint, 673-735. Libri quatuor in principium Genesis. English. Book 1. III. Severian of Gabala, fl. 398-408. In cosmogoniam. English.
BS1235.53.C655 2010
222'.1107—dc22

2010024971

P	24	23	22	21	20	19	18	17	16	15	14	13	12	11	10	9	8	7	6	5	4	3	2	1
Y	31	30	29	28	27	26	25	24	23	22	21	20	19	18	17	16	15	14	13	12	11	10		

CONTENTS

GENERAL INTRODUCTION

The Ancient Christian Texts series (hereafter ACT) presents the full text of ancient Christian commentaries on Scripture that have remained so unnoticed that they have not yet been translated into English.

The patristic period (A.D. 95-750) is the time of the fathers of the church, when the exegesis of Scripture texts was in its primitive formation. This period spans from Clement of Rome to John of Damascus, embracing seven centuries of biblical interpretation, from the end of the New Testament to the mid-eighth century, including the Venerable Bede.

This series extends but does not reduplicate texts of the Ancient Christian Commentary on Scripture (ACCS). It presents full-length translations of texts that appear only as brief extracts in the ACCS. The ACCS began years ago authorizing full-length translations of key patristic texts on Scripture in order to provide fresh sources of valuable commentary that previously was not available in English. It is from these translations that the ACT Series has emerged.

A multiyear project such as this requires a well-defined objective. The task is straightforward: *to introduce full-length translations of key texts of early Christian teaching, homilies and commentaries on a particular book of Scripture.* These are seminal documents that have decisively shaped the entire subsequent history of biblical exegesis, but in our time have been largely ignored.

To carry out this mission the Ancient Christian Texts series has four aspirations:

1. To show the approach of one of the early Christian writers in dealing with the problems of understanding, reading and conveying the meaning of a particular book of Scripture.

2. To make more fully available the whole argument of the ancient Christian interpreter of Scripture to all who wish to think with the early church about a particular canonical text.

3. To broaden the base of biblical studies, Christian teaching and preaching to include classical Christian exegesis.

4. To stimulate Christian historical, biblical, theological and pastoral scholarship toward deeper inquiry into early classic practitioners of scriptural interpretation.

For Whom Is This Series Designed?

We have selected and translated these texts primarily for general and nonprofessional use by an audience of persons who study the Bible regularly.

In varied cultural settings around the world, contemporary readers are asking how they might grasp the meaning of sacred texts under the instruction of the great minds of the ancient church. They often study books of the Bible verse by verse, book by book, in groups and workshops, sometimes with a modern commentary in hand. But many who study the Bible intensively hunger to have available to them as well the thoughts of some reliable classic Christian commentator on this same text. This series will give the modern commentators a classical text for comparison and amplification. Readers will judge for themselves as to how valuable or complementary are their insights and guidance.

The classic texts we are translating were originally written for anyone (lay or clergy, believers and seekers) who would wish to reflect and meditate with the great minds of the early church. They sought to illuminate the plain sense, theological wisdom, and moral and spiritual meaning of an individual book of Scripture. They were not written for an academic audience, but for a community of faith shaped by the sacred text.

Yet in serving this general audience, the editors remain determined not to neglect the rigorous requirements and needs of academic readers who until recently have had few full translations available to them in the history of exegesis. So this series is designed also to serve public libraries, universities, academic classes, homiletic preparation and historical interests worldwide in Christian scholarship and interpretation.

Hence our expected audience is not limited to the highly technical and specialized scholarly field of patristic studies, with its strong bent toward detailed word studies and explorations of cultural contexts. Though all of our editors and translators are patristic and linguistic scholars, they also are scholars who search for the meanings and implications of the texts. The audience is not primarily the university scholar concentrating on the study of the history of the transmission of the text or those with highly focused interests in textual morphology or historical-critical issues. If we succeed in serving our wider readers practically and well, we hope to serve as well college and seminary courses in Bible, church history, historical theology, hermeneutics and homiletics. These texts have not until now been available to these classes.

Readiness for Classic Spiritual Formation

Today global Christians are being steadily drawn toward these biblical and patristic sources for daily meditation and spiritual formation. They are on the outlook for primary classic sources of spiritual formation and biblical interpretation, presented in accessible form and grounded in reliable scholarship.

These crucial texts have had an extended epoch of sustained influence on Scripture interpretation, but virtually no influence in the modern period. They also deserve a hearing among modern readers and scholars. There is a growing awareness of the speculative excesses and spiritual and homiletic limitations of much post-Enlightenment criticism. Meanwhile the motifs, methods and approaches of ancient exegetes have remained unfamiliar not only to historians but to otherwise highly literate biblical scholars, trained exhaustively in the methods of historical and scientific criticism.

It is ironic that our times, which claim to be so fully furnished with historical insight and research methods, have neglected these texts more than scholars in previous centuries who could read them in their original languages.

This series provides indisputable evidence of the modern neglect of classic Christian exegesis: it remains a fact that extensive and once authoritative classic commentaries on Scripture still remain untranslated into any modern language. Even in China such a high level of neglect has not befallen classic Buddhist, Taoist and Confucian commentaries.

Ecumenical Scholarship

This series, like its two companion series, the ACCS and Ancient Christian Doctrine (ACD), are expressions of unceasing ecumenical efforts that have enjoyed the wide cooperation of distinguished scholars of many differing academic communities. Under this classic textual umbrella, it has brought together in common spirit Christians who have long distanced themselves from each other by competing church memories. But all of these traditions have an equal right to appeal to the early history of Christian exegesis. All of these traditions can, without a sacrifice of principle or intellect, come together to study texts common to them all. This is its ecumenical significance.

This series of translations is respectful of a distinctively theological reading of Scripture that cannot be reduced to historical, philosophical, scientific, or sociological insights or methods alone. It takes seriously the venerable tradition of ecumenical reflection concerning the premises of revelation, providence, apostolicity, canon and consensuality. A high respect is here granted, despite modern assumptions, to uniquely Christian theological forms of reasoning, such as classical consensual christological and triune reasoning, as distinguishing premises of classic Christian textual interpretation. These cannot be acquired by empirical methods alone. This approach does not pit theology against critical theory; instead, it incorporates critical historical methods and brings them into coordinate accountability within its larger purpose of listening to Scripture.

The internationally diverse character of our editors and translators corresponds with the global range of our audience, which bridges many major communions of Christianity. We have sought to bring together a distinguished international network of Protestant, Catholic and Orthodox scholars, editors, and translators of the highest quality and reputation to accomplish this design.

But why just now at this historical moment is this need for patristic wisdom felt particularly by so many readers of Scripture? Part of the reason is that these readers have been long deprived of significant contact with many of these vital sources of classic Christian exegesis.

The Ancient Commentary Tradition

This series focuses on texts that comment on Scripture and teach its meaning. We define a commentary in its plain-sense definition as a series of illustrative or explanatory notes on any work of enduring significance. The word *commentary* is an Anglicized form of the Latin *commentarius* (or "annotation" or "memoranda" on a subject or text or series of events). In its theological meaning it is a work that explains, analyzes or expounds a biblical book or portion of Scripture. Tertullian, Origen, John Chrysostom, Jerome, Augustine and Clement of Alexandria all revealed their familiarity with both the secular and religious commentators available to them as they unpacked the meanings of the sacred text at hand.

The commentary in ancient times typically began with a general introduction covering such questions as authorship, date, purpose and audience. It commented as needed on grammatical or lexical problems in the text and provided explanations of difficulties in the text. It typically moved verse by verse through a Scripture text, seeking to make its meaning clear and its import understood.

The general western literary genre of commentary has been definitively shaped by the history of early Christian commentaries on Scripture. It is from Origen, Hilary, the *Opus imperfectum in Matthaeum*, John Chrysostom and Cyril of Alexandria that we learn what a commentary is—far more so than in the case of classic medical, philosophical or poetic commentaries. It leaves too much unsaid simply to assume that the Christian biblical commentary took a previously extant literary genre and reshaped it for Christian texts. Rather it is more accurate to say that *the Western literary genre of the commentary (and especially the biblical commentary) has patristic commentaries as its decisive pattern and prototype.*

It is only in the last two centuries, since the development of modern historicist methods of criticism, that modern writers have sought more strictly to delimit the definition of a commentary so as to include only certain limited interests focusing largely on historical-critical method, philological and grammatical observations, literary analysis, and socio-political or economic circumstances impinging on the text. While respecting all these approaches, the ACT editors do not hesitate to use the classic word *commentary* to define more broadly the genre of this series. These are commentaries in their classic sense.

The ACT editors freely take the assumption that the Christian canon is to be respected as the church's sacred text. The reading and preaching of Scripture are vital to religious life. The central hope of this endeavor is that it might contribute in some small way to the revitalization of religious faith and community through a renewed discovery of the earliest readings of the church's Scriptures.

An Appeal to Allow the Text to Speak for Itself

This prompts two appeals:

1. For those who begin by assuming as normative for a commentary only the norms considered typical for modern expressions of what a commentary is, we ask: Please allow the ancient commentators to define *commentarius* according to their own lights. Those who assume the preemptive authority and truthfulness of modern critical methods alone will always tend to view the classic Christian exegetes as dated, quaint, premodern, hence inadequate, and in some instances comic or even mean-spirited, prejudiced, unjust and oppressive. So in the interest of hermeneutical fairness, it is recommended that the modern reader not impose on ancient Christian exegetes modern assumptions about valid readings of Scripture. The ancient Christian writers constantly challenge these unspoken, hidden and indeed often camouflaged assumptions that have become commonplace in our time.

We leave it to others to discuss the merits of ancient versus modern methods of exegesis. But even this cannot be done honestly without a serious examination of the texts of ancient exegesis. Ancient commentaries may be disqualified as commentaries by modern standards. But they remain commentaries by the standards of those who anteceded and formed the basis of the modern commentary.

The attempt to read a Scripture text while ruling out all theological and moral assumptions—as well as ecclesial, sacramental and dogmatic assumptions that have prevailed generally in the community of faith out of which it emerged—is a very thin enterprise indeed. Those who tendentiously may read a single page of patristic exegesis, gasp and toss it away because it does not conform adequately to the canons of modern exegesis and historicist commentary are surely not exhibiting a valid model for critical inquiry today.

2. In ancient Christian exegesis, chains of biblical references were often very important in thinking about the text in relation to the whole testimony of sacred Scripture, by the analogy of faith, comparing text with text, on the premise that *scripturam ex scriptura explicandam esse*. When ancient exegesis weaves many Scriptures together, it does not limit its focus to a single text as much modern exegesis prefers, but constantly relates it to other texts, by analogy, intensively using typological reasoning, as did the rabbinic tradition.

Since the principle prevails in ancient Christian exegesis that each text is illumined by other texts and by the whole narrative of the history of revelation, we find in patristic comments on a given text many other subtexts interwoven in order to illumine that text. In these ways the models of exegesis often do not correspond with modern commentary assumptions, which tend to resist or rule out chains of scriptural reference. We implore the reader not to force the assumptions of twentieth-century hermeneutics on the ancient Christian writers, who themselves knew nothing of what we now call hermeneutics.

The Complementarity of Research Methods in this Series

The Ancient Christian Texts series will employ several interrelated methods of research, which the editors and translators seek to bring together in a working integration. Principal among these methods are the following:

1. The editors, translators and annotators will bring to bear the best resources of *textual criticism* in preparation for their volumes. This series is not intended to produce a new critical edition of the original-language text. The best Urtext in the original language will be used. Significant variants in the earliest manuscript sources of the text may be commented on as needed in the annotations. But it will be assumed that the editors and translators will be familiar with the textual ambiguities of a particular text and be able to state their conclusions about significant differences among scholars. Since we are working with ancient texts that have, in some cases, problematic or ambiguous passages, we are obliged to employ all methods of historical, philological and textual inquiry appropriate to the study of ancient texts. To that end, we will appeal to the most reliable text-critical scholarship of both biblical and patristic studies. We will assume that our editors and translators have reviewed the international literature of textual critics regarding their text so as to provide the reader with a translation of the most authoritative and reliable form of the ancient text. We will leave it to the volume editors and translators, under the supervision of the general editors, to make these assessments. This will include the challenge of considering which variants within the biblical text itself might impinge on the patristic text, and which forms or stemma of the biblical text the patristic writer was employing. The annotator will supply explanatory footnotes where these textual challenges may raise potential confusions for the reader.

2. Our editors and translators will seek to understand the *historical context* (including socioeconomic, political and psychological aspects as needed) of the text. These understandings are often vital to right discernment of the writer's intention. Yet we do not see our primary mission as that of discussing in detail these contexts. They are to be factored into the translation and commented on as needed in the annotations, but are not to become the primary focus of this series. Our central interest is less in the social location of the text or the philological history of particular words than in authorial intent and accurate translation. Assuming a proper social-historical contextualization of the text, the main focus of this series will be on a dispassionate and fair translation and analysis of the text itself.

3. The main task is to set forth the meaning of the biblical text itself as understood by the patristic writer. The intention of our volume editors and translators is to help the

reader see clearly into the meanings which patristic commentators have discovered in the biblical text. *Exegesis* in its classic sense implies an effort to explain, interpret and comment on a text, its meaning, its sources and its connections with other texts. It implies a close reading of the text, utilizing whatever linguistic, historical, literary or theological resources are available to explain the text. It is contrasted with *eisegesis*, which implies that interpreters have imposed their own personal opinions or assumptions on the text. The patristic writers actively practiced intratextual exegesis, which seeks to define and identify the exact wording of the text, its grammatical structure and the interconnectedness of its parts. They also practiced extratextual exegesis, seeking to discern the geographical, historical or cultural context in which the text was written. Our editors and annotators will also be attentive as needed to the ways in which the ancient Christian writer described his own interpreting process or hermeneutic assumptions.

4. The underlying philosophy of translation that we employ in this series, like that of the Ancient Christian Commentary on Scripture, is termed *dynamic equivalency*. We wish to avoid the pitfalls of either too loose a paraphrase or too rigid a literal translation. We seek language that is literary but not purely literal. Whenever possible we have opted for the metaphors and terms that are normally in use in everyday English-speaking culture. Our purpose is to allow the ancient Christian writers to speak for themselves to ordinary readers in the present generation. We want to make it easier for the Bible reader to gain ready access to the deepest reflection of the ancient Christian community of faith on a particular book of Scripture. We seek a thought-for-thought translation rather than a formal equivalence or word-for-word style. This requires the words to be first translated accurately and then rendered in understandable idiom. We seek to present the same thoughts, feelings, connotations and effects of the original text in everyday English language. We have used vocabulary and language structures commonly used by the average person. We do not leave the quality of translation only to the primary translator, but pass it through several levels of editorial review before confirming it.

The Function of the ACT Introductions, Annotations and Translations

In writing the introduction for a particular volume of the ACT series, the translator or volume editor will discuss, where possible, the opinion of the writer regarding authorship of the text, the importance of the biblical book for other patristic interpreters, the availability or paucity of patristic comment, any salient points of debate between the Fathers, and any special challenges involved in translating and editing the particular volume. The introduction affords the opportunity to frame the entire commentary in a manner that will help the general reader understand the nature and significance of patristic comment on the biblical texts under consideration and to help readers find their critical bearings so as to read and use the commentary in an informed way.

The footnotes will assist the reader with obscurities and potential confusions. In the annotations the volume editors have identified Scripture allusions and historical references embedded within the texts. Their purpose is to help the reader move easily from passage to passage without losing a sense of the whole.

The ACT general editors seek to be circumspect and meticulous in commissioning volume editors and translators. We strive for a high level of consistency and literary quality throughout the course of this series. We have sought out as volume editors and translators those patristic and biblical scholars who are thoroughly familiar with their original language sources, who are informed historically, and who are sympathetic to the needs of ordinary nonprofessional readers who may not have professional language skills.

Thomas C. Oden and Gerald L. Bray, Series Editors

VOLUME EDITOR'S INTRODUCTION

The importance of the first three chapters of Genesis to early Christian theological reflection is profound and must not be underestimated. The creation story occupied a central place in the thought of many of the great exegetes of the early church. They discerned fundamental patterns of Christian theology by reading these narratives within the framework of the gospel of the risen Christ, through whom all created things found their existence. These texts affirmed creation to be essentially good and created by God's Word from nothing. Likewise, the early exegetes found in these opening passages of Genesis a theological anthropology grounded in humanity's creation "according to the image and likeness of God."

A popular form of early Christian commentary, the *Hexameron*, limited itself to comments on the first six days of creation. The two commentaries presented in this volume technically do not fall within this genre because they include commentary on the paradise narrative (Gen 2:4–3:24) and investigate the expulsion of Adam and Eve from Paradise.

The exegetes translated in this volume derive from very different contexts. Severian of Gabala was a Syrian bishop who became a celebrated preacher in the court of Constantinople at the beginning of the fifth century. Severian's popularity is confirmed by the fact that his works survived in Greek, Armenian, Ethiopian and possibly Arabic. Following the condemnation of the non-Chalcedonian Severus of Antioch in 536, Severian's homilies, probably because of name confusion, were often transmitted under the name of John Chrysostom. The irony and significance of the preservation of these homilies under the name of Chrysostom should not be lost on the modern reader.

It is important to avoid the error of understanding Severian according to simplistic divisions of Greek versus Latin, Eastern versus Western Christianity. Severian was from the Syrian margins of Hellenistic society and, through his engagement with the Greek philosophical tradition and the Hebrew Scriptures, challenged Hellenistic assumptions by reading Genesis as the sole source for understanding the world and living in it correctly. Severian favored Genesis as the source material for many of his homilies and engaged this material through his Syrian sensibilities in contrast to the Hellenistic inspired exegetes of the Alexandrian school.

Bede the Venerable is so closely identified with the English people that the fact of his descent from the Germanic warriors who conquered Christian Britain has been all but forgotten. Writing at the end of the age of the Fathers, Bede lived at the margins of the "civilized" world. Unlike Severian, Bede studied, taught, preached his homilies and wrote his commentaries near his birthplace. The audience of his homilies and commentaries, the twin monastic community of Wearmouth-Jarrow in the northeastern corner of Britain, was a world and age away from Severian's congregation in the new imperial city, Constantinople. As Joseph Kelly states, Bede was "a scholar on the brink between two worlds, an ancient one he knew only from books but which he still loved dearly, and a modern one, which he frequently criticized, but whose inhabitants, the English, the newest of God's elect peoples, he also loved dearly."[1]

Though these commentators labored in vastly different contexts, they held a number of similar views. Both accepted that their readings of the first chapters of Genesis were built on the profound learning of others who preceded them. Severian acknowledges, albeit conventionally, that his comments were only a slight addition to the traditional body of knowledge. Bede, on the other hand, does not admit to adding to tradition but only to setting down the meaning of the early fathers. Most of the time he lets them speak in their own words, but sometimes, if only for the sake of brevity, he employs his own words as the appropriateness of the topics dictate. In both cases, these writers received the teaching of their predecessors and translated those ideas into a new cultural context and historical situation. Bede became particularly important, as a scholar on the brink between two worlds, as a receiver and translator of ancient ideas and values for the medieval church. His success was such that his work at times obscured the patristic sources from which he drew his most important insights.

Both writers express a deep respect for the Christian Scriptures, which they considered central to the Christian life. Both were concerned about those under their care and oriented their exegesis for the benefit of their flock. Severian said, "Our soul's improvement is the whole purpose of religious devotion; all the lessons stemming from religious devotion have regard to this business of saving our souls. . . . Everything in fact that is done for us and on account of us has for its purpose that in moving to improvement we may be found worthy of religious devotion. So all the holy Bible has our salvation as its theme."

Substantial differences also exist between these writers. Perhaps most significantly, they held different translations of the Hebrew Scriptures to be authoritative. Severian, as did most early Christian scholars, regarded the Greek Septuagint as the authoritative text of the Old Testament. Bede preferred Jerome's Latin translation of the Hebrew, later known as the Vulgate, to the *Vetus Latina* or *Old Latin*, the Latin translation based on

---

[1]Joseph F. Kelly, "1996 NAPS Presidential Address on the Brink: Bede," Journal of Early Christian Studies 5 (1997): 85.

the Septuagint. The first early church commentator to regularly use Jerome's translation in his commentaries, Bede promotes the Hebrew ideal by employing Jerome's term *Hebraica veritas* at a number of points in his commentary *On Genesis*.

Severian and Bede also held dissimilar views of the earth. Ancient authors asked what the shape of the sky is: is the sky like a globe on every side, or like a lid that covers it on one side? Severian argued for a flat earth structured like a tent: the floor was flat with a domed canopy over it. Thus, the earth was constructed according to the plan of the tabernacle of Moses. Creation was not simply arranged for life; it was a setting for communion with God similar to the Mosaic tabernacle. Severian, similar to the later writer Cosmas Indicopleustes, argued against "pagan" opponents who believed that the earth and the surrounding heavens were spherical.

Bede argued that the earth was a stationary sphere around which the moon, stars and sun revolved. In addition, a spherical, crystalline-like firmament made of congealed water separated the highest of heavens from the earthly heavens. Bede's presentation of a spherical earth contradicts versions of history which claim that under the "darkness" of ecclesiastical Christianity the Western world was held captive by a flat-earth mythology until Renaissance scholars revived classical notions of a spherical earth. Clearly this was not the case.

Severian and Bede shared a similar opinion of a two-tiered heaven which formed a unified edifice. There were two heavens: a higher and lower heaven; the former was the heaven of heavens, the invisible abode of angelic beings, while the latter extended from the ethereal to the lower atmosphere of birds. Severian states "Just as in a house with two levels there is a platform in-between them, so the Lord created the world like a single house and inserted heaven as a platform in-between, placing the waters above it."

Bede cites Pseudo-Clement's *Recognitiones* to demonstrate that his view of creation was in accordance with earlier authorities, thereby implying that it was in harmony with the apostolic vision, "In the beginning when God had created the heaven and earth as one house . . . the water which was within the world in that middle space of the initial heaven and earth expanded, congealed like ice and solidified like crystal. The space in the middle of the heaven and earth was enclosed by a firmament of this sort, and the Creator called the firmament 'heaven,' so called from a name of that ancient times, and he divided the fabric of the whole world into two parts, although it was one house. The reason for this division, moreover, was so he could present the upper region as the habitation for angels, the lower one for men."

Though he preferred to interpret these passages figuratively, Augustine argued earlier that both interpretations were logically possible and did not necessarily contradict each other at a literal level. Bede affirmed the compatibility of these two views but offered a more naturalistic interpretation without being pressed into either literalism or allegory.

About the Translators

The late Robert C. Hill, a founder and Honorary Fellow at Australian Catholic University's Centre for Early Christian Studies, published over thirty translations, most of which were commentaries or homilies on the Old Testament by ancient Antiochene exegetes. Regrettably, his translation of Severian of Gabala's *Homilies on Creation and Fall* (his only published translation of Severian) will be his last published translation. Dr. Hill died in 2007.

Well aware that this translation would not be released until much later, Dr. Hill expressed his preference that Severian's *Homilies* be included in the series because "exegetically they are significant and distinctive, and deserve publication." The editors of Ancient Christian Texts and InterVarsity Press would like to express our gratitude for the significant contribution Dr. Hill made to the study of early Christian exegesis and to those readers who wish to reflect and meditate on the Christian scriptures with the great minds of the early church.

We would also like to express our gratitude to Carmen S. Hardin for her diligence in producing a very readable translation of Bede's *Commentary on Genesis*. Though Dr. Hardin served as one of the volume editors for *Psalms 1–50* in the Ancient Christian Commentary on Scripture, this is her first publication of a full-length translation.

Michael Glerup

ABBREVIATIONS

ACW	Ancient Christian Writers
BAC	Bible in Ancient Christianity
CCL	Corpus Christianorum: Series latina
CCG	Corpus Christianorum: Series graeca
CPG	Clavis patrum graecorum
FC	Fathers of the Church
Gen. litt.	*De Genesi ad litteram*
Gen. Man.	*De Genesi contra Manichaeos*
GenComm	Gerhard von Rad, *Genesis: A Commentary*. Philadelphia: Westminster, 1972.
Gk	Greek
GO	Göttinger Orientforschungen
HeyJ	*The Heythrop Journal*
Lat	Latin
LCL	Loeb Classical Library
LXX	Septuagint
NPNF	A Select Library of the Nicene and Post-Nicene Fathers of the Christian Church
OCA	*Orientalia christiana analecta*
OCP	*Orientalia christiana periodica*
PG	Patrologia graeca
PL	Patrologia latina
RSV	Revised Standard Version
SBL	Society of Biblical Literature
SC	Sources chrétiennes
StudP	*Studia patristica*
TRE	*Theologische Realenzyklopädie*
Vg	Vulgate
WGRW	Writings from the Greco-Roman World

Severian of Gabala

Homilies on Creation and Fall

TRANSLATED WITH AN
INTRODUCTION AND NOTES BY
ROBERT C. HILL

TRANSLATOR'S ACKNOWLEDGMENTS

If Severian of Gabala tragically abused the hospitality of John Chrysostom in Constantinople all those years ago, he is still repaying the debt. The modern reader who would access his homilies on creation and fall must consult the works of his erstwhile host in the seventeenth- and eighteenth-century editions of Henry Savile and Bernard de Montfaucon, where they are to be found safely and ironically preserved under the name of the Golden Mouth. For assistance in accessing the former edition I am indebted to Lenore Rouse, director of Rare Books and Special Collections in the Mullen Library, Catholic University of America, to Severian scholar Robert E. Carter, to Father Miltiades Chryssavgis of Rose Bay, Sydney, and to Patrick Klein of Warrimoo NSW, to all of whom I express my thanks.

Robert C. Hill
September 14, 2007
Sixteenth centenary of the death of John Chrysostom

TRANSLATOR'S INTRODUCTION

Perhaps because of the supposed involvement of Severian in the downfall, exile and death of John Chrysostom—the crimes of the guest against his host, of the interloper from the provinces against the bishop of Constantinople[1]—there is a difference of opinion also on the former's abilities as preacher, exegete and interpreter of Scripture. The fact that these homilies on creation and fall were not originally acknowledged as Severian's but included among the works of Chrysostom is itself significant.[2] The seventeenth- and eighteenth-century editors Henry Savile and Bernard de Montfaucon, who accepted earlier recognition of their independence, were at one in maintaining (quite stridently in the latter's case) their obvious inferiority.[3] Of more recent commentators, Johannes Quasten denies Severian originality and declares his biblical interpretation to be naive, unscientific and literal,[4] whereas he is "a first-rate biblical scholar" in the view of biographer of Chrysostom J. N. D. Kelly, "an accomplished preacher" "with a fine command of Scripture" whose works "have often been underrated by critics." Even Kelly, however, is prepared to see the bishop of Gabala (modern Jeble, 15 miles [25 km] south of Laodicea, modern Latakia) as "an ambitious social climber."[5]

Severian's Indebtedness to Chrysostom

Of particular relevance here is Severian's degree of success in the six homilies now listed as *In Cosmogoniam*[6] in treating the Priestly account of creation in Genesis 1, his stated intention. What immediately becomes obvious, however, is that he is obliged by an inability to plumb the material in depth to extend his attention to the following two (Yahwist) chapters of Genesis that include life in the garden and the Fall, in the course of which,

---

[1]S. J. Voicu, "Séverien de Gabala," *Dictionnaire de spiritualité* (Paris: Beauchesne, 1990), 14:752, notes that the ancient historians generally (Socrates, Sozomen, Palladius, Photius) refer to Severian only in the context of his period in Constantinople. Significantly, Severian has not been accorded an entry in the *TRE*; Voicu's article is a worthy substitute for providing what is known of his life and works.

[2]Voicu, "Séverien de Gabala," 753, finds no obvious reason for this inclusion.

[3]PG 56:429-30, where Montfaucon quotes Savile's words. The text of the six (listed as CPG 4194, *In Cosmogoniam*) appears in cols. 429-500. Details of the seventh are given below.

[4]Johannes Quasten, *Patrology* (Westminster, Md.:Newman Press, 1960) 3:484.

[5]J. N. D. Kelly, *Golden Mouth: The Story of John Chrysostom, Ascetic, Preacher, Bishop* (Ithaca, N.Y.: Cornell University Press, 1995), 183, 173.

[6]CPG 4194.

it has been argued, he proceeds to preach a seventh homily.[7] Nowhere in these homilies does Severian refer explicitly to his host, John, but he pays him the sincerest form of flattery in what appear to be a dozen or so instances of imitation or borrowing from the celebrated series of homilies and sermons on Genesis delivered in Antioch.[8] He can even chide his anonymous mentor for mistaken interpretation. Severian concedes at the outset that he is not the first to treat of the topic.

> The treatment by the Fathers, far from being rejected, is transmitted in our treatment. Even if theirs is wonderful and ours insignificant, it is nonetheless all of a piece with theirs; just as a tiny stone laid in support will strengthen a mighty stone in the form of a cube that is fitted into a building and is slightly unstable, so too the statements of the Fathers make the building of the church better when in receipt of a slight addition.[9]

To an extent, this is a conventional acknowledgment of tradition, like Theodoret's classing himself in the field of Pauline commentary as a mosquito buzzing about the apostolic meadows in the company of bees.[10] Severian further claims that "there is a common source, in fact, and all the gifts are set before us in common, provided we are willing to make the effort with complete enthusiasm." What is of relevance here is the extent to which he does seem to call on Chrysostom's previous exercises of commentary, leading us to wonder how he might have fared without access to them; only in the third homily does this indebtedness not appear, and there as elsewhere we regret that his congregation had not been treated to some "golden age" insights to supplement his "iron age" treatment (in Savile's terms), such as by an accent on the goodness of creation, conspicuously missing before Homily Four but an accent to be found in this "source."

While an instance of verbatim quotation seems to occur in Homily Six in the reference to the serpent in the garden as the devil's "ideal instrument" (epitēdeion organon), Severian appears to be influenced by Chrysostom's earlier treatment also in that well-worn question of absence of mention of creation of the angels, the Jewish nomination of angels as the addressees of "let us make" (Gen 1:26), the meaning of a scribal misreading of aoristos as aoratos in Genesis 1:2, the introduction of Luke's brigand on the cross in a discussion of paradise in the fifth homily, Adam's enjoyment of divine inspiration in bestowing names on the animals, places being named after events (to account for naming the tree of knowledge of good and evil), the tree resembling an imperial effigy (or decree,

---

[7]CPG 4195, which bears the title Adamus (Quomodo animum acceperit).

[8]For the text of the homilies, see PG 53; 54 (R. C. Hill, trans., St. John Chrysostom: Homilies on Genesis, FC 74, 82, 87); of the sermons, the critical edition by L. Brottier, Jean Chrysostome: Sermons sur la Genèse, SC 43 (R. C. Hill, trans., Eight Sermons from the Book of Genesis [Brookline, Mass.: Holy Cross Orthodox Press, 2004]).

[9]PG 56:430.

[10]PG 82:37. C. Datema, "Severian of Gabala: A Modest Man?" StudP 22 (1989): 107, concludes, "Severian was decidedly not a modest man."

in John's earlier image), the introduction of King Uzziah of 2 Chronicles 26 (inaccurately transmitted by Severian) in Homily Two and the citation of Isaiah 9:6 on Genesis 1:26. He also seems familiar with Chrysostom's commentary on Psalms in Homily Four.

Severian seems to have Chrysostom's Homily Sixteen in mind in faulting a "pious" interpretation of Genesis 3:9, where Chrysostom had labored the losses that the Fall entailed, by comparison with his own "true" one.

> Many people have taken that in a pious manner, but we must give it careful attention; I accept their interpretation since it is pious, and I state this one because it is true. *Adam, where are you?* Where have you been? Where have you come from? From what glory have you fallen? I really accept the interpretation as pious, it is proper and attractive; but I am looking for the movement of thought.[11]

While one commends him for adopting here precision, *akribeia*,[12] as a hermeneutical principle (less so "movement of thought," *akolouthia*, which had proved insufficient for previous interpreters like Diodore and Theodore to supply for exegetical limitations),[13] one laments time and time again that that principle had not been combined with one that so enhances Chrysostom's interpretation, *synkatabasis*, divine considerateness in biblical discourse that makes unnecessary for a commentator a precision that takes textual details in a fundamentalist manner[14]—ad nauseam, as Montfaucon laments of Severian (*akribologia* in Theodore's slighting remark that is pertinent here, as in the case of the talking serpent in Homily Six).[15] One also notes Chrysostom's greater ability to find in the days of creation and the Fall enough stimulating material for his congregations, which is never in danger of being exhausted. However, one appreciates the relatively less severe attitude adopted by Severian toward the woman as the guilty party in the Fall (because, one wonders, of his warmer relations with the empress?), where Chrysostom's strictures in his Homily Sixteen are scathing. Finally, however, Severian agrees with the author of the Pastorals (1 Tim 2:14) that, unlike Eve, Adam was not deceived, only beguiled.

Circumstances of Delivery of the Homilies

If these six homilies (or seven)[16] lay for so long embedded in the Chrysostomian corpus,

---

[11]PG 56:493. Cf. Chrysostom's comments (PG 53:131, 133).

[12]The term is often rendered "accuracy," but as Severian's usage illustrates, precision can sometimes be inaccurate. See R. C. Hill, "*Akribeia*: A Principle of Chrysostom's Exegesis," *Colloquium* 14 (October 1981): 32-36.

[13]See R. C. Hill, "His Master's Voice: Theodore of Mopsuestia on the Psalms," *HeyJ* 45 (2003): 40-53. Voicu, "Sévérien de Gabala," 760, notes that Severian follows Diodore's terminology.

[14]See R. C. Hill, "On Looking Again at *synkatabasis*," *Prudentia* 13 (1981): 3-11.

[15]The term is used by Theodore of attempts by commentators to locate the Tarshish mentioned in Jonah 1:3 (H. N. Sprenger, ed., *Theodori Mopsuesteni commentarius in XII prophetas*, GO, Biblica et Patristica 1 [Wiesbaden: Otto Harrassowitz, 1977], 178).

[16]The homily listed as CPG 4195, *Quomodo animum acceperit Adam*, appearing only in the 1613 Eton edition (*S. Joannis Chrysostomi Opera*, in Collegio regali, excudebat Joannes Norton) by Savile, 5:648-53, is also a Lenten homily that is part of a series. On the basis of work by J. Zellinger, *Die Genesishomilien des Bischofs Severian von Gabala*, Alttestamentliche Abhandlun-

it would not be surprising if we could not now detail precisely the circumstances of their delivery. Severian, Syrian by birth, had come to Constantinople soon after Chrysostom's consecration as bishop (this much we know from Socrates[17] and Sozomen[18]) and as a fellow bishop was given preaching opportunities, such as the other series that year,[19] on the incarnation, to which he refers in Homily Five. As it was Lent, that provided the occasion in the Eastern church for commentary on this traditional material also in the case of Chrysostom's several extant series, and so Severian refers at the outset to the liturgical season and its concomitant practice of fasting: "We are aware, then, that these matters of detail seem tedious to the minds of the general run of people; but there is need to speak of deeper issues to people when they are alert in the period of fasting in particular."[20] It is, however, an accent that is not sustained. Severian seems to be delivering the homilies to a congregation on more or less successive days; while the term *prōēn* is used ambiguously as "the day before yesterday" or "the other day" and "yesterday," it seems clear that more than one day intervened before the sixth homily. More than once we are told that the day is coming to an end and are left to presume that the occasion for the homilies is a non-eucharistic evening synaxis, with no other speaker involved.[21]

As to the nature of the congregation or congregations, though Severian never has to chide those present for the failings of the absent, as does Chrysostom in his Homily Six devoted to lamenting the absence of people who have chosen to patronize the race track in Antioch, they are more than once flattered by the preacher with some knowledge of the Scriptures. It is presumed that they already know the story of Rahab from Joshua 2 and the incident of water from the rock in Exodus 17. While it may be a mannerism on the preacher's part, they have to be called to "pay attention" at frequent intervals: do they find his style unappealing? Is that another reason why they find his lengthy invocation of natural science, *physiologia*, less than engaging (a fault for which Montfaucon also chides him)?[22] He begins Homily Five by admitting of his previous

---

gen 7.1 (Münster: Aschendorffschen, 1916), who claims it follows "immediately" on Homily Six, R. E. Carter, "The Chronology of Twenty Homilies of Severian of Gabala," *Traditio* 55 (2000): 1-17, painstakingly constructs the chronology of Severian's preaching in Constantinople, dating the seven homilies to Lent 401. On the evidence of Gennadius of Marseille, we know that Severian died sometime after 408.

[17]Socrates *Historia Ecclesiastica* (PG 67:697).

[18]Sozomen *Historia Ecclesiastica* (PG 67:1541).

[19]Carter, "Chronology," 10-11, 17, assigns the series on the incarnation to January 401.

[20]Montfaucon speaks of Quadragesima for this Lenten period, though we know from Chrysostom's *Homilies on the Statues*, for example, that Lent in Antioch lasted eight weeks, leading Carter, "Chronology," 3, to presume that length also in the case of Constantinople.

[21]Carter, "Chronology," 14-17, sees Severian possibly speaking twice a day, taking the references to voice problems to be consequent "hoarseness." Even in the seventh homily Severian complains about "the instrument that is our voice" (Savile, 5:648). Zellinger, *Die Genesishomilien*, 46, places the seventh homily on a Friday on the basis of Severian's beginning (Savile, 5:648) with the statement that it was "the day God formed [Adam]." In that homily Severian concludes by making way for a *leitourgia*—a liturgy of the Eucharist?

[22]PG 56:429-30: *Rerum naturalium perquisitionem plerumque aggreditur, et ad nauseam usque explorat, suoque more, nimirum inepte, edisserit* ("He frequently pursues an investigation of natural science and explores it to the extreme, and would have continued it in his usual manner, namely, ineptly"). The call to attention is made also in the seventh homily, a feature that

day's comments on lights in the firmament (Gen 1:14-15), "I heard some people's fault finding, What use is it to mention fire and water and the fact that fire screams when water is thrown on it? It is not *physiologia* we are anxious to learn, they say, but the true doctrine of God (*theologia*)." In the fourth and fifth (and seventh) homilies he also seems to be struggling with his voice—or is he only conceding his failure to match the oratory of the Golden Mouth?[23]

As Severian closes his sixth homily, he sums up his homilies in the words, "We have gone through paradise (or the garden)[24] with you," which is not what he originally intended, a study of "the book of creation, *dēmiourgia*." He was not quite up to the latter challenge. From a modern standpoint we may venture the observation that, if the more anthropomorphically-minded Yahwist, to whom Severian in his literalism and dramatic interest warms in Genesis 2 and Genesis 3, had composed also Genesis 1, the commentator would have found more in creation that was grist to his mill.

Severian's Approach to the Task of Commentary

In commenting on Genesis, *Kosmopoiia* or "the book of *dēmiourgia*," Severian seems to be reading the form of the Greek version used also by Chrysostom, the Antiochene or Lucianic text.[25] The only departure from it may occur in Genesis 1:9, "Let the water be gathered together," where there seems to be no appearance of the explanatory sentence found in some Hebrew manuscripts, in Chrysostom's text and the Septuagint generally as Genesis 1:9b, "The water under heaven was gathered together into its masses, and the dry land appeared." We can never be sure of this identity of form of the text in the case of other books, since Severian can be guilty of loose recall. As he would have found in Chrysostom and his fellow Antiochenes, an author's purpose, *skopos*, is immediately to be identified by the commentator; and Severian follows suit: "Now, what was the purpose of the inspired composer? Moses had two concerns, to develop teaching and to foreshadow lawgiving; though a lawgiver, he took as his point of departure not lawgiving but creation." His opening remarks also imply a pastoral concern.

> Our souls' improvement is the whole purpose of religious devotion; all the lessons stemming from religious devotion have regard to this business of saving our souls.

Zellinger, *Die Genesishomilien*, and Carter, "A Greek Homily on the Temptation (CPG 4906) by Severian of Gabala: Introduction, Critical Edition and Translation," *Traditio* 52 (1997): 47-71, note along with other recurring phrases to confirm its authenticity.

[23]Cf. Kelly, *Golden Mouth*, 183: "Although [Severian] had a harsh voice and spoke with a strong Syrian accent, [his sermons] evidently went down well with popular audiences." Carter, "Chronology," 15, attributes the comments to a hoarse voice arising from preaching twice daily.

[24]The use of the Persian loan word *paradeisos* is ambiguous. The seventh homily continues commentary on life in the garden until expulsion by the cherubim with the flaming sword (Gen 3:24).

[25]For the characteristics of this text and for recent scholarship identifying them, the reader may consult N. Fernández Marcos, *The Septuagint in Context: Introduction to the Greek Versions of the Bible* (Boston and Leiden: Brill, 2001), 223-38, and R. C. Hill, *Reading the Old Testament in Antioch*, BAC 5 (Leiden and Boston: Brill, 2005), 47-61.

The word of God, for instance, is also concerned with this, the law of Moses supplies a basis for it, the spiritual statements of the Old Testament authors proclaim it, the New Testament authors cry aloud about it with mouths that are never silent—everything in fact that is done for us and on account of us has for its purpose that in moving to improvement we may be found worthy of religious devotion. So all the holy Bible has our salvation as its theme, as I said above.

Though this pastoral manifesto seems to be observed more in the breach than in the observance, we note here an accent on the orality of Scripture and on the harmony of the Testaments—"the two Testaments are sisters," he will say shortly after; but again neither accent predominates. Also like those Antiochene predecessors, and perhaps in imitation of them, he sees comprehension of the text as his primary goal, "the purpose being that with the help of God's grace the treatment may be made perfectly clear to the best of our ability—not from our own reasoning but from what we have been taught." This goal he does strive for, with questionable success.

Not that Severian does not try hard. It may be that his formation as a commentator is at fault. His specifically exegetical skills are limited, as were those of Chrysostom and his peers.[26] He has no Hebrew; attempts at etymology of Hebrew terms limp. He gets into his head that the Hebrew for "human being" means "fire" and justifies it thus:

Since God foreknew, then, that from one human body the ends of the earth is filled (one lamp lights so many wicks, west and east, north and south), he imposed a name suited to the reality. Hence he gave it the name *Adam* as a pledge for the world; intending to fill the four quarters from him, he imposes the name *Adam*: A for east (*anatolē*), D for west (*dysis*), A for north (*arktos*), M for south (*mesēmbria*). The name with its four letters confirms the human being's destiny of filling the world. Hence its Hebrew name "fire".[27]

Montfaucon is left aghast at the naiveté, which we shall see is a characteristic of Severian's hermeneutic, too. As with his predecessors, the psalm titles (done less than justice by the LXX, admittedly) are beyond his understanding, as he shows in citing Psalm 75 at the end of the first homily. While help with textual obscurities was at hand in the alternative versions associated with the names of Aquila, Symmachus and Theodotion, which were available in a copy of the Hexapla, they are invoked here only twice.[28]

Severian is slow to admit that the scriptural text offers problems (*ta aporoumena, ta zētēmata*); he both affirms and denies it in the opening pages of Homily Six. We have seen that his response to textual challenges includes precision, *akribeia* (found both in the text

[26]Kelly, *Golden Mouth*, 94, appositely reminds us that "neither John, nor any Christian teacher for centuries to come, was properly equipped to carry out exegesis as we have come to understand it."
[27]PG 56:474.
[28]PG 56:441, 459.

and in the commentator), and movement of thought, *akolouthia*. He is tireless in noting items that occur or even do not occur in the text. He notes a morphological discrepancy in the divine declaration of goodness in the case of the great lights and in the case of the sea monsters (accent on their goodness being in a minor key).

> *God made the huge sea monsters,* then, *and God saw that they were all good* (Gen 1:21). Why did he say *good* in the plural, and not in the singular for the multitude? When he made the stars and sun and moon, however, with many things made, he says, *God saw that it was good* (Gen 1:18). There were many stars, their vast number beyond counting, and he did not say, God saw that they were good, but It was good. Why? Because even if there were many stars, they came from one light, and all met the same need, being assigned to providing light. In this case, since there was a great variety of creeping things, winged things and swimming things (there being a different basis to creeping, winged and swimming), and since there were many and varied species in each genus, he says, *God said that they were good.* There is commendation also for the variety of the works.[29]

The trouble is—and it may account for the frequent calling of the congregation to pay attention—that Severian does not know when to admit that enough is enough: *ad nauseam* in Montfaucon's phrase. He is not content to cite one example when three are available. Often this leads him to start hares; the text is already clear when Severian must persist and raise a nonexistent problem. In Homily Three he illuminates the text by explaining the reference to "times" in Genesis 1:14, distinguishing helpfully between *kairos* and *chronos*: "There is a difference between this *time* and another: *chronos* suggests measurement, *kairos* suitability. No one says, It is *chronos* for harvesting; no one says, It is *chronos* for the maiden to marry—rather, It is *kairos* for the maiden to marry, *kairos* for sowing, *kairos* for reaping." But not knowing when to stop, Severian has to go on and berate heretics, who, we shall see, include anyone not agreeing with his point of view, who cannot explain how rain is not salty, which is hardly pertinent to the biblical text: "Why does he do it? How do the clouds send rain? He made the clouds like wineskins, and through them he draws up the seawater, which is salty, fills the clouds, transforms the water and gives the earth a drink. Let them [the heretics] explain how what is heavy is lifted on high, how it is drawn up, how the clouds are drawn up. Far from being immediately emptied, they travel long distances wherever the Lord bids, and it is due to a command of God like shackles imposed on them that he does not allow them to rain until he wills."[30] No wonder the congregation needed calling to attention.

Severian does have the ability to dramatize biblical scenes; in his view, "many things

---

[29]PG 56:459. In the seventh homily he makes much of the distinction between Adam's being "formed" and Eve's being "fashioned" and urges his listeners to note that Mary's child-to-be (Lk 1:35) will be "born" (*gennēthen*), not "made" (*genēthen*).
[30]PG 56:451, 454.

are transmitted by imagining them rather than by speaking of them," as he says in explaining what *firmament* means in Homily Two. Adam's naming of the animals receives attention from him that is sustained and graphic.

> So pay attention. It was a remarkable thing to behold, Adam standing there and God like a servant bringing them to Adam; *God brought the animals*, the text says.[31] Pay attention to this, not to the text but to the notion. Imagine God standing there and Adam assessing them; God parades them all and says to Adam, Come now, say what you think this one should be called. Let its name be lion; God so determined, the text says. Next, this one: Let its name be bull. Good choice. In a similar fashion God confirmed each of the names.[32]

His use of imagery can likewise be both plus and minus; the images can be contrived and clumsy but at times effective, so that one wonders if he came across them somewhere. Severian develops the notion of the animals in the garden as Adam's pets, his intention being to prepare the congregation for the entry of the talking serpent as just one such creature that mimics human beings. The preparatory Homeric simile is truly dismal, atypical of the pedestrian pedant: does its source lie elsewhere?

> When God sees a soul that is weary, he consoles it with what is pleasant, as also happens in our case. Often on returning from the marketplace a person is stressed in mind with countless worries, often experiencing depressing sights and encountering unbearable misfortunes and losses; but on reaching home he derives consolation from his child, and the tender thoughts alleviate the harshness of work. You see, when his wife does not approach him in his discouragement by way of comfort since her consolation would be untimely, and no servant presumes to offer encouragement, God introduces the simplicity of nature to offer pardon for what it is unaware of, and by this means soothes the soul wearied by labor. If a servant laughs, he is thought to be mocking the master's moods; if the wife jokes, she is thought to be insensitive to the misfortune; the child is not suspected of flattery in its natural guilelessness. It often happens that what friends did not manage with their advice or sages with their suggestions, a child by merely giggling succeeds completely in solving the problem. At this point, at the very climax of distress, on seeing the child he spurns its advances and rebuffs its consolation as untimely; but by its persistence he is won over, and to its frequent glances his mind capitulates. He then picks up the child, dismisses his distress and says, God gives me only this, and I have no concern for anything else. Do you see how even from chance events God prompts

---

[31]Gen 2:19.

[32]PG 56:480. The soldier piercing Jesus' side in the seventh homily is another such example. R. F. Regtuit, "Severian's Charm: The Preaching of Severian of Gabala," *StudP* 27 (1993): 202-8, who accords Severian the status of "an entertaining preacher" (208), notes this interest in dramatization and use of imaginary dialogues.

comfort for the soul? Since Adam was by himself in the garden, therefore, with no friend, no neighbor, no kith and kin, God presented him with the animals for his consolation—for example, as is the case today, the animals that mimic.[33]

There are other times where Severian presents what appears to be prepackaged material (noted in the text below), suggesting an arsenal into which he, like many another preacher, dips at will.

Though Severian does not moralize—something that may account for his relative difficulty, by comparison with a Golden Mouth, in making his material go the distance—he is ever the churchman. Indeliberately he sheds light on church life and practice of his day. He gives us an insight into church liturgy and discipline, for instance, in reporting in Homily Two a current issue regarding the wording of the Sanctus (the use of the trisagion from Isaiah 6:3 in the eucharistic prayer).

> Today a certain heretic came to us in the presence of holy men and Fathers and said (I mention it in case the report in any way should be relayed differently and cause different feelings of alarm), Father, Son and Holy Spirit are one divinity, one power, one kingdom; and we must ensure the removal from our soul, not to say from the altar, of the expression used in the *Sanctus*, "Holy, holy, holy, Lord sabaoth." Unless you abolish it, he said, you are not Christians. Do you see the awful madness of the devil he was perpetrating? Do you see the root of hostility to God? Do you see the enormity of blasphemy? He wanted to decapitate piety, paralyze the Eucharist, abolish faith, uproot its foundations.[34]

Despite Severian's ever-ready application of "heretic" to a divergent thinker, and his excessive response, he seems to be documenting a community practice of raising issues in public, this one evincing opposition to use of a Hebrew term, "sabaoth," in Christian worship. He can also be found referring to the sacraments of initiation, to catechumens, neophytes, initiated.

Interpreting Creation and Fall

We noted above that, while Severian felt free to draw on earlier treatment of this part of the Bible by Chrysostom and may even have moderated an excessive reaction of the latter to the woman's role in the Fall, he never grasped one of the latter's key hermeneutical principles, *synkatabasis*, that would ensure that a commentator does not fall into the danger of literalism. Chrysostom's term is not in Severian's vocabulary; the principle rarely receives attention. The closest he comes to showing acceptance of it is in his single warning to his congregation about interpreting anthropomorphisms in Homily Five.

---

[33]PG 56:485.
[34]PG 56:445.

Let us make a human being in our image (Gen 1:26). Many people who were simple and uninstructed in spiritual matters had the idea that the human being was made in God's image in the sense that God has a nose, eyes of the same kind, ears of the same kind, a mouth of the same kind. This notion, however, is flawed and inappropriate. Even to this day there has been a heresy claiming that the divinity has a human form; since they heard, "The eyes of the Lord," "The ears of the Lord," "The Lord smelled," "The mouth of the Lord said," "The hand of the Lord did," "The feet of the Lord stood,"[35] they depicted what is incorporeal with limbs, not realizing the inappropriateness of the notion. God says this for you to learn that a human being bears no resemblance to God as far as bodily appearance goes; I do not cancel the statement that says, *Let us make a human being in our image.* Instead, he shows what *in our image* means. "I shall fill heaven and earth, says the Lord"; and again, "Heaven is my throne and earth a footstool for my feet."[36] Are we to follow the text? Are we to adhere slavishly to the expression? On the contrary, the movement of thought forbids me.[37]

Even here it is *akolouthia* that urges caution, not *synkatabasis*. Acceptance of the latter, demonstrated eminently by his host in Constantinople, would have helped Severian recognize the nature of the material to be found in the differing accounts of creation and fall in those opening chapters of Genesis. While we may debate the assertion made even of Chrysostom by his biographer Kelly, that he "could not be expected to understand the nature of Old Testament writings,"[38] its truth in the case of Severian is patent. Though he begins by stating of Genesis 1:1 that "it is not as a historian (*historiographos*) that Moses said this but as an inspired author (*prophētēs*)," the result of his inspired work being *prophēteia*, he soon (on Gen 1:20) slips into referring to Moses as just such a *historiographos* and his work a historical record; and in describing details of the garden (Gen 2:12) he commends this *historiographos* for showing the same *akribeia* as he as a commentator appreciates. From inspired composition the work has become a textbook—for example, a surgical textbook on the removal of a rib from Adam in Genesis 2:22 to make the woman, whereas for someone like Didymus in Alexandria it is an ascetical manual. And so Severian complacently concludes his commentary (at least in Homily Six) with the assurance that he has conducted the congregation through the "royal records," *hypomnēmata*. He has turned the composer(s) into an image of himself.

The result of this fatal failure to recognize the genre of the material in these chapters of the Bible, where divine considerateness in language is so eminently demonstrated (Chrysostom rightly claims), is on Severian's part an acceptance of biblical flat-earth cos-

---

[35]Ps 34:15; Gen 8:21; Is 1:20; Job 12:9; Ps 132:7.
[36]Jer 23:24; Is 66:1.
[37]PG 56:474.
[38]Kelly, *Golden Mouth*, 94.

mology and a chase after detail, *akribologia*. As his eighteenth-century editor Montfaucon feelingly lamented, *De mundo, quem rotundum esse negat, de igne, di aqua, plus quam satis esset agit.*[39] Figurative and apocalyptic statements of biblical authors are adduced in confirmation of such a cosmology; anyone who offers a less literalistic view is a heretic.

> He did not create heaven as a sphere, as the idle talkers claim; he did not make it as a sphere moving on its axle. Rather, as the prophet asks, what course does the sun follow? "He arches the heaven like a curved roof and extends it like a tent."[40] None of us is so impious as to be convinced by the idle talkers. The biblical authors say that heaven has a beginning and an end; hence the sun does not climb—it travels. Scripture says, "The sun had emerged upon the earth when Lot entered Zoar";[41] so it is obvious that the sun emerged, as Scripture says, and did not climb. And again, "From the furthest point of heaven was its emergence,"[42] not its ascent: if it were a sphere, it would not have a furthest point; what is the furthest point of something completely circular? Surely it is not only David who says this, therefore, or even the Savior? Listen to his words, "When the Son of man comes in his glory, he will send his angels with a loud trumpet call, and they will gather his elect from one end of heaven to the next" (Mt 24:31).[43]

Where Savile was prepared merely to class this as an example of "iron eloquence" from a "golden age," Montfaucon in the next century dismissed the apologetic, classing such texts instead as "nonsense," *phlyaria*. There are countless examples of naiveté in the commentator, like that bestowal of the name Adam as an anagram for the four quarters of the earth.

And yet, for all his literalism, Severian can show an openness to other levels of meaning in the biblical accounts that he would not have found in the great Antiochenes who were pupils of Diodore; he must have been reading commentators from elsewhere. He evinces a readiness to recognize typology; when in Genesis 2:8 Eden is said to be "in the east (the dawn)," Severian comments, "Adam traveled to the west and set in a grave; things of earth followed him and were buried with him as he set. Christ came and caused the one who had set to rise."[44] And on the previous verse, where God breathes life into the man, Severian in this Homily Five develops the christological parallel at greater length: "When creation had lost its original vigor, Christ renewed it at the incarnation. Adam was formed from the earth, Christ formed the eyes of the blind from mud so that you might

---

[39]PG 56:429-30: "He goes on to extremes about the world, which he refuses to accept is round, about fire, about water."
[40]Is 40:22.
[41]Gen 19:23.
[42]Ps 19:6.
[43]PG 56:452. Cf. Voicu, "Sévérien de Gabala," 759: "Il est aussi parmis les tenants d'une sort de fondamentalisme biblique."
[44]Cf. Voicu, "Sévérien de Gabala," 760: "Sévérien accorde une préférence de principe au sens littérale du texte biblique, mais souvent il fait intervenir des interprétations symboliques."

come to recognize the one who took dust from the earth and formed you. God breathed a breath of life into the face of Adam; Christ breathed on the face of the apostles and said, 'Receive a Holy Spirit' (Jn 20:22)"—and he continues the parallel until his voice gives out. In Homily Five he sees in John 19:34, the piercing of Jesus' side (*pleura*), a reference to the removal of Adam's rib, *pleura*, in Genesis 2:21, and develops the parallel at length in the seventh homily. By contrast, the bishop does not recognize sacramental overtones to the text with the frequency we later find in the bishop of Cyrus; the contrast of the fruit occasioning the Fall with the eucharistic bread in Homily Six is a rare reference.[45]

If Severian has imbibed from other sources a sensitivity to spiritual meanings in a text that Diodore would not have sanctioned, however, the term "allegory" still rings for him the same alarm bells it did for the founder of the school of Antioch and his pupils.[46] A celebrated instance, documented also from Theodore and Theodoret, is the "spiritual (*pneumatikos*) interpretation" given to the garden by "the allegorists," such as Origen and Didymus,[47] which he roundly condemns in Homily Six. Instead of invoking the principle of *synkatabasis* as Chrysostom did in his Homily Thirteen, Severian, typically but ill-advisedly, takes them on at a literalistic level.

> Let the allegorists be confounded in their teaching that paradise is in heaven and is spiritual. What does a fig tree produce in heaven? But granting that paradise is in heaven: whence come the rivers—not from earth? If paradise is on high, it follows that the rivers also flow from on high; surely Scripture did not say as much, that a river flows down from Eden? That is only playing with words. The allegorists mock us with the taunt, *God clad them in garments of skin*: surely he did not slaughter oxen and sheep, open a tannery and perform the work of a tanner? Our reply is that he produced the animal fully grown, without breeding, without copulation. He made what did not exist: surely he is not incapable of making part of what does exist? Conceding that for the time being, nevertheless God never makes part of an animal, God makes nothing incomplete. He hears the word *skin* and looks for the source; I

---

[45]In the seventh homily Severian cites the baptismal formula to support his argument for the creative role of the Spirit.

[46]Cf. Diodore's introduction to his commentary on the Psalms (CCG 6:7): "One thing alone is to be guarded against, however, never to let the discernment process be seen as an overthrow of the underlying sense, since this would no longer be discernment but allegory: what is arrived at in defiance of the content is not discernment but allegory." Though we do find Johannes Quasten, *Patrology* 2:121-23, speaking in a local and physical sense of "the school of Antioch founded by Lucian of Samosata" in opposition to the "school of Caesarea," Origen's refuge after his exile from Egypt, I prefer to use the term only of a fellowship of like-minded scholars joined by birth, geography and scholarly principles, even if some members did exercise a magisterial role in regard to others. (Diodore's editor, J.-M. Olivier, CCG 6:ciii, will maintain rather that it was he who was "le véritable fondateur" of the school of Antioch, conceding only the term "initiateur" to Lucian.)

[47]On Gal 4:24 (according to the fifth-century Latin version edited by H. B. Swete, *Theodori Episcopi Mopsueteni in epistolas B. Pauli Commentarii* I [Cambridge: Cambridge University Press, 1880], 74-75), Theodore commented, "When they turn to expounding divine Scripture 'spiritually'—spiritual interpretation is the name they would like their folly to be given—they claim Adam is not Adam, paradise is not paradise, the serpent is not the serpent. To these people I should say that if they distort *historia*, they will have no *historia* left." When Theodoret in his *Questions on the Octateuch* is confronted with the question (25), "Some commentators claim that the garden is in heaven," he replies that "it is very presumptuous to follow one's own reasoning when the Spirit has imparted the doctrine to us" (*Theodoreti Cyrensis Quaestiones in Octateuchum*, 29).

hear of blood in Egypt and look for the way he turned the Nile into blood, the great number of animals he slaughtered. The river turned into blood, and no animal was slaughtered; there were two skins, and he wonders about the number of animals they came from—yet in that case as well there was skin without an animal.[48]

Whether this distinction was of help to his congregation, it would have confirmed the allegorists in their approach.

With his openness to other levels of meaning, however, Severian is not sure whether spiritual meanings and allegory are always unacceptable. If he can find a connection with the facts, *historia*, or some support in Scripture, he invokes the latitude allowed by Diodore,[49] as in comment on Genesis 1:20 in Homily Four:

> *And on the earth birds flying across the firmament of heaven*: on earth because of the body, in heaven because of the way of life (Phil 3:20). It is not to indulge in allegory that we introduced this; rather, we found this spiritual interpretation (*theōria*) in the facts (*historia*). It is one thing to force an allegorical interpretation on the facts; it is another to retain the facts and arrive at a spiritual interpretation.[50]

However, he is unhappy with the spiritual meaning given by Origen and Didymus to the darkness in Genesis 1:2 as the devil and to the deep as demons.

Theological and Polemical Concerns

Even if Severian passes up the frequent opportunities offered by the text to endorse the goodness of created things, he does close his series of six homilies on an upbeat: "To the best of our ability, therefore, with the grace of the Holy Spirit we have gone through paradise with you, we have read aloud the royal records, we have seen the freeing of the guilty, the judge's lovingkindness." Eastern optimism is again reflected. There is, however, a polemical edge to much of his commentary. Admittedly, he is ready to cry "heretic" if someone does not agree with his point of view, even on a matter like the formation of the lower heaven from water, a notion he supports from Psalm 33:6. "Do you see God's creative activity? Do you see how he stops the mouths of heretics, who are ignorant of creation and yet pry into the creator? All things obey God's law: heaven stood still, not under pressure from its own force but set firm by a divine law. Whenever you are uncertain as to how heaven was solidified from water, in fact, blessed David resolves your uncertainty

---

[48]PG 56:492-93. His argument here is as heated as that of an Alexandrian like Didymus is to the opposite effect when dismissing the validity of factual interpretations. In fact, there are several indications that Severian has been in contact, if not with Didymus's earlier work, at least with his principal source, Origen.

[49]"We shall not stand in the way of a spiritual and more elevated sense. The historical sense (*historia*), in fact, is not in opposition to the more elevated sense (*theōria*); on the contrary, it proves to be the basis and foundation of the more elevated ideas" (CCG 6:7).

[50]PG 56:459.

in the words, 'By the word of the Lord the heavens were set firm.' "[51]

While Severian feels that he can do justice to the biblical account(s) of creation at his own literalistic level, then, he does not extend that liberty to others, accusing them of "prying" into "divine incomprehensibility," an Anomean failing he would have found Chrysostom castigating. Only occasionally will he admit defeat and invoke this doctrine, as on the creation of light in Genesis 1:3: "While he mentioned what had been made, he did not make mention of the manner, nor did he understand it; the fact that the light was made I am aware of, he says, but how it was made I do not grasp." The Anomeans are not his principal target, however, this distinction going to the Arians and their subordinationist errors; he is upholding the position of councils of Nicaea and Constantinople, especially their insistence of the *homoousion* of Father and Son, as he implies in listing current heresies in Homily Four.

> God in his wisdom has allowed heresies to get a name for their teachings from their originators so that it may be clear that what is decreed by them is not God's teaching but man's invention—Macedonians from Macedonius,[52] Arians from Arius, Eunomians from Eunomius, and likewise the other heresies. But wishing to preserve the faith of the apostles intact, he did not allow them to be named after a man; even if they call us Homoousiasts, they are not referring to a man but proclaiming the faith.[53]

If the text of Genesis was not these groups' staple ammunition, Severian obliges by being prepared to leave it for more favored New Testament loci, as he says after noting the frequency of occurrence in Genesis 1 of the verb "made" in Homily Four.

> It would take a long time at this stage to review everything made by the Word; leaving behind the account of creation in the Old Testament, let us move to the account in the New of what was made by him through the Word alone. He it was, in fact, who created things of old and made new things, according to John's account, "Everything was made by him, and without him not one thing was made" (Jn 1:3).[54]

Texts that speak of generation like Genesis 1:24, "Let the earth bring forth a living being," prompt the question of the relationship of Father to Son; and time and again Severian jousts with the Arian claims of subordination.

Note the knavery: when they raise questions, they speak on the basis of human

---

[51]PG 56:455.

[52]Macedonius was a fourth-century homoeousian bishop of Constantinople who actively campaigned against the Arians. He, like other homoeousians, denied the divinity of the Holy Spirit. The name Macedonians originally applied to homoeousian groups associated with Macedonius in and near Constantinople, but after 380 the term expanded to cover all non-Arian groups who would not affirm the divinity of the Holy Spirit. Severian appears in many ways to be similar to Macedonius. Both are anti-Arian and support ascetical ideals, such as fasting, yet they differ in their profession of the Holy Spirit as divine.

[53]PG 56:470.

[54]PG 56:457.

reasoning, as in saying, Everything generated has a beginning to its existence. How so? Their response is immediate: When you were born, did you not have a beginning? your father? your grandfather? If you present them with a different argument that is based on their own arguments and capable of overturning their folly, they immediately mince words, The discussion is about God, and are you presenting me with human arguments? On the one hand, they develop the root of the problem from common reasoning, and on the other they refuse to accept the demolition of the problem on the basis of the same reasoning.[55]

The plural verb in Genesis 1:26, "let us make," gives rise here, as in other commentaries of the period, to an endorsement of trinitarian faith after lengthy discussion and rejection of the nomination of angels as God's associate, which Severian attributes to the Jews.

Note the beam of orthodox faith ever resplendent; the sun in its shining joined its own beam. *Let us make a human being in our image and likeness.* He retained the order of the persons (*hypostases*) and the unity of being. *Let us make a human being in image*, not in images: it is not the case that the Father has one image, the Son another. *Let us make* (the purpose being to bring out the plurality of persons) *in our image* (to explain the oneness of being, *homoousion*). Who is an associate in this marvelous address and remarkable creation? Jews voice opposition and are embarrassed to be reduced to silence; heretics indulge in frenzy, truth opposes them, the cause of religion delivers an unassailable confession.[56]

As we noted Severian's openness to hermeneutical approaches not thoroughly Antiochene, so he can also be found eulogizing Mary as *Theotokos* and *Kyriotokos* to a degree not found in Chrysostom or his peers. One occasion is the text's focus on Eve's role in the Fall, where Severian duly highlight's Mary's role to the opposite effect. After agreeing with the position taken by the author of the Pastorals (1 Tim 3:11-15) on the basis of the text of Genesis 3:16, that women have forfeited the role of teaching and holding authority, he concludes, "So what? Has the female sex been subjected to condemnation and left to suffer pain, without the bondage being undone? Christ came, and he undid the bondage. The bearer of the Lord (*Kyriotokos*) appeared for the defense of her sex, the holy Virgin in place of the virgin, Eve also being a virgin when she sinned; she abolished the pain and the labor of the condemned one."[57]

Severian as Expositor of Creation and Fall

Of the sixty or so extant homilies of Severian judged to be authentic (all from his first

---

[55]PG 56:461.

[56]PG 56:465. The "breathing" of the soul into the man in Gen 2:7 leads in the seventh homily to a sustained defense of the creative role of the Holy Spirit in opposition to heretics.

[57]PG 56:.497. Voicu, "Sévérien de Gabala," 760, notes that Severian frequently makes the parallel between Mary and Eve.

four or five years in Constantinople), those surviving under the rubric *In Cosmogoniam* of 401 (to which arguably should be added a seventh) probably suffice to exhibit his exegetical, hermeneutical and homiletic skills, on which such a wide variety of opinion has been formed. For readers to arrive at a verdict on these features, it is ironic that the figure of Chrysostom proves his nemesis, just as Severian did in regard to his host in more vital matters. It can be admitted from the outset that Severian is no Golden Mouth. For one thing, in a comment on Genesis 1 he finds the carefully layered, repetitive, undramatic presentation of the Priestly author that leads to a sabbatical climax not sufficiently stimulating, unlike Chrysostom's more expansive if moralistic treatment. As the anthropomorphic Yahwist appeals to him more, he readily moves, despite his initial resolve, to focus on Adam's life in the garden and the Fall in Genesis 2 and Genesis 3. Second, and more significantly, he never achieves a sense of that key hermeneutical principle of *synkatabasis*, divine considerateness for human limitations revealed in biblical discourse, that is a feature of Chrysostom's exposition, which, though literal, is rarely literalistic[58] and is so necessary for interpreting this part of the Hebrew Scriptures in particular. Comparisons, if odious and perhaps unfairly drawn to Severian's detriment, are thus in this case inevitable.

We know nothing of the formation of the bishop of Gabala; he seems to have had a liking for the accents and the terminology that pupils in Diodore's *askētērion* in Antioch imbibed, while also displaying a refreshing openness to levels of meaning that those alumni, especially Theodore, did not exemplify. His strictly exegetical skills are no better or worse than theirs, and he shares with them an accent on comprehension on the Antiochene biblical text and its "precise" details. But he would again earn Theodore's censure for *akribologia*, a chase after such details when a commentator with a keener sense of the nature of biblical communication would leave well alone. As a result, he starts down a rabbit trail, and in pursuit he seems to have irritated his listeners,[59] despite his gift for dramatizing scenes between key characters—in the garden, for instance.

Diodore would have commended the respect shown by Severian for the hermeneutical principles outlined in the former's classes on the Psalms, at least in his spirited rejection of the attempt by allegorists to locate the garden in heaven; what he has to say on the illegitimacy of a spiritual interpretation of it is vintage Theodore. If he stands at one extreme of interpretation of the creation story, one has to concede that an allegorical and philosophical commentator like Didymus, familiar with Origen's treatment, hardly does it more justice.[60] Yet what earns the ire of a reader like Montfaucon in particular is

---

[58]For Chrysostom, A. C. Thiselton remarks (*New Horizons in Hermeneutics* [London: Harper & Collins, 1992], 173), "the 'literal' may include the use of metaphor or other figures of speech, if this is the meaning which the purpose of the author and the linguistic context suggest." Severian, by contrast, suffers from the basic incapacity to recognize genre.

[59]Regtuit, "Severian's Charm," 206, observes, "Severian's homilies are on the whole not well structured. His train of thought seems to be determined by association rather than logical coherence."

[60]Cf *Didyme l'Aveugle. Sur la Genèse*, ed. P. Nautin, SC 233, 244. For instance, where for Severian the firmament of Gen 1 is "a

Severian's literalistic approach to the primeval story; though beginning by doffing his cap to Moses as *prophētēs*, he soon treats him as *historiographos* and his work less as text than as textbook; anyone who contests his flat-earth cosmology is a heretic. Though Severian lets slip occasional glimpses of church life, liturgy and discipline, he has not the sensitivity to a sacramental dimension to the text to the degree that will be shown by his fellow Syriac-speaking bishop, Theodoret of Cyrus. Ever ready to forsake his text for anti-Arian theological polemic, however, in this work at least Severian hardly deserves the epithet Quasten accords him as "full of hatred."[61]

What this first English translation of the homilies *In Cosmogoniam* of Severian of Gabala may contribute is a glimpse of a commentator at work on a most challenging biblical text (if traditional Lenten reading), using exegetical and hermeneutical skills that could, like any virtue, fail by both excess and defect.[62] Close perusal of them may allow for an assessment less partial than one arrived at under the influence of regrettable historical events.

Select Bibliography

Brottier, L. *Jean Chrysostome: Sermons sur la Genèse*. SC 433. Paris: du Cerf, 1998.

Carter, R. E. "The Chronology of Twenty Homilies of Severian of Gabala." *Traditio* 55 (2000): 1-17.

———. "A Greek Homily on the Temptation (CPG 4906) by Severian of Gabala: Introduction, Critical Edition and Translation." *Traditio* 52 (1997): 47-71.

———. "An Index of Scriptural References in the Homilies of Severian of Gabala." *Traditio* 54 (1999): 323-51.

Datema, C. "Severian of Gabala: A Modest Man?" *StudP* 22 (1989): 104-7.

Fernandez Marcos, N. *The Septuagint in Context: Introduction to the Greek Versions of the Bible*. Boston and Leiden: Brill, 2001.

Hill, R. C. "*Akribeia*: A Principle of Chrysostom's Exegesis." *Colloquium* 14 (October 1981): 32-36.

———. *Diodore of Tarsus: Commentary on Psalms 1-51*. WGRW 9. Atlanta: SBL, 2005.

———. "His Master's Voice: Theodore of Mopsuestia on the Psalms." *HeyJ* 45 (2003): 40-53.

———. "On Looking Again at *Synkatabasis*." *Prudentia* 13 (1981): 3-11.

---

crystal-like fixture, raising half the water on high, and leaving half below," for Didymus it is the faculty of reason distinguishing good from evil (SC 233:62).

[61] By Severian's proclivity to class all adversaries as heretics, one is reminded of F. M. Young's remark about Athanasius (*Biblical Exegesis and the Formation of Christian Culture* [Cambridge: Cambridge University Press, 1997], 167), that on the one hand "the writings of Athanasius make it absolutely clear that the Arian controversy was about exegesis," while on the other "of course, Athanasius cannot admit to a genuine controversy about exegesis."

[62] Voicu, "Séverien de Gabala," 760, concedes that there has been no detailed study of Severian's exegesis and presumably hermeneutics—a lacuna this work may help to fill.

————. *Reading the Old Testament in Antioch*. BAC 5. Leiden and Boston: Brill, 2005.

————. *St. John Chrysostom: Commentary on the Psalms*. 2 vols. Brookline, Mass.: Holy Cross Orthodox Press, 1998.

————. *St. John Chrysostom: Eight Sermons on the Book of Genesis*. Brookline, Mass.: Holy Cross Orthodox Press, 2004.

————. *St. John Chrysostom's Homilies on Genesis*. FC 74, 82, 87. Washington, D.C.: Catholic University of America Press, 1986, 1990, 1992.

————. *Theodore of Mopsuestia: Commentary on the Twelve Prophets*. FC 108. Washington, D.C.: Catholic University of America Press, 2004.

————. *Theodoret of Cyrus: Commentary on the Letters of St. Paul*. Brookline, Mass.: Holy Cross Orthodox Press, 2001.

————. *Theodoret of Cyrus: Commentary on the Psalms*. 2 vols. FC 101, 102. Washington, D.C.: Catholic University of America Press, 2000.

Kelly, J. N. D. *Early Christian Doctrines*. 5th ed. New York: Harper & Row, 1978.

————. *Golden Mouth: The Story of John Chrysostom, Ascetic, Preacher, Bishop*. Ithaca, N.Y.: Cornell University Press, 1995.

Nautin, P., ed. *Didyme l'Aveugle: Sur la Genèse*. 2 vols. SC 233, 244. Paris: du Cerf, 1976, 1978.

Olivier, J.-M., ed. *Diodori Tarsensis Commentarii in Psalmos 1, Commentarii in Psalmos I-L*. CCG 6. Turnhout: Brepols, 1980.

Paverd, Frans van de. *The Homilies on the Statues: An Introduction*. OCA 239. Rome: Pontifical Institute of Oriental Studies, 1991.

Quasten, Johannes. *Patrology 2, 3*. Westminster, Md.: Newman, 1953, 1960.

Regtuit, R. F. "Severian's Charm: The Preaching of Severian of Gabala." *StudP* 27 (1993): 202-8.

Sáenz-Badillos, A. *Theodoreti Cyrensis Quaestiones in Octateuchum*. Textos y Estudios Cardenal Cisneros. Madrid: Consejo Superior de Investigaciones Cientificas, 1979.

Sprenger, H. N., ed. *Theodori Mopsuesteni Commentarius in XII Prophetas*. GO, Biblica et Patristica 1. Wiesbaden: Otto Harrassowitz, 1977.

Thiselton, A. C. *New Horizons in Hermeneutics*. London: Harper & Collins, 1992.

Uthemann, K.-H. "Severian von Gabala in Florilegien zum Bilderkult." *OCP* 66 (2000): 4-47.

Voicu, S. J. "Sévérien de Gabala." *Dictionnaire de spiritualité* 14:752-63. Paris: Beauchesne, 1990.

Young, F. M. *Biblical Exegesis and the Formation of Christian Culture*. Cambridge: Cambridge University Press, 1997.

Zellinger, J. *Die Genesishomilien des Bischofs Severian von Gabala*. Alttestamentliche Abhandlungen 7.1. Münster: Aschendorffschen, 1916.

SEVERIAN OF GABALA
Homilies on Creation and Fall

Homily One

On the first day of creation[1]

Our souls' improvement is the whole purpose of religious devotion; all the lessons stemming from religious devotion have regard to this business of saving our souls. The Word of God, for instance, is also concerned with this, the law of Moses supplies a basis for it, the spiritual statements of the Old Testament authors proclaim it, the New Testament authors cry aloud about it with mouths that are never silent[2]—everything in fact that is done for us and on account of us has for its purpose that in moving to improvement we may be found worthy of religious devotion. So all the holy Bible has our salvation as its theme, as I said above. Now, the book of creation itself is the beginning, source and power behind everything in the Law and the Prophets: just as it is impossible for a house to stand if no foundation is laid, so the beauties of creation could not shine forth, either, if creation itself had not had a beginning.

I am aware, then, that many of the holy Fathers, in composing a treatment of creation, uttered many wonderful and admirable sentiments to the degree that the grace of the Holy Spirit was conferred on them. Despite the many wonderful and marvelous statements previously expressed, there is nothing to prevent words being expressed by us as well on condition that the grace of the Holy Spirit is made available. After all, just as people before us were not discouraged by those before them, neither are we by those before our generation; it is the same grace of the Holy Spirit that makes available the ability to them as well as to us and those before them. Scripture says, remember, "All this is activated by one and the same Spirit, who allots to each one individually just as the Spirit chooses."[3] Accordingly, the treatment by the Fathers, far from being rejected, is transmitted in our treatment. Even if theirs is wonderful and ours insignificant, it is nonetheless all of a piece with theirs; just as a tiny stone laid in support will strengthen a mighty stone in the form of a cube that is fitted into a building and is slightly unstable, so too the statements of the Fathers make the building of the church better when in receipt of a slight addition.[4]

Now, I urge your good selves to pay heed to the thinking in what is said, concerned not with any novelty but with its truth; not that truth lies completely in what is customary, nor is novelty false—rather, the object of inquiry at

---

Homily One   [1]*Kosmopoiia*, the term Diodore had used for the first book of the Pentateuch, whereas we find *Ktisis* in Theodore and Genesis elsewhere. Severian proceeds to speak also of "the book of creation, *dēmiourgia*." The manuscripts and Savile and Montfaucon speak of them as homilies on creation, as does Severian, but he finds that topic insufficient for his needs and proceeds to Gen 2 and Gen 3. [2]The whole of the Bible (which is primarily oral for Severian), both Old Testament authors (*prophētai*) and New Testament (*apostoloi*), is salvific in purpose.   [3]1 Cor 12:11.   [4]Severian's self-effacing comparison with his predecessors is probably a convention (he may have Chrysostom's various series of homilies on Genesis in mind); Theodoret in the preface to his commentary on Paul compares himself with a mosquito buzzing about the apostolic meadows in the company of bees.

every point is whether the statements are true or false. I ask you not to pay me the compliment as a friend of accepting my words unquestioningly, nor as an enemy to reject what I say as unusual, but to observe at every point whether truth gives the nod to what is said. *In the beginning*, the text says, *God made heaven and earth.*[5] While the story is a composition of Moses the lawgiver and is a revelation of the Holy Spirit, it describes the creation performed by the power of God and revealed to Moses by the charism of inspiration; it is not as a historian that Moses said this but as an inspired author.[6] In fact, he told what he had not seen and described what took place when he was not an eyewitness; just as we previously mentioned three forms of prophecy—the first form of prophecy being in word, the second in deed and the third in deed and word—so in this case as well there are three parts to inspired composition—composition about the present, composition about the future, composition about the past. For example, no prophet was present—Isaiah, to cite one—when this happened in the case of Moses; but since the spirit of Moses was in him, it was inspired composition for the events to be revealed to him.[7] Now, there is also inspired composition in the case of present events, so that even if someone at the time of the inspired person wanted to hide something in his mind, the inspired person would rebuke him, as Elisha did Gehazi in predicting the future and unveiling what was hidden.[8]

Moses mentioned what had previously happened, others what was to come; this is therefore the way to approach this account, not as a record but as a truthful inspired composition uttered with the help of the Holy Spirit. Now, what was the purpose of the inspired composer?[9] Moses had two concerns, to develop teaching and to foreshadow lawgiving; though a lawgiver, he took as his point of departure not lawgiving but creation. Now, why did he choose first to present God as creator and Lord of all? So that he might be presented as God, giving laws not for other peoples but for his own; if he had not first presented God as creator of the world, he would not have emerged as a trustworthy lawgiver for the world. After all, giving laws to other people requires obligation, whereas instructing one's own is a matter of consensus. It was like John the Evangelist, who did not give pride of place to Christ's lawgiving before mentioning his lordship in the words, "In the beginning was the Word, and the Word was with God, and the Word was God. All things came into being through him, and without him not one thing came into being. In him was life, and the life was the light of all people. He came to what was his own, and his own people did not receive him."[10] It was only after saying God is maker and creator that he introduced him as teacher and lawgiver of all.

Moses in turn had a different purpose: why did blessed Moses mention heaven, earth, sea, waters and what came from them but not mention angels and archangels, seraphim and cherubim?[11] Because he was also adapting the

---

[5]Gen 1:1. [6]Severian had begun by speaking of Old Testament authors (as distinct from New Testament) as *prophētai*, a term where the accent falls on divine inspiration (not that New Testament authors were not inspired, but they were working in the light of the incarnation). A mere historian (*historiographos*, as here, or *syngrapheus*) or sage (*sophos*) was not generally classed as a *prophētēs* because not requiring that charism to the same extent, though in Homilies Four and Five Moses is called *historiographos*. Severian proceeds to speak of *prophētai* as commenting on past and present, though the word is most frequently used of those Old Testament authors whom the Hebrew Bible styles Latter Prophets, including Isaiah, who also foresaw the future, whereas it calls Former Prophets those commentators who reviewed the present, like Elisha. [7]Severian seems to cite the case of Isaiah as one, like Moses, who though not an eyewitness delivered a midrash of the creation and exodus story in Is 40. [8]2 Kings 5:26-27. [9]As an Antiochene, Severian identifies the author's purpose, *skopos*, as he will below as well. [10]Jn 1:1, 3, 4, 11. [11]Quasten remarks of Severian's work on Paul, "Most remarkable is his strong opposition to veneration of the angels which endangers the central position of Christ in the Church and in the universe. He blames especially the Christian converts from paganism for substituting the angels for the pagan gods which they adored before and for

lawgiving to his own times, aware as he was that the people he was speaking to had come out of Egypt after learning the error of the Egyptians, sun and moon and stars, rivers and springs and waters. So he omitted the creation of invisible things and confined his treatment to visible things so as to persuade people adoring those things to think of them not as gods but as works of God. In fact, it was not necessary at that time to draw their attention to angels and archangels in case he should likewise promote that failing in them; if they made that claim without seeing them, much more would they have thought angels and archangels to be gods if they heard them mentioned. Instead, he mentions heaven and earth, mountains and waters and everything that came from them, his purpose being to explain what was invisible from what was visible and present the architect from consideration of his works. The three youngsters in Babylon also did likewise; since they were living among that nation that was hostile to God and had no knowledge of God, instead worshiping idols; they said when in the furnace, "Bless the Lord, all you works of the Lord."[12] Why was it that, instead of saying, Angels, heavens, earth, fire, water, cold, heat and all such things, they listed the individual elements of creation? So that they might cleanse the whole of creation, purify all created things, and leave unquenched no spark of impiety. You see, just as in this case Moses also wanted to drive out of the Jews the Egyptian error, so he made mention of heaven and earth as things that were created, his purpose being to highlight what was made and mention the maker, saying, *In the begin-*

ning God made heaven and earth.

Now for some of my observations. I marvel at the way John and Moses used the same introduction, one saying, *In the beginning he made*, the other saying, "In the beginning he was."[13] Yet while the latter was pastorally minded, the former used precision; where creation was in focus, Moses put *he made*, whereas when it was the Creator, the Evangelist put "he was." Now, there is considerable difference between *he made* and "he was": what did not exist was *made*, whereas what has always been in existence "was." *In the beginning he made* and "in the beginning he was"; whereas being in existence is proper to God, being made is proper to created things, a distinction the Evangelist also observes, saying of the Savior, "In the beginning was the Word, and the Word was with God, and the Word was God. He was in the beginning. In him was life, and the life was the light of all people." He uses the word "was" six times so as to explain what was in existence.[14]

Now, after proclaiming the one who is and moving to the servant John, he said of him as of an attendant, "There happened to be a man."[15] God was in existence, whereas "there happened to be a man." If, however, they presume to claim also of the Savior that the Savior also "happened to be" and is no different from the earth, take heed, I beg you. If the heretic claims that Christ happened to be and did not exist before being made, in what way is he more than the earth? After all, Moses also said of the earth, *Now, the earth was;*[16] so if they take the phrase "in the beginning he was" in the sense of being made and not indicating

---

regarding them as mediators between God and creation" (*Patrology* 3:486). Here the danger of angel worship is presented rather as a relic of the Egyptian captivity, the point made also by Chrysostom in his first sermon on Genesis in 386 (probably known to Severian), as also to Theodoret in the several questions devoted to the subject at the beginning of his work on the Octateuch. In his *Commentary on Colossians*, Theodoret would also mention the wide extent of the cult of the angels in Christian churches in Phrygia, from where Severian hailed. [12]Pr Azar 35. Severian is probably citing the version of Theodotion (Dan 3:57). [13]Jn 1:1. [14]The commentator's precision, *akribeia*, in dealing with items in the text would, in the mind of an Antiochene, reflect the precision in the text itself—an example of what Chrysostom would call divine considerateness, *synkatabasis*. Every virtue can fail by excess; literalism is always a danger. [15]Jn 1:6. Severian is probably relaying the manipulation of certain biblical texts by Arians—in this case the occurrence of ἐγένετο for ἦν in the sense of "existed" when it can also have the meaning "was made"—to build a case for subordination of the Son. [16]Gen 1:2.

eternal by nature, he is nothing more than the earth: God the Word was in existence, and the earth was in existence. In the one case, however, he was in the beginning, not made, eternally existing, whereas the earth was in existence after being made. The lawgiver, note, did not say, *Now, the earth was,* prior to his saying, *In the beginning God made heaven and earth:* first *he made* and then *it was.*

We are aware, then, that these matters of detail seem tedious to the minds of the general run of people, but there is need to speak of deeper issues to people when they are alert in the period of fasting in particular.[17] "In the beginning he was" and *in the beginning he made;* hence his making the same introduction, "in the beginning" and *in the beginning,* the purpose being that the one basis of religious devotion should emerge, instructing the lawgiver in one case and enlightening the theologian in the other. The two Testaments, after all, are sisters, sprung from one Father; hence the teaching they offer is also in harmony, being as it were the same "image and likeness."[18] In other words, just as in sisters born of the one father there occur identical characteristics, so since the two Testaments were born of the one Father, they bear a close resemblance. Of course, in the Old Testament the Law takes precedence and the Prophets follow, and in the New it is the gospel that takes precedence and the apostles follow. In the former there are twelve prophets, each of them a member of the Twelve, the Twelve being of the company of Hosea; and there are four—Isaiah, Jeremiah, Ezekiel, Daniel. In the New there are twelve apostles and four Evangelists. In the former, likewise, God's first calling began with brothers, since he took Moses and Aaron as the first heralds; and in the Gospel he gives the first call to Peter and Andrew. And while in the former there is single grace, in the latter it is twofold; in the former two brothers, Moses and Aaron, were called, whereas in the latter there was a doubling of two brothers, Peter and Andrew, James and John.[19] Since the Savior wanted to prefigure to us the love according to the Holy Spirit and make brethren by disposition and spirit, he took nature as the foundation, attached natural emotion, and on that he laid the foundation of the church. The first sign in the Old was the turning of the river into blood; the first sign in the New was the turning of water into wine.

This is not the time, however, to develop the complete similarity; let us return to the text. *In the beginning God made heaven and earth.* In six days God made everything, but the first day is different from the others after it; on the first day God made things from what did not exist, whereas from the second day God made nothing from what did not exist, instead changing things at will from what he made on the first day. You for your part, if you consider and examine this and find it to be true, express your agreement; if you do not find it to be true, register your criticism, and I shall accept it. It gives me grounds for a lengthy defense. While on the first day, then, God made the materials of creation, on the other days he did the shaping and development of created things. For instance, he made heaven when it did not exist—not this one but the upper one; this one was made on the second day. God made heaven above, of which David also says, "The heaven of heaven is the Lord's."[20] This one is the firmament; just as in a house with two levels there is a platform in between them, so the Lord created the world like a single house and inserted this heaven as a platform in between, placing the waters above it. Hence David says, "He covers his platform with waters."[21] So he

---

[17]Commentary on Genesis was the traditional Lenten fare in the early Eastern church. [18]Gen 1:26. Chrysostom can also be quoted for the harmony of the Testaments. [19]In his LXX Bible, the Twelve Prophets stand ahead of the Major Prophets; to complete the comparison in moving to the New he is forced to invoke the twelve apostles rather than simply biblical authors. [20]Ps 115:16. [21]Ps 104:3. Severian subscribes to biblical cosmology.

made heaven when it did not exist, earth when it did not exist and the deeps when they did not exist, winds, air, fire, water—on the first day he made the matter of everything that has been made.

Someone may possibly say, however, While Scripture says that he made heaven and earth, it does not mention water and fire and air.[22] First, then, from his mention of the creation of heaven and earth he implied the contents from what contained them; by saying, *God made the human being by taking dust from the earth*,[23] he referred to the shaping without listing the organs or saying, God made the eyes, ears, nose, including all the organs by mention of the human being. Likewise in saying, *God made heaven and earth*, he included everything and implied the making of the darkness and the deeps; the text says, *Darkness was over the deep*.[24] Now, by *deep* is meant the mass of waters; the fact that deeps also were made Scripture confirms in the words, "Before the making of the deeps, before the earth was made"[25]—and so deeps also were made. Next, for the time when the air was made, listen to the text: *And the spirit of God moved over the waters*.[26] Now, it is not the Holy Spirit that he refers to here—the uncreated is not listed along with creation; instead, by *spirit* he refers to the movement of the air. Just as it is written in Elijah the prophet, "The heavens were darkened with cloud and wind,"[27] so in this case as well by *spirit* he refers to the element of air.

It now remains to show where fire was made. God said, *Let there be light*,[28] and the element of fire was made; it is not only our fire that is fire—the powers above are also fire, and the fire above has a kinship with ours. Now, the question arises why it is that while one kind is extinguished, the other is not extinguished. Because God also made the angels spirits, and our souls spirits, but he put our souls in bodies while making the angels without bodies. What he did in the case of souls and angels, therefore, you can see also in the case of fire. The fire on high is independent of matter, whereas the fire below depends on matter; the fire on high has a kinship with them, just as our soul also has a kinship with angels—as the latter are spirits, the former too are spirits, as the three youngsters also say, "Bless him, spirits and souls of the righteous," and again, "He makes his angels spirits."[29] A soul is not visible without a body, then, nor can fire be seen without straw or kindling or some other material. Now, in case an impression is given that fire comes from some outside source, creation gives a lesson. It frequently happens, remember, that many people make use of the sun to start a fire; if it came from some other source, how would what is foreign be taken from it? This is especially the case with the fire in heaven that is independent of matter and so great that fire appeared also on Mount Sinai; it did not spring from a base of timber—instead, God brought it into view from a fire quite independent of matter. Just as you would say our fire is tiny by comparison with that great one, so Moses also says, "From heaven he made his voice audible, and God gave a glimpse of his great fire,"[30] his purpose being to show ours to be tiny. Everything, therefore, is fire—lightning, the stars, the sun, the moon—and akin to our fire. Consider how lightning is akin to stars at the level of terminology: *astrapē* and *astra*. To bring out that fire and lightning have kinship, the Savior says in the Gospel, "The eye is the lamp of the body; so if your eye is full of light, your whole body will be full of light." These are the words of the Savior, who then adds, "As when the lamp gives you light with a flash of light," calling the

---

[22]Severian treats the creation story as a literalistic record. His cosmology is that of his time; his respect for it is unquestioning, whereas Chrysostom at this point might invoke the principle of *synkatabasis* to excuse departures from literalistic adherence. [23]Gen 2:7. [24]Gen 1:2. [25]Prov 8:24, 26. [26]Gen 1:2. [27]1 Kings 18:45. [28]Gen 1:3. [29]Pr Azar 64; Ps 104:4. Severian's approach to creation could hardly be called lyrical, his preference going to pedantry rather than poetry. Intertextuality is limited to proof texting. [30]Deut 4:36.

lamp's beam a lightning flash.[31]

Everything was made, therefore: fire was made, the deeps were made, winds, the four elements—earth, fire, water, air; whatever he omitted, as it were to our surprise, Moses included in his summary, "In six days the Lord made heaven and earth and everything in them."[32] Just as in the case of the body he did not mention all the items, so there was no listing in the case of creation, either, even if everything was made along with the world. If there were no fire on the earth, people would not today ignite fire from rock or from sticks; sticks produces fire when rubbed together. So be careful to pay attention. *Darkness was over the deep*, the text says. Surely, you ask, God did not make darkness, then? We admit that it is a profound idea, but since we often find ourselves in a group composed both of those listening loyally and of those inclined to take exception, we are obliged to avoid leaving the text without scrutiny lest there be little fulfillment of a lavish promise. So where did darkness come from? God did not make it, you say, since God in your view is not the maker of darkness or gloom. What, then, is darkness? Many people have taken the point of view that it is the obscuring of heaven; as the upper heaven was made and the upper lights yet to come, the earth was left naked and darkness occurred. But the upper heaven is full of light, not dark; and even if it did not have the sun or the moon and stars, it did have its very nature to give light. So if heaven was set in place and earth laid out—one giving light from on high and the other being enlightened below—where did darkness come from? In my view, then, when water covered the surface of the earth,

mist and gloom gathered around the waters, as happens even today on the rivers; mist gave rise to gloom in forming clouds, and the clouds cast shadows and produced darkness. The fact that clouds give rise to darkness Scripture states, "The heavens were darkened with cloud."[33]

Now, we should not be unaware of the heretics' allegories, either. Some heretics presumed to claim that the devil is darkness and the demons the deep,[34] and when God said, *Let there be light*—namely, the Son[35]—he was not only equal to him in status but also senior. While we should not even mention this impiety, however, we parade their arguments to prevent your being unaware of them. Accordingly, the darkness at that time came from the clouds. There was likewise darkness also in Egypt, not because it was night but because mist fell; there was likewise darkness also on Mount Sinai, not because night fell but because a cloud overshadowed it; there was likewise darkness also at the crucifixion of Christ, not with the coming of night but because shadows and opposition were generated. One should not idly assail the divine sayings in this way.

And the spirit of God moved over the waters.[36] By *spirit* he means the wind, as it says elsewhere: "With a violent wind you will shatter the ships of Tarshish,"[37] by "wind" referring to the movement of the air. Do not think, in fact, that air and wind are different things: when moved, the air itself causes wind, as is confirmed by experience. We often therefore move with a fan or cloth the air when it is still and by the movement cause a breeze. So to make it clear by mention of the *spirit* that the wind is a movement of air, he accordingly said *moved*;

---

[31]Mt 6:22; Lk 11:36. Severian is still responding to the reason for the text's failure to account for all four elements. He invokes any and all evidence, including lexical items, such as the similarity of the terms for lightning and stars and a New Testament statement (where his text of Mt is idiosyncratic or perhaps adjusted, "if your eye is full of light"). [32]Ex 20:11. [33]1 Kings 18:45. [34]Origen's position, Montfaucon says. In Antioch, the term "allegory" betokened an approach to the biblical text that took no account of its literal sense; Eustathius and Diodore had associated it with Origen. [35]Montfaucon appends an addition occurring in the Savile text: "That is, he referred to the Son being made. They did not blush to say the devil was senior to the Son. After all, if a demon is the deep, and the devil darkness, it was afterwards that God said, Let there be light, that is, the Son." [36]Gen 1:2. [37]Ps 48:7.

it was due to wind that there was movement in creation.

God said, Let there be light.[38] Why did Moses not say, God said, Let there be heaven, let there be sea, instead of saying in that case *he made* and in this *he said*, since with us word precedes action—that is, first we speak, and then we act? In his wish to show God first acting, so as to present creation as occurring more rapidly than any word. When he uses materials through power, he says *he made*, whereas when he was on the point of developing the whole world, and light was the beginning of the world, he inserts an appropriate word. And furthermore, since light was God's first work and the human being God's final work, God first makes the light with a word and later the human being with an action, completing light with light.

To learn how a human being is also light, listen carefully. Light shows what is in existence; the human being is the light of the world, and at his entrance he showed you a light of artifice, a light of knowledge. The light showed grain, intelligence made bread; the light showed grapes of the vine, the light of understanding showed the wine in the grapes; the light showed wool, the human's being light showed clothing; the light showed a mountain, the light of understanding showed stonecutting. This is the reason why the Savior also calls the apostles light in saying, "You are the light of the world."[39] Why does he call them light? Not only for you to honor them but also to show the hope of resurrection. In other words, just as the light fades at evening without being lost, and instead is hidden, only for what is hidden to appear again, so too the hu-

man being is consigned to the grave in a kind of fading but in turn is kept alive by the dawn of resurrection.

Let there be light. While he mentioned what had been made, he did not make mention of the manner, nor did he understand it; the fact that the light was made I am aware of, he says, but how it was made I do not grasp. This is the reason the Savior also said to the apostles, "It is not for you to know the times or the periods that the Father has set by his own authority." It is not for you to know times and periods at a later stage or to grasp the Lord of times and the maker of ages with human reasoning.[40] *God said, Let there be light, and there was light.* O that holy and marvelous power! *There was light, and God called the light Day, and the darkness Night.*[41] Why did he call it day? Since everything was bright and cheerful, it is called mild.[42] Hence we also call lovingkindness mildness, and we call tame animals mild. *And God called the light Day, and the darkness Night.* Why night? Because it evokes in the sleeping human being a reminder of death, as if to say, Be mindful, mortal, of who you are: you are mortal, in thrall to sleep. Why get ideas above yourself? Night, after all, brings compunction—hence David's saying, "Have compunction on your beds for what you say in your hearts."[43] Of course, a human being lies prostrate at night, neither dead nor alive. Ask a heretic this question: What is it to be, dead or alive? If he says, Alive, ask him, Why, then, is there no sense of people talking or walking around? If he says, Dead, ask, Why are you breathing? A breathing person is not dead; a person without sensation is not alive. You are not conscious of yourself—instead, you have ideas above yourself.

---

[38]Gen 1:3. [39]Mt 5:14. A more christologically-minded commentator (beyond Antioch) might have moved to the Johannine form of the dominical saying, "I am the light of the world" (Jn 8:12), to develop a christological sense of the pregnant verse from Genesis. Severian's development is more pedestrian. [40]Acts 1:7. The dangers of Anomean temerity discourage Antiochene commentators from prying into divine transcendence; Chrysostom had made a similar abdication when dealing with Isaiah's vision of the Lord (Is 6:1) in his homilies on that passage. [41]Gen 1:3, 5. This exclamation of wonderment at the divine power revealed in creation is rare in the homilist's mouth. [42]Though Eustathius had chided Origen for playing with words instead of getting down to the facts in the biblical text, we have seen Severian indulging in some less profound wordplay. Here he relates "day" (*hēmera*) to the adjective "mild" (*hēmeros*). [43]Ps 4:4.

So much for the first day, however; evening has fallen, and, just as in that case, we have exhausted the contents of the first day as far as possible, despite the ideas being profound as well. It is for believers to ponder what was said and examine the account.[44] Beneficiaries of holy fasting as we are, and enjoying heavenly things thanks to bodily deprivation, let us be zealous in observing the holy fast. Scripture says, remember, "Make holy a fast." Are we making it holy, or being made holy by it? The prophet meant by this for us to keep it holy, just as we pray, "Hallowed be thy name"[45]— not that we are praying for his name, since his name hallows everything; instead, since his name is invoked on us, being called Christians after Christ,[46] it means, May your name be hallowed in our case. After all, with the Holy One everything is holy, nothing unholy coming near God; God, who is holy, rests in holy people. Even his heaven is holy; Scripture says, "He will hearken to him from his holy heaven." The angels are holy: "When the Son of man comes in his glory with his holy angels." The land where there is divine worship is holy: "He will wish to overthrow a covenant in his holy land."[47] David says that his court is holy: "Adore the Lord in his holy court"; Isaiah, the temple is holy: "Holy is your temple, wonderful in righteousness." The irrational sheep that are sacrificed are said to be holy: "Like holy sheep in Jerusalem." The covenant is holy: "He will confirm his holy covenant with many." This city was said to be holy: "And on the holy city of your ancestors, Jerusalem." Nothing that is not holy, in fact, has access to God— hence Paul's remark, "Holiness, without which no one will see God."[48]

We fasted from bread; let us fast also from iniquity. Are you not eating bread? Do not eat the flesh of the poor, lest God say of you as well, "They eat my people in consuming bread." Are you not drinking wine? Let anger not intoxicate you, lest you hear from the lawgiver, "Their anger is like that of a snake," and again, "Their wine is the anger of dragons"[49]—in other words, when you abuse and oppress the poor, in God's eyes you will be convicted of eating bread won by sweat and tears. This is the reason that God also says, "Cover my altar with tears." So God reproves those weeping on the altar, saying, "Enter, priests, weep"—but his reproof is not for their weeping but because the wronged, orphans and widows, chanced to be there at the altar. And in order to bring out that it is to them that he refers, he went on, "With weeping and wailing and crying."[50]

It is worthwhile having an eye to your sacrifices. The Word of God is therefore a table laid for your soul. A body that is fasting is made holy, whereas a soul that is starved perishes; may it be your good fortune that the body fasts from sins and treats the soul to the divine teachings. You cannot eat the bread of Christ and the bread of tears; as Paul says, "You cannot partake of the table of Christ and the table of demons."[51] So the person who is fasting ought to keep away from food, and first from sins; every day angels keep a note of who proposes to abstain from avarice, impurity and injustice, the angels recording this fasting and God keeping a register of it. In other words, just as it is from the records that the rulers report everything to the emperor, so too the angels report to God everything that happens,

---

[44]Severian feels that he has done justice to the Genesis account of the first day and that he has even achieved profundity. The goodness of creation has escaped attention, however. [45]Joel 1:14; Mt 6:9. [46]See Acts 11:26, "It was in Antioch that the disciples were first called Christians." [47]While this citation is unclear, the previous two are from Ps 20:6; Mk 8:38. [48]Ps 95:9 LXX; not Isaiah but Ps 64:5 LXX; Ezek 36:38; Dan 9:27, 24 (approximating to the Theodotion version); Heb 12:14. Compared with a discourse that has to this point been rather bare of scriptural documentation, a tissue of texts has now come with a rush, though embroidering a point—the holiness of God and everything associated with him—that is not the speaker's focus at the moment. Has he just tapped a familiar battery of citations? [49]Ps 14:4; 58:4; Deut 32:33. [50]Mal 2:13; Joel 1:13; 2:12, the latter two loosely recalled. [51]1 Cor 10:21.

not as though informing someone unaware but in performance of a ministerial role for creation. For my part, I would have declared countless times more blessed the one who eats than the wrongdoer who fasts. I say this not to undermine fasting but to uphold religious values; it is not eating that is wrong but committing sin, as God says of a righteous person, "Your father did not eat but did my will." Likewise elsewhere as well, "The fast of the fourth month, the fast of the fifth and the fast of the tenth will bring you happiness, rejoicing and happy festivals; love the truth."[52]

The visible light has shone, however, so that the Creator of the light may be proclaimed, and evening has fallen to set the seal on the course of the day; let what made a good beginning come to a close. Instead of resisting it with ill will, listen to David, "To the end, do not destroy."[53] May God enlighten you all with this light, in word, law, faith, righteousness, self-control, in Christ Jesus our Lord, through whom and with whom be the glory to the Father together with the Holy Spirit, for ages of ages. Amen.

Homily Two

On the second day of creation,
and in response to the person who claims
we Christians should not say in the
Sanctus,[1] Lord Sabaoth

The Word of God arouses the soul's desire and envelops it in joy like a kind of lamp, so as to bring luster to its reasoning, cheer its thinking, cleanse it of sin and enlighten its ideas. That is what the Word of God is like: what a whetstone is to a blade, the Word of God is to the soul. It is not a single benefit that the whetstone brings to the blade; instead, it first has the effect of expunging rust from it, then it thins its thickness, sharpens it when blunt, brightens it when dull, cleanses, brightens and sharpens. So this is what the Word of God is like, causing the soul to expunge the rust of sin, sharpening it when blunt, thinning it when thick, brightening it when dull. The Word of God wants us to shine with the apostles' condition described in these terms, "holding fast to the word of life so as to be like stars in the world." Note the brightness: it wants us to be not blunt but sharp; it says, remember, "The Word of God is living and active, sharper than any two-edged sword."[2] It wants us not to be thick; instead, our mind should be thin in its ideas; wherever there is thickness there is alienation from God, whereas thinness of mind is in keeping with the law of God. Hence Scripture says in reference to thickness, "Jacob ate, was filled, became sleek and thick, and put on weight, abandoning God who made him."[3]

So come now, let the Word of God shed light on our minds, too, especially at the time of this holy fast, which thins our bodies and sharpens our thinking. Fasting, after all, is both the nurse of all sanctification and the mother of a pious mind. It is not a question only of how we are to fast but how piously we are to fast; many people fast through pressure of affairs, but it is not reckoned to them as fasting, since judgment is made on the intention, awards not going to sheer necessity. It was with this saintly disposition that blessed Moses on the mountain was instructed in the Law and was taught about creation. Yesterday, therefore, it was said by us that on the point of giving the Law through Moses God first presented himself as creator and then as lawgiver. How would the Jews have been able to believe that God made heaven and earth and everything in them if he had not first worked

---

[52]Zech 8:19. The preceding citation is obscure.   [53]The LXX has not helped Severian and his peers to see in this title to Ps 75, like others, a cue for the musicians to a familiar melody.   **Homily Two** [1]The Sanctus verse, or *trisagion* (uttered by the seraphim in Is 6:3, "Holy, holy, holy, Lord Sabaoth"), ushers in the eucharistic prayer.   [2]Phil 2:15-16; Heb 4:12. The analogy of the Word of God as whetstone seems original, if not subtle.   [3]Deut 32:15.

the miracles in Egypt that revealed him to be creator of the world? In our case we teach in order to persuade; God persuades in order to teach.[4] When Moses was about to expound and declare that God made heaven, earth, sea and everything in them, unless he had first worked the miracles in Egypt and shown that he is maker of all created things, the people would not have believed that God made heaven and earth. Unless Moses had first raised his hands to heaven and brought down hail and fire, and the people learned through the faithful servant that this mortal hand, when moved by the word of God, disturbed heaven and upset creation, much more was it the hand of God, who did the bidding, that set heaven in place and established earth; after all, no one moves creation without having first made it. Demonstration was therefore required that God made the earth; Moses extended his hand over the earth, and out came gnats. Demonstration was likewise required that God made fire; Moses took soot from a furnace, scattered it and filled the bodies of the Egyptians with ulcers burning like flame. Demonstration was required that God made the water; the water was changed into blood. Demonstration was required that he made the sea; the sea turned to stone, and the people passed over.[5] So first he demonstrated through the works that he is Lord, and then through the works he led to the conclusion that he is creator.

In similar fashion, too, the Savior in the Gospel did not teach before working miracles. In his first sign he changed the water into wine and is not presented as teaching before this sign; it was necessary that the work should precede and the word follow. Hence the historian says, "I wrote the first book, O Theophilus, about all that Jesus began to do and to teach."[6] How did the Savior mean to

teach that he is maker of the world? Unless he had brought light to the eyes of the blind, in fact, he would not have been believed when he said, "I am the light of the world." If he had not raised Lazarus, they would not have believed him when he said, "I am the resurrection and the life." If he had not made a paste out of mud and smeared the blind man, there would have been no belief that he is the one who took the dust of the earth to make Adam. If he had not walked on the sea, he would not have been recognized as Lord of the sea. If he had not threatened the wind, he would not have been proved to be Lord of the winds.[7] This is the reason that while being visible as man, he was acknowledged and glorified as God through the miracles. The Savior astounded the disciples, for instance, and they said, "What sort of man is this, that the winds and the sea obey him?"[8] He first showed the elements obeying him and then through the works led them to the conclusion that everything was made through him. He first showed them obeying him; if creation had not been first shown obeying him, John the Evangelist would not have been believed when he said, "Everything came into being through him."[9] How could the apostles have been believed when in their peculiar dialect they made assertions about the Word of God, creator, savior, sage and teacher? The miracles, however, served as language for the apostles; the apostles' mouth was a dead man raised, a lame man walking.

Now, the fact that faith follows miracles Scripture confirms in the words, "Many signs and wonders were done among the people through the apostles. Everyone was amazed, and more than ever each day great numbers of men and women joined them."[10] The miracles first shed their light, and the teachings fol-

---

[4]In other words, as Severian goes on to demonstrate, we rely for conviction on words, whereas God achieves that end by action. [5]Ex 8; 9; 14. [6]Jn 2; Acts 1:1, Luke in this capacity writing as a historian, *syngrapheus*. While one could debate Severian's point that the Gospels consistently present Jesus doing before teaching (to document his point that in the Bible creation precedes lawgiving), it resonates with another maxim that in the Bible, gospel precedes law. [7]Jn 9:5; 11:25; 9:6; Gen 2:7; Jn 6:19; Mt 8:26. [8]Mt 8:27. [9]Jn 1:3. [10]Acts 5:12, 14; 2:7.

lowed. Likewise also in the case of the Law, the miracles in Egypt came first, presenting God as creator. In his goodness, however, God did not wish reverence to be shown only to him; instead, he shared the glory with Moses. When God became visible in what he did, remember, Moses also was conspicuous in the glory he received; when he came down after receiving the Law, in case they should regard him only as a mere mortal, God suffuses his face with glory so as to complement the deficiencies of nature with the abundance of grace.[11] They considered, in fact, that a glorified countenance is not in opposition to God; the Savior likewise also made the face of the protomartyr Stephen shine. Now, why did he make Stephen's face shine? Since he was about to be stoned as a blasphemer for saying, "I see the heavens opened, and the Son of Man standing at the right hand of God,"[12] in anticipation God crowned his face with an angelic appearance so as to make those ingrates realize that if he were a blasphemer, how could he be glorified?

Yesterday, therefore, it was said by us that on the first day God made what exists from what did not exist. The marvel is that the works not only demonstrate God's creation but also rebuke the heretics' impiety. My question is, in fact, How did what did not exist come to be when they raise the question about the one who exists, how was he generated? If what did not exist had no existence, they say, how did he come to be if he did not exist? What does not exist has not been made, as far as human reasoning goes, but not in terms of divine power. Sometimes the heretic says, God spoke, and it was made. But in this case you mentioned the fact, not the manner. "God said, Let there be light";[13] what did not exist came into being. A word was transformed into a real thing,

like the term itself being uttered and becoming light; so it does not derive from what did not exist but from what exists. I mean, who presumes to claim that the Word did not exist? So he made nothing from what did not exist, but from him; and created things are found to be of the same being as him, and what they avoided in the case of the Son they apply to created things.[14]

Under pressure, however, they likewise make the claim, The will of God produced what did not exist; but will makes what does not exist; so nature does not generate what exists. That is remarkable. Let me cite an example, taking the case of a spring and a rock: which is easier, for the spring to generate water, or the rock? If the spring generates it, it brings forth what it has, whereas the rock does so from what it does not have. Thus, while the rock generated what did not exist from what it did not have, did not the spring generate a spring it had in itself? How was what did not exist made—surely not by accident? Is it not merely a name and nothing else? Do not get the idea, I say in the case of what does not exist, that what does not exist has any existence. Since then you cannot explain how what exists was made from what did not exist, will you presume to pry into the way the one who exists was generated from the one who exists? Far from existing from the beginning, all created things were made; the only-begotten Word and creator of the world was not made in the beginning: he was in existence. The former did not exist and were made; the latter existed in the beginning without being made, whereas they were made in the beginning after not existing.

Now, the earth was invisible, the text says. What is the meaning of *invisible*? I know that many of the holy Fathers have said, The earth

---

[11]Ex 34:29. [12]Acts 7:55. Have we strayed from Severian's original point? [13]Gen 1:3. Severian has left his point about creation preceding lawgiving in Genesis and, before continuing his commentary, has engaged subordinationist heretics in debate about the procession of the Son. [14]In other words, the heretics, who hesitate at applying the conciliar term *homoousios* to the Word, find themselves applying it to created things.

was invisible because it was covered in water.[15] While many ideas are pious, they are not true—for example, the three friends of Job, who saw him in his trials but condemned the holy man for the sufferings due to him and claimed, If you had not caused widows distress and oppressed orphans, God would not have inflicted this on you. Yet since they were ignorant of God's purpose, they chose rather to condemn him for sufferings due to him than to arrive at a contrary verdict against God for unduly inflicting them. They acted on behalf of God, and God rebuked them, "Why did you say what is not right against my servant?"[16] While the intention was pious, therefore, it was not correct. What, then, is the meaning of *Now, the earth was invisible and unfinished?* The translators translated it clearly, "Now, the earth was an empty void."[17] *Invisible* means not that it had not appeared but that it was so to say unadorned; it was not yet bedecked with plants, not yet wreathed in crops, not yet girded with rivers and springs, not yet enriched with various attractions of other kinds—just *invisible,* still unfinished as far as suitability for production goes. Scripture says of a brave and handsome man, "Did he not fell the Egyptian, a striking [visible] man?"[18] So can a man be *invisible?* He means worth looking at. Just as he said the Egyptian was a striking man in the sense of worth looking at, so he referred to the formless land as *invisible.*

On the second day God said, *Let there be a firmament in the middle of the water, and let it separate the water from the water.*[19] So he made this heaven, not the one above it but the visible one, making it out of water to be solid like crystal. I want to depict the arrangement for you; many things are transmitted by imagining them rather than by speaking of them. This water rose up over the earth, so to say, thirty cubits. Then God said, *Let there be a firmament in the middle of the water,* and from then on in the middle of the waters there was set a crystal-like fixture, raising half the water on high and leaving half below, as the text says, *Let there be a firmament in the middle of the water, and let it separate the water from the water.* Now, why does he call it *firmament?* Because he made it firm by comparison with the insubstantial and flowing water; hence David also says, "Praise him in the firmament of his power."[20] And to use another example: just as smoke that rises from wood and fire is less substantial and dense and on reaching the heights is reduced to the consistency of a cloud, so God elevated the waters that were naturally less substantial and fixed them on high. The truth of the example Isaiah confirms in saying, "Heaven was set firm like smoke." Being fixed in the middle of the waters, then, heaven raised half the waters on high. Why were there waters on high? For what purpose—for drinking, for sailing? In fact, that there are waters on high David confirms in saying, "And the water above the heavens."[21]

Note in this case the wisdom of the Creator: the crystal-like heaven set in place was made from the waters; since it was due to be the object of the flame of the sun and moon

---

[15]Gen 1:2. Severian realizes that he had not commented on every detail of the account of the first day and returns to this clause. Chrysostom in his third homily on Genesis (but not in his first sermon) had addressed this puzzling form *aoratos,* which seems a copyist's error for *aoristos,* one of the two terms the LXX employs to render the Hebrew phrase suggesting a formless waste; he accounts for it by the cover of water, as Severian says, and darkness. Theodoret will also take this position in his Q.5 on Genesis. [16]Job 42:7. [17]Severian refers to the alternative versions associated with the names Aquila, Symmachus and Theodotion, which were available in a copy of the Hexapla. Being Jewish, they often get closer to the meaning of the Hebrew than does the LXX. [18]2 Sam 23:21, the LXX term being *oratos,* which is perhaps best rendered here "striking" rather than "visible," even though Severian's contrast is thus lost. [19]Gen 1:6. [20]Ps 150:1. Severian depicts the cosmology of the biblical author without submitting it to critique. [21]Is 51:6; Ps 148:4. Severian's understanding of a physical firmament is at the opposite extreme from that of Didymus, who took the firmament to be reason distinguishing between right and wrong. Chrysostom eschewed a decision: "No sensible person would be rash enough to make a decision on it. Instead, it is better to be quite grateful and accept what it told us and not reach beyond the limits of our own nature by meddling in matters beyond us." (*Homilies on Genesis* 4.7).

and limitless number of stars and to be totally filled with fire, to avoid its being dissolved or burned by the heat, he spread those oceans of water on the surface of heaven so as to soothe and cool its surface and thus resist the flame and avoid scorching. You have an example as well: just as today if you put a pot on the fire with water above it, it resists the fire, whereas if it is not there, it is dissipated, so God placed the water to offset the fire so that it may have an adequate buffer from the waters on high cooling it. Consider the remarkable fact: there is such an abundance of moisture in the heavenly body under assault from so much fire that it can even lend it to the earth. Whence comes the dew? With clouds nowhere in evidence, the air lacks water; clearly, the heaven from its abundance lets drops fall on it. This is the reason also that the patriarch Isaac in blessing Jacob said, "May God give you of the dew of heaven, and of the fatness of the earth."[22]

Now, it is said that on the day of judgment the water above will recede, heaven will be dissolved through not having the support of the waters and stars will fall as a result of not having a path or station. Far from our saying this idly, it is the teaching of Scripture: "Heaven will roll up like a scroll—that is, be scorched, since what is scorched rolls up—and the stars wither like leaves on a vine."[23] Now, pay attention, I beg you, to something else of value as well: the waters above the heavens not only support heaven but also direct downwards the flame of the sun and the moon; if heaven were transparent, all the brilliance would escape upwards, since fire moves upwards and would leave the earth desolate. The reason, for example, why he compressed the upper heaven with unlimited water was that concentrated brilliance should be directed downwards. Observe the skill of the craftsman. In yourself, however, you also have an image of the crafts-

man's skill; God made in you as well the image of the four elements. Pay attention, I ask you: think of the heaven above as the head, what is above the tongue the other heaven, namely, the firmament—hence its name "ceiling"; above, invisible in the unseen parts, is the brain, below and visible is the tongue. So just as the heaven above is in the unseen parts and the world in what is described, and just as in the elements you find earth to be heavy, and water to be lighter than earth but heavier than fire, and in turn air to be lighter than water and heavier than fire, so too in ourselves the senses—taste, smell, hearing, sight—are not all equal. In proof of that, if you want to taste something, unless you place it near the tongue, you will have no sense of what is tasted; it is insensitive and cannot operate when at a distance. Smell, by contrast, operates from afar; for example, moving through the house you smell incense, though not seeing it. Sight in turn is more sensitive than smell; it sees a broad plain from a mountain.

The mind in turn is sharper than sight; it ponders heaven, earth, sea, and is found everywhere. Hence the mind is also an image of God; the mind ponders and immediately within itself creates marketplaces, depicts a crowd, a mob. Let heretics beware: if the mind is responsible for such actions, does not the mind's craftsman, who is more sensitive than any sense of smell, have a more speedy operation, a more ready power of creation, an incomprehensible nature? Now, I want to mention to you something novel as far as impiety goes but related to the faith when subjected to scrutiny, for you to learn what awful fads the devil comes up with, what he devises, what he suggests to the heretics—or, rather, they suggest to him. Today a certain heretic came to us in the presence of holy men and fathers and said (I mention it in case the report in any

---

[22]Gen 27:28. [23]Is 34:4. Severian strikes one as a rather naive transmitter of fanciful notions, content to find confirmation of them in colorful scriptural statement.

way should be relayed differently and cause different feelings of alarm), Father, Son and Holy Spirit are one divinity, one power, one kingdom; and we must ensure the removal from our soul, not to say from the altar, of the expression used in the *Sanctus*, "Holy, holy, holy, Lord sabaoth." Unless you abolish it, he said, you are not Christians.

Do you see the awful madness of the devil he was perpetrating? Do you see the root of hostility to God? Do you see the enormity of blasphemy? He wanted to decapitate piety, paralyze the Eucharist, abolish faith, uproot its foundations. Note as well the devil's dire purpose: he persuaded him to say, Father, Son and Holy Spirit, one faith, one power, one kingdom. He tempered the poison with honey, as falsehood always does when it wants to be believed; it is not believed unless it lays a foundation of seeming truth. How so, listen; it is not quite the same, but I shall tell it. When the prostitute Rahab admitted the spies and was asked, "Did the men enter your place?" she replied, "Yes," which was half true, adding, "but they left," which was false;[24] if she had said, They did not leave, the house would have been searched. She told the truth to win their confidence; she added the falsehood to deceive them. This man was like that, too: when we asked, Why are we to eliminate the *Sanctus*? he replied, You say "Lord sabaoth," which is not the name of God, it is the name neither of Christ nor of the Father. Do you see his vile and sacrilegious mouth? He was unaware in his simplicity that "sabaoth" is not a term for

God but a term for the hosts—in other words, Lord of hosts. Now, I mention also his fault; but before finishing I bring you also the good news: he repented, he prostrated himself, he cursed the devil, he prayed for forgiveness, he was welcomed back.[25]

Pay attention, then; since the topic has intruded itself, we ought also explain the occasion when blessed Isaiah heard this blessing addressed to God. Isaiah was a remarkable man, filled with zeal, a man of initiative, but an initiative based not on impudence but on zeal. At that time there was a king, Uzziah by name, who along with his royal office wanted to assume priesthood as well. Though the priests were aware of the consequences, for the most part they did not want to gainsay the king, out of respect for his office, regard for the throne and fear of the army. Isaiah himself also kept silence and did not oppose the king. When God saw the fear of the priests, the reluctance of the prophet and the temerity of the king, he afflicted him with leprosy on his forehead for presuming to touch the holy things; he was then expelled not only from the priesthood but also from royal office and remained a leper. Now, while God did what was proper, he was angry with the priests and especially with the prophet for betraying true religion, though present. God therefore observed silence toward the prophet and did not communicate with him until the transgressor died. When the impious one finally died, then God set aside his anger and was reconciled with the prophet.[26]

Accordingly, Isaiah says, "In the year that

---

[24]Josh 2:4, 5. Severian flatters the congregation with knowing the context of the story of Rahab and the spies. [25]We have strayed some distance from the day's topic; perhaps Severian had little more to say on the subject, having already discoursed on the elements. As he hinted at the end of the first homily, he is preaching late in the day, following an earlier *synaxis* (perhaps eucharistic, with clergy present). This incident, which may likewise have been introduced to fill out the homily, illustrates contemporary community processes for allowing exposition of heterodox views and readmitting their authors, unlettered or otherwise. This particular malcontent seems to have problems with the use of Hebrew (= Jewish) terminology in Christian liturgy. [26]Like Chrysostom in his homilies on these opening verses of Is 6 (consequently known as *In Oziam*), where the temerity of King Uzziah is the focus of attention, Severian cites the incident in 2 Chron 26 where the king tries to wrest priestly office and is punished with leprosy. Does Severian know these homilies (belonging, it seems, to Chrysostom's earlier ministry in Antioch)? Unlike John, he proceeds to embroider the text from Chronicles: Isaiah is said to be present, the priests offer no resistance (cf. 2 Chron 26:18); but like him he sees a penalty for the community in the cessation of prophetic inspiration.

King Uzziah died, I saw the Lord seated on a throne that was lofty and exalted." Why was God "seated on a throne that was lofty and exalted"?[27] God is invisible, whereas by being visible the king inspired fear. He gives the prophet a glimpse of heavenly glory so as to convince him of the kind of throne they were scorning and the kind of throne they were respecting, the kind of retinue, heavenly and angelic, they were failing to respect and take into account out of regard for a human retinue. "And the house was full of his glory," the text says, "and the seraphim were in attendance round about him."[28] The cherubim are his throne, the seraphim his retinue; cherubim means nothing else than complete wisdom.[29] Just as this throne here or some other one supports the person seated and offers honor and support, so too God's throne is wisdom, and by it God is supported; hence David says, "You are seated on the cherubim," that is, supported by complete wisdom.[30] This is the reason why the cherubim are full of eyes, on their back, head, wings, feet, chest—all filled with eyes; since wisdom gazes out from all quarters, its eye is open in all directions. "Each with six wings," the text says; "with two they covered their faces, with two their feet, with two they were flying. Each cried out to the other, Holy, holy, holy, Lord sabaoth," that is, Lord of hosts.[31]

"Each with six wings": eight keep quiet, four call out. So what does Scripture teach us? Not to practice any reasoning about God—rather, to proclaim some things silently, and in faith to glorify others and develop true doctrine about God. Now, why do they cover feet and head? Because there

is no beginning or end. With two they cover their head and with two their feet, obviously flying with the wings in the middle, not the ones above or below; in speaking about God we need to say what is central, that he is God, that he is creator, that he is Lord, that he is benefactor—all the central ideas. If you were to pose the question, How did he generate? you would uncover the head, which the cherubim cover. If you were to ask, Where is the end of God? you would bare the feet, which the cherubim cover. Now, they cover the head and the feet, not to conceal them but to convey that they are beyond scrutiny, that they are beyond comprehension. Adopt also a typological explanation: there were six plus six, twelve wings; eight keep still, four move—a type of the apostles, twelve apostles but four Evangelists calling out.[32] And what do they call out? The phrase that Satan was anxious to cancel. Pay attention, I beg you; it was not without purpose that they said, as we do, "Holy, holy, holy"; instead, they responded to one another, as the text says, "Each cried out to the other." It means, We ought to say Holy once; a second one says, Holy; then another, Say Holy a third time. Do not think, then, that because we have counted three, there are three gods. What does it mean, then, "Holy, holy, holy Lord"? One Lord, one faith, one baptism.[33] And just as in recitation of the psalms we direct the verses to one another, so the powers above recite in choir and utter the doxology as though it were the song's antiphon.[34]

It goes on to say, "The house was full of his glory. The lintel was lifted up with the sound of their cry, and the house was filled with

---

[27]Is 6:1. [28]Is 6:1-2. Similar to Eusebius (PG 24:125), Severian thinks there are more than two seraphim surrounding the throne. [29]Severian offers a typical Antiochene interpretation of visions of the temple. The numerous seraphim stand near, and the higher powers, the cherubim, are figuratively described as the throne of God (see Chrysostom *Against the Anomoeans* 3:24 [FC 72:106]). [30]Ps 80:1. See also Pr Azar 32 for reference to cherubim as throne. [31]Is 6:2-3. See Ezek 10:5 for reference to wings of the cherubim. Severian conflates eyes on the bodies of the cherubim described in Ezek 10:12 with the angelic powers of Is 6:2. "Each had six wings" refers to two cherubim. [32]While congregations in Antioch and Constantinople would resist allegory, as Chrysostom said in the first of his homilies on this Isaian passage, a rare recourse to typology was acceptable for a commentator. [33]Eph 4:5—a helpful reference for the *trisagion*? [34]Severian's church was accustomed to the rhythm of psalmody in use in monastic choirs today.

smoke."[35] A strange thing! From the doxology it was necessary to move to the glory;[36] what existed disappeared, and smoke made its appearance. Now, smoke is an image of desolation. So what does it mean? The Holy Spirit knew in advance that the phrase "holy, holy, holy" was applicable to the world, thanks to the apostles' preaching, and it was not the temple of the Jews that was its object. So he means that after the preaching of the gospel, the synagogue is filled with desolation and smoke. Now, it was not the door that was lifted up but the lintel. Take note: every door has a threshold placed under it and a lintel resting on the doorposts; doorposts cannot stand without a threshold, nor can they be set firmly and unshakably in place without a lintel. So the previous form of the synagogue was removed—not the synagogue in its entirety, which had doors, but in not having a lintel, the lintel being the influence previously exercised. With the removal of the lintel it was bereft of grace; with the removal of the lintel the doorposts were necessarily shaken even by a chance hand. As a result, every hand shakes Judaism. This is also the reason why a certain prophet said, "I shall make Jerusalem like a shaken threshold."[37]

"The house was filled with smoke." Where had the glory gone? Pay attention, I beg you. Isaiah had said, "The house was full of his glory," and then he says, "It was filled with smoke." So with the entry of the smoke, the glory had to move. To where did it move? Not to a single house; instead, it filled the churches throughout the world. And to show where the glory in the temple had gone, the cherubim say, "The whole earth is full of his glory." One nation was bereft, and the ends of the earth were enlightened. The devilish mouth said, Remove from the altar this holy phrase of the Lord, this kingly hymn of praise, this inspired instruction.

The fact that the blasphemy is directed against Christ the text makes clear. Whom did Isaiah see on the throne? He says, remember, "I heard the voice of the Lord saying, Whom shall I send? and who will go to this people?"[38] While he was reconciled with his servant, he still bore him the ultimate degree of displeasure. Just as in our case, if we are reconciled with a servant, instead of immediately gracing him with our complete attention, we slightly avert our gaze, so when God is unwilling to display his face completely, he says when the person stands before him, "Whom shall I send?" Just as if there were servants standing before the master and he wanted to chide them for their laziness, he would say, Whom shall I send? I have no one for this task—not that he has no one, but he has no one willing. Likewise God, too: Whom shall I send instead of him, the one who kept silent when the man assailed the priesthood? So what was Isaiah's response? Like a servant who has been found wanting, he is remorseful and anxious to make up for his former failings: "Here I am, send me." How, then, are we to prove that the glory was Christ's? John the Evangelist says, "Although Jesus had worked such wonderful signs, the Jews did not believe him, the purpose being to fulfill the saying in Isaiah, You will continue to listen but not understand. He said this when he saw his glory and spoke about him."[39] Do you see the peak of our salvation, the Sanctus? If the Sanctus is not said, the Eucharist is not celebrated, either. In this you have a figure: the cherubim simply said, "Holy, holy, holy Lord," and the sacrifice was sanctified. The text goes on, "One of the cherubim was sent to me holding a burning coal, which he had taken from

---

[35]Is 6:3-4. The day's theme continues to be sidelined; perhaps, as before with the tissue of texts about holy things in Homily One, Severian is tapping into a different topic on which he has ready-to-hand material. [36]That is, from the *doxologia* to the *doxa*. [37]Zech 12:2. The application of the Isaian verse to the synagogue, if original (like others), is contrived. [38]Is 6:8. [39]Jn 12:37-38, 40-41.

the altar with a pair of tongs."[40] He did not receive it until he was sanctified; the text says, "He touched my lips." Why his lips? The vestibule of the sacraments. What do we faithful say? This sacrament removes sins. The cherubim also said, "Lo, I have removed your sins."[41] Do you recognize the type? Do you recognize the splendor of truth?

Accordingly, let us not cease to declare holy him who is on a throne that is lofty and exalted. Instead, let us also give thanks for a soul that was ensnared,[42] that the wolf seized but the shepherd rescued, that the devil seized but the loving Lord saved, in order that every heretical voice and every tongue guilty of blasphemy in its frenzy may sing the praises of Father, Son and Holy Spirit forever. Amen.

Homily Three

On the third day of creation, and about resurrection[1]

The world's craftsman bedecked heaven with sun, moon and stars, wreathed the earth in flowers and plants and lent all creation variety. Our task is to resume the account of creation, admiring what was made and adoring the craftsman. After all, it was composed for us not only to learn that it was made but also to admire the maker. We were told that on the first day he produced the materials of created things, and on the second how he established the firmament from naturally insubstantial water—hence its name firmament. This is also the reason why when the whole world was insubstantial and enervated, dissipated with various forms of the error of polytheism, he gathered people together and made a single faith, and the apostle calls it firmament in the words "according to the firmament of faith in Christ." Accordingly, the deep waters were divided, there being deeps that remained below and deeps that were elevated on high. How is that so? David says, "Deep calls upon deep at the sound of your cataracts."[2] So the deeps were separated, and a firmament was made.

God said, Let the water under heaven be gathered together into one mass, and let dry land appear.[3] Since the wretched heretics make it their intention to examine everything and scrutinize the ways of the one who is by nature incomprehensible, let them explain how the water was gathered together, where it was gathered together and where it went once gathered together. In your view, after all, it is not simply statements that should be followed; it is the facts that must be looked for. *God said, Let the water under heaven be gathered together.* Where was it gathered together? In the sea; was not the sea then filled? The land was filled, and definitely also the sea. So how was it gathered together? People who are incapable of grasping what is invisible though close at hand pry into impenetrable depths, the incomprehensible depths of divinity, nor does the sea's incomprehensibility dissuade them from conducting a scrutiny of the craftsman. Hence let the prophet also say to the heretics, Let heretics be ashamed, said the sea, as in fact he did say, "Be ashamed, Sidon, the sea has spoken."[4]

How, then, were the waters gathered to-

[40]See 1 Kings 6:23-27. Why the substitution of cherubim for seraphim? Some modern interpreters suggest that the cherubim of the temple when exposed to sunlight appear as fire, or as the seraphim, the "burning ones." [41]Is 6:6-7. The phrase from the eucharistic rite, "This sacrament removes sins," is recited today, even if in a slightly different form. [42]Since much of the homily is taken up with this question of an objection to the form of the Sanctus that would have impaired the celebration of the Eucharist, *eucharisteō* here may have the sense not just of giving thanks but celebrating the Eucharist. **Homily Three** [1]The homily titles, which would not be Severian's, do not necessarily reflect the contents reliably; this one is a case in point. [2]Col 2:5; Ps 42:7. In immediately offering an allegorical approach to details of creation, Severian is departing from normal Antiochene hermeneutical practice. He shows himself also more literalistic than most Antiochenes in adducing David as cosmologist. [3]Gen 1:9. [4]Is 23:4. The lack of respect for the incomprehensibility of God (the topic of a series of a dozen homilies by Chrysostom, some delivered in Antioch, some in Constantinople, and an issue also in the homilies *In Oziam*, which Severian seems to have known) was the heresy of the Anomeans, who also denied the oneness of being of

gether? Listen. When God made the earth, the mountain hollows were not yet in existence; instead, as soon as he said, *Let the water be gathered together*, the earth was split and valleys were made.[5] The facts confirm that the earth has been sundered, there being islands and mountains in between. And the reason why God left the islands and the mountains was for you to understand that originally they were joined together but the word of God separated them: *Let the water be gathered together*, the earth was laid bare. Now, it should be realized that what we call earth today was not the earth that God made, nor did he give it such a name; instead, the name of creation from the beginning was dry land, as David says, "The sea is his, and he made it, and his hands formed the dry land."[6] The dry land was formed and was called earth, just as this firmament was made and was called heaven. With the division of the waters, therefore, the dry land emerged; bearing the appearance of land awash, for the waters had just receded.

As the earth was laid bare, therefore, the Creator gave orders: *Let the earth put forth a crop of vegetation, plants yielding seed, each according to its kind and likeness, and fruit trees bearing fruit with seed inside, each according to its kind and likeness.*[7] Not even this causes shame in the heretics. Plants and trees and grass generate according to their likeness, and yet God generated someone not of his being? And when in turn the four-footed animals, serpents and birds were made, God says, *Let the waters produce reptiles with living souls, and birds flying on the earth, each according to its kind.*[8] The animals, the reptiles, the birds, the swimming creatures, the plants, the grass, the trees generate according to kind and likeness, and only God generated someone not of his being? And when God created us, he said, *Let us make a human being in our image and likeness:*[9] the work bears a likeness, and the craftsman is not of the same being?

Note the remarkable feature, however; often the heretical vice finds a den. If you claim, they say, that the Son is in his likeness, we accept that, too; likeness in nature is one thing, likeness in grace another. We are in his likeness, he is his likeness; "whoever has seen me has seen the Father," remember,[10] whereas we are in his likeness. God's servants, however, need to inquire into the differences in the terms. God says, *Let the earth put forth a crop of vegetation, and fruit trees bearing fruit.* Then he says, *Let the earth bring forth four-footed creatures and animals.*[11] Why *put forth* in the former case and *bring forth* here? The plants and trees and fruit produce a yield annually. So since they were meant to remain on the earth and emerge from it, accordingly *let it put forth*, but *let* the living beings *bring forth* for the reason that once they sprang from the earth, they no longer depended on the earth, being given birth by natural succession.

And so it was: the word took effect, the earth was adorned; now the heaven also needed to be adorned. Why does he attend to adornment of the earth before that of heaven? Because of the likely emergence of the error of polytheism in regard to sun, moon and stars. *God said, Let lights be made in the firmament of heaven.*[12] Why did he not make sun and moon on the first day? Because at that stage there was no firmament in which he meant to fix

Father and Son (*an-homoios*). It would seem that Severian would class as heretical anyone wishing to evaluate the Genesis story at a level beyond the merely literal(istic).   [5]Severian's text seems not to include the explanatory sentence added to Gen 1:9, found in some Hebrew manuscripts, in Chrysostom's text and the LXX generally, "The water under heaven was gathered together into its masses, and the dry land appeared."   [6]Ps 95:5. Severian's naiveté appears also in this matter of the names, where he finds two terms in the LXX. It reminds one of Chrysostom's comment on Adam's naming the animals in Gen 2:19: "Those names he imposed on them remain up to the present time."   [7]Gen 2:11. Again no attention is drawn to the clause "and God saw that it was good."   [8]Gen 1:20.   [9]Gen 1:26.   [10]Jn 14:9.   [11]Gen 1:24.   [12]Gen 1:14. The bulk of the homily moves on to other matters. It had taken Chrysostom ten homilies of the larger series to exhaust Gen 1.

them. And not only for that reason, but also because at that stage there was no fruit that needed ripening, the fruit being produced on the third day. And in case you should think that they were produced naturally by the sun when creation was completed, it was at that time that God finally makes sun, moon and stars. From what did he make them? It was said, remember, that on the first day he made all the things from what did not exist and on the other days from what was in existence.[13] So from what did he make the sun? From the light that was made on the first day, which the craftsman transformed as he wished, adapting it to various appearances, in the former cases the material of light, in this case the stars; just as if someone produced a nugget of gold and later minted coins, so he would arrange for the ornamentation of light. In other words, just as he divided the single mass of deep water in the beginning into seas, rivers, springs, lakes, swamps, so too the light, originally one and with a single aspect, the craftsman diversified, dividing it into sun and moon and stars.

Now, I want to inquire how it was that God made the lights; he seems to have made them away from heaven and then to have fixed them above. Just like a craftsman finishing a picture and then fixing it to the wall, so God first made the lights away from heaven and then fixed them above, like a craftsman, as Scripture confirms: *God made the two lights and set them in heaven.* So how did he fix them? Surely the two were not fixed together? That would make no sense. What, then? By fixing them, according to the statement of God: *God set the lights, the greater light to rule the day, and the lesser light to rule the night.*[14] When the sun was set in the east, the moon was set in the west, since the latter was bidden rule the night and the former the day. So the moon was made, and on the first day full moon occurred; it was not appropriate for the new creation to be deprived of its fullness immediately—instead, the light needed to be shown as it was made, whereas later by its changing shape it indicated times and seasons and different weather. So as the sun ran its proper course toward the west, the moon immediately moves from its rising so as to fulfill the command *to rule over day and night.*[15]

A question now arises: Why did God make the moon full? Pay attention; it is a profound explanation. It had to be produced on the fourth day if the fourth quarter was to be revealed; but if in turn it was the fourth quarter, it would not have reached the furthest point west. It was therefore in excess by eleven days; it was the fourth quarter, but it gave the appearance of being at the fifteenth day. The moon now had a surplus of eleven days compared with the sun, not in creation but in brightness. As a result, the extra days the moon then had it restored to the sun; the number of days each month that the moon had was twenty-nine and a half, which in twelve months of the year amounts to 354. In other words, if you count twenty-nine and half days as a month, 354 days make a year, and so each year the moon restores to the sun the days it has in excess. If you can count, count them.[16]

Let there be lights in the firmament of heaven to shine on the earth.[17] Since fire naturally rises, God put a curb on its nature to ensure that its brightness went not upwards but downwards,

---

[13]A problem emerges for any commentator (Chrysostom included, who responds in similar terms) from the creation of the great lights after light itself. Von Rad remarks, "The Oriental did not consider the remarkable separation of light and stars as something that could not be performed, because he did not think of light and darkness exclusively in connection with the heavenly bodies (Job 38:19-20). But this separation could also be connected with conspicuously stripping the stars of mystical connotations and thereby depriving them of every creative dignity." [14]Gen 1:16. [15]Gen 1:18. [16]It is a contrived argument for supporting Severian's contention that the moon was full on the day it was created and to account for the lunar cycle. He is going to great trouble to vindicate all details of the Genesis account instead of leaving it be and moving on. [17]Gen 1:14-15. As though the Genesis account did not raise difficulties, Severian, who likes gilding the lily, embroiders it with other quirks of nature.

fire tending to move not downwards but upwards. If you have a torch, turn it downwards, and you will notice that despite your directing the appliance, the flame heads upwards. Since he knew this to be its nature, therefore, he constrained it so that it should not shine naturally but by command. Let one of you observe the way fire lays hold of oil in the lamp: the oil is forcefully drawn down whereas fire naturally moves upwards and emits a cry as though the object of force; if fire is obliged to move against its tendency, it releases a sound as though the victim of force, as though going against nature. After all, whenever something happens to an element against its nature, it cries out. Why? Whenever oil is put on fire, it makes no sound, whereas if water is put on it, it screams. One is a liquid, and the other is a liquid; but since the former comes from a tree as a food and the olive tree bears it, and fire is generally fond of wood, it is glad to welcome what comes from its kith and kin. If, however, water is put on fire, it screams, being hostile to its opposite. Fire is at ease with air, for they are related; if you blow on a lamp, the air turns the fire to smoke, because its kith and kin has gone.

Behold the wisdom of the craftsman, behold his power. He set the lights in heaven to shine on the earth. *And let them be for signs and days and years.*[18] What is the meaning of *for signs?* Astrologers raise false expectations by giving impossible interpretations. The fact that it is impossible to give interpretations bearing on people's lives Isaiah confirms in the words, "Let astrologers arise who scan the heavens, and let them tell you what is going to happen."[19] So heaven gives no sign about people's lives. Do you want to know what his signs mean? They signify heavy rain, winds, tempests, fair weather. The stars convey this meaning, a result of God's lovingkindness, so that the sailor may see the sign and avoid danger, the farmer may see the onset of a storm and take the initiative in plowing the land. It is a sign both of war and of peace. The Savior confirmed that they are obvious and require no careful study, saying to the Jews, "Hypocrites, if you see a cloud rising in the west, you say, A storm is coming, and it comes. And if you see a red sky in the evening, you say, Fair weather, and it is fair. And if you see a threatening sky in the evening, you say, A storm is coming." He then went on, "Do you know how to read the face of heaven, and cannot interpret this time?"[20] It is possible to observe these signs that betoken no danger—heat, storms, rain, fair weather—that are not irrelevant to religion and are related to God.

Now, it would be possible to extend at length the treatment of astrology; but there is need of a restrained coverage and a delivery that is not tedious; the mind keeps pace with the commentary, and reasoning fails at the same rate as the tongue. Let us proceed, therefore, to less complicated things. *Let them be for signs and times.* There is a difference between this *time* and another: *chronos* suggests measurement, *kairos* suitability. No one says, It is *chronos* for harvesting; no one says, It is *chronos* for the maiden to marry—rather, It is *kairos* for the maiden to marry, *kairos* for sowing, *kairos* for reaping. Solomon says, "A *kairos* for giving birth, a *kairos* for dying, a *kairos* for building, a *kairos* for pulling down,"[21] by *kairos* meaning a suitable time. This is what the stars signify—for example, the rising of the Pleiades the beginning of harvest; the setting of the Pleiades the beginning of sowing. While this is unrelated to impiety, it is related to religion, such times also being called festivals of God; God says, "Three times a year you will observe a festival for me: the festival of unleavened bread, the festival of Pentecost, the festival of Tabernacles"[22]—

---

[18]Gen 1:14. [19]Is 47:13. [20]Cf. Mt 16:2-4; Lk 12:54-56. [21]Eccl 3:2. It is wise of Severian to withdraw from further complexities and attend to a helpful distinction between two similar but distinct terms for time.

three times. Note, *signs and times*. Similarly, the moon is responsible for sabbath days and months. The sun maintains the seasons of the year—spring, equinox,[23] summer, autumn. The norms remain unshakeable: he spoke, and they were fixed; he ordered, and they were established.

Now for the spiritual meaning:[24] who is the craftsman behind this, who created it—the Father? No one gainsays that. The Son? Heretics join in unison but to ill effect, claiming that the Father made the Son and the Son made everything. Am I to admit the impiety? Since he seals the reasoning of the heretics with indissoluble bonds, let us ask the inspired authors: Does the one who made everything have someone greater, or is he above everyone? They fall victim to their own first principle. They claim that the Son made everything but the Father made him—pardon the blasphemy: repeating the words of the impious wretches is in truth horrifying. Nevertheless, let us imitate surgeons who insert their hands into incisions so as to cleanse the ulcers. The apostle was also obliged to mention vile practices, not for the sake of polluting his tongue but to cleanse the sins. They claim that the Son made everything but the Father made him. I shall ask the authors who made heaven and what is his status. The prophet Isaiah replies, "Thus says the Lord, who made heaven and established it, who laid the foundations of the earth and what is in it, who gives breath to the people that are on it and spirit to those who walk on it. I am the Lord: before me there is no god, and after me there is no god. I am, and there is no other." It is the one who made heaven and earth who says this, the Only-begotten, who according to the heretics was made and he then created. But in the words of his lips, "The wicked is ensnared."[25]

Blessed Jeremiah says, "Say this"—to whom? To the pagans—"gods who did not make heaven and earth will perish from the earth." The Lord, "who by understanding made heaven," is the one who is the living and true God. If the one who made heaven and earth is true God, and even the heretics confess that it is the Son who made heaven and earth, what contest is there when Christ says, "In order that they may know you, the only true God, and Jesus Christ, whom you have sent"? When the Savior said this either through the biblical authors or in his own person, he did not say by way of contrast with himself, "In order that they may know you, the only true God," but by way of distinction from the false gods. Hence Paul also says, "You were converted from idols to serve the living and true God." He calls him "true" to refute the false ones and "living" to insult the dead idols. I think—or, rather, I am convinced—that our dead would be angry with us if they heard that we call the idols "dead"; you insult our condition, they would say: we are called dead after once being alive, whereas "gods who did not make heaven and earth are to perish."[26]

It is the Lord "who by understanding made heaven" who is the living and true God. Who is the living God? The one who made heaven. Surely the heretics' definitions do not stand up. Does not their impiety fall? Is not their godliness found wanting? Is not their knavery undone? You are unable to comprehend the works of the Creator and pry into the craftsman and search him out. What is David's cry? "How your works are magnified, O Lord! You made everything in wisdom."[27] Biblical authors magnify the works; heretics diminish the craftsman. He is the one who is mighty in counsel and powerful in deeds; I do not stop marveling. It is composed of water, and it bears water; it was composed of water, and it carries

---

[22]Deut 16:16.   [23]Montfaucon notes that a different edition had replaced "equinox" with "winter."   [24]Severian, whom we have seen ready to offer allegorical interpretations, now proceeds from a close literalistic study of the text to a spiritual meaning, *nous*.   [25]Is 42:5; 43:10-11; Ps 9:16. As in the previous homily, Severian digresses to an anti-subordinationist argument that seems intentional and indebted to a ready-to-hand arsenal of texts.   [26]Jer 10:11; Ps 135:5; Jn 17:3; 1 Thess 1:9.   [27]Ps 104:24.

the deeps—the marvel is completely unparalleled. Have you seen sheets carried from the water, carrying snow from on high? Winter was responsible; is it not God who is responsible?

He did not create heaven as a sphere, as the idle talkers claim; he did not make it as a sphere moving on its axle. Rather, as the prophet asks, what course does the sun follow? "He arches the heaven like a curved roof and extends it like a tent." None of us is so impious as to be convinced by the idle talkers. The biblical author says that heaven has a beginning and an end; hence the sun does not climb—it travels. Scripture says, "The sun had emerged upon the earth when Lot entered Zoar"; so it is obvious that the sun emerged, as Scripture says, and did not climb. And again, "From the furthest point of heaven was its emergence,"[28] not its ascent: if it were a sphere, it would not have a furthest point; what is the furthest point of something completely circular? Surely it is not only David who says this, therefore, or even the Savior? Listen to his words: "When the Son of man comes in his glory, he will send his angels with a loud trumpet call, and they will gather his elect from one end of heaven to the next."[29]

Now, let us inquire where the sun sets and where it travels at night. According to the pagans, under the earth; according to us, since we claim heaven is a tent, where? Pay attention, I beg you, as to whether that view is false; if you have a guarantee confirmed by the truth, the place is consistent with the expression. Think of it in terms of a curved roof superimposed: east is in one direction, as the pattern requires, north another, south another, west another. When the sun rises and is destined to set,

instead of setting under the earth it proceeds to the ends of heaven, travels to the northern regions, concealed as it were by a wall since the waters prevent its course being visible, traverses the northern regions and reaches the east. How is this known to us? Blessed Solomon says in Ecclesiastes, a text that is authentic, not spurious, "The sun rises, and the sun sets; on rising, it travels to its setting, and goes around to the north. It goes round and round, and rises in its place."[30] Note its traveling south and turning north in the period of winter; since it does not rise due east but verges to the quarter of the south and follows a shorter route, it produces a briefer day, and on setting in due course it travels in a circle and produces a longer night. We know that the sun does not always emerge at the same point; so how are the days briefer? Its rising verges towards the southerly quarter; then, instead of going to the heights, it reduces its course and makes the days short. On setting at the furthest point of setting, conversely, it has to cover all the west and all the north in its circle through the night to reach the furthest point of the south, the inevitable result being a long night. When, by contrast, the course is of equal length and the journey equal, it produces days of average length. Likewise, when it turns towards the north, as in winter it turns towards the south, it mounts to the furthest point of the north, is elevated and produces a day of great length, whereas when its circle is short, it produces a night that is brief.[31]

The pagan savants did not teach us this, nor is that their view; rather, they claim that the stars and the sun travel under the earth. Our Scriptures, the divine teacher, the Scriptures teach us, enlighten us. He then created the

---

[28]Is 40:22; Gen 19:23; Ps 19:6. [29]Mt 24:31. We have seen Severian not only prepared to accept biblical cosmology without question but also —unwilling to let sleeping dogs lie—anxious to pursue the implications of its flat-earth view of the universe. [30]Eccl 1:5-6, a proto-canonical Wisdom book that Severian presumes his listeners will find unimpeachable, in a form that departs from others of the LXX or is just the result of Severian's loose recall of Scripture. These verses do not get a mention in Chrysostom's commentary on Ecclesiastes. [31]Severian is dogmatic in his astronomical views, making the same points more than once. He proceeds to claim the Scriptures as his teacher in cosmology.

sun, an unfailing light, the moon, which doffs its beauty and in turn dons it. He brings out the achievement of the craftsman; the craftsman is indefatigable, his achievement eternal, the light of the moon never consumed, only concealed. Now, this is also an image of us mortals. Consider how many ages it has been rising; and if it is the first quarter, we say, Today the moon is born. Why? Because it is an image of our bodies: it is born, it waxes, it becomes full, it wanes, it diminishes, it sets; and we likewise are born, we grow, we reach maturity, we pass our prime, we fail, we become old, we die, we set. But in due course it is born, as we too are destined to rise and another birth awaits us. This is the reason why, in his wish to bring out that, as we were born here, we shall again be born, the Savior says, "When the Son of man comes at the rebirth."[32] The moon gives a pledge of resurrection, saying, Note the way I am concealed and in turn brought to light, and do you forsake hope for yourselves? Was not the sun made for our sake? the moon for our sake? everything that was made? In fact, what is there that does not give a pledge of our resurrection? Is not night an image of death? Bodies are felled by darkness; do you not discern outlines? Often with your hand you grope the faces of those asleep, unaware which face is which, asking questions so that their voice may be a herald of those concealed in darkness. Just as night conceals our outlines, therefore, even if we are all the same and no one knows anyone else, so death comes and obscures outlines, so that no one knows anyone else. You wander among the graves; if you see many skulls in a tomb, do you know whose they are? But the one who shaped them knows, the one who took them is aware whence these forms developed. Are you not in admiration of God's creative power? In so many forms among such countless numbers there are none identi-

cal; even if you travel to the ends of the world, you will not find two alike—and even if you did find a likeness in nose or eye, it would be extraordinary. Twins come forth from a single womb, and the likeness is terminated.

Further, is not the one who produced so many forms when they did not exist capable of renewing them when he dissolves them? Wretched mortal that you are, do not measure God's power by your own reasonings; do not get the idea that God's power is limited by the limitations of your reasoning. If his power had the limits of my thinking, I would dare to say that God is far smaller; after all, it was my mind that set his limits. But if he outstrips our thinking and surpasses our reasoning, the Creator is unsearchable and his works incomprehensible. Let questions be put to heretics by what is visible so that they may realize their own uncertainty. Since God said, *Let a firmament be made,* and immediately the word took effect, he left it as a guarantee for us that it was he who made it. Today we leave the sky clear at evening time, and on getting up in the morning we find another firmament fixed in the clouds. There are individual guarantees after the first, when you see the sky darkened and another firmament from the clouds.[33] The one who now makes clouds in a brief moment shows how he then in a brief moment made the sky.

Why does he do it? How do the clouds send rain? He made the clouds like wineskins, and through them he draws up the seawater, which is salty, fills the clouds, transforms the water and gives the earth a drink. Let them explain how what is heavy is lifted on high, how it is drawn up, how the clouds are drawn up. Far from being immediately emptied, they travel long distances wherever the Lord bids, and it is due to a command of God like shackles imposed on them that he does not

---

[32]Mt 19:28. [33]Montfaucon notes that this sentence occurs in parentheses in Savile's earlier edition, perhaps suggesting that it seems an intrusion.

allow them to rain until he wills. Now, that they are wineskins David confirms: "He who gathers seawater like a wineskin."[34] Observe the marvel: he gathers the water, the undying and invisible hand rests on it, not allowing it to be emptied all at once, only gradually. Just as a woman develops a fine thread and divides the wool into many different strands, so he apparently separates the immense depths of the sea into drops and thus releases it on the earth.

The remarkable thing, however, is this: if it is let go, why is it not emptied all at once? If it is held up, why does it flow? While the example you have is limited, it is still able to convince you. Did you see one who laid hold of the water? Did you see how it was perforated from below? The hand resting on it holds the load, and it is blocked below on account of what is resting on it above. This is the way God's undying finger rests on the clouds, releasing as much as it wants and holding as much as it wants, the purpose being to dispatch the gift throughout the whole earth. He does this particularly in late rainstorms, when he floods the whole earth, giving a drink at one time to this region, at another time to another. Hence the author says, "He will rain on one city and not rain on another city; one part gets rain, and another part where there is no rain will dry up." It is not the finger of God that rests on it, however, but the dispatch; I used the figure as a type of our situation. He gives instructions, and they do not rain. Scripture says as much: "I shall instruct the clouds not to send rain."[35]

"How your works are magnified, O Lord! You have made everything in wisdom." Do you see God's creative activity? Do you see how he stops the mouths of heretics, who are ignorant of creation and yet pry into the Creator? All things obey God's law: heaven stood still, not under pressure from its own force but set firm by a divine law. Whenever you are uncertain as to how heaven was solidified from water, in fact, blessed David resolves your uncertainty in the words, "By the word of the Lord the heavens were set firm."[36] Why "set firm"? Because they are made of water; nowhere is what is set firm said to be firm. No one can say, The rock is set firm; it is one thing to be firm, another to be set firm. It is set firm when what is insubstantial and flimsy is fixed—hence Peter's saying when he cured the paralytic, "You Israelites, why do you wonder at this, or why do you stare, as though by our own power or piety we had made him walk? The God of our fathers, the God of Abraham, Isaac and Jacob, has glorified his servant Jesus, and it was by faith in his name that his name has made firm this man whom you see and know."[37] He made firm the paralytic; hence "by the word of the Lord the heavens were set firm." From the insubstantial and flowing waters by the word of the Lord the clouds are raised on high. Take note, I ask you: the bitter water is transformed; the clouds are drawn up from the sea, and they make what is bitter on being drawn up from the depths sweet and potable. Christ raised us from the depths, and we do not lay aside our bitterness.

Who is it who created heaven and earth? For me the answer is, Christ. How do I arrive at that? Because unless he were Lord of all, in the Gospel he would not have worked miracles involving all created things. In fact, he worked through all elements—earth, sea, air, fire—so as to be shown to be Lord of all created things. The light of evening succeeded to the light of day. Sun shines, and a lamp

---

[34]Ps 33:7. Having left commentary on the text behind him, Severian moves to still another polemical rebuttal of a scientific explanation, evaporation of salty seawater that falls as fresh water on the land. [35]Amos 4:7; Is 5:6 (the term "dispatch" between these two citations troubling all editors). Again Severian has started a hare, raising the question of persistent showers instead of instant release of all the rain. [36]Pss 104:24; 33:6. Severian starts another hare; he would seem inclined to be contentious. His imaginary opponents are heretics many and varied: those who see the Son as a creature, those who pry into creation, those who contest Severian's flat-earth cosmology and his views on the nature of the firmament and the source of fresh water. [37]Acts 3:12-13, 16.

carries a torch; end of day and beginning of night. But in your case, when you see lamp and sun, say, "Yours is the day, and yours the night, you produced light and sun." The torchbearer does not dispute the command; the sun must run its course at his bidding ("The sun knows its setting," remember) to provide proof that Christ is the Lord of all created things. John proclaims that "all things were made through him, and without him not one thing came into being," yet he had to shine not only in word but also in deed. He says to the sea, "Peace, be still";[38] it was still, the artifact acknowledging the artificer. He spoke to the sea, note, and it was silent, he spoke to the wind, and it was still. If it had not obeyed, he would not have made it; if he were not Lord of the water, he would not have changed the water into wine; if he were not Lord of heaven, a star would not have announced him from heaven; if he were not Lord of the sun, he would not have been enveloped in darkness on the cross. Christ was on the cross, and the sun was darkened—what a portent! Not even creation could bear the insult to the Lord. The sun was darkened for you to recognize the Lord even on the very cross; the earth was shaken for you to learn that it was of him that David said, "He who gazes on the earth and makes it tremble"; the rocks were split for you to learn of whom the prophet said, "His anger wastes principalities, and the rocks were cracked by him."[39] The tombs opened for the resurrection to be apparent and for God in raising him to be resplendent in everything.

We need, however, to provide also a moral comment. The lamp prompts us to say, "Your word is a lamp for my feet and a light for my paths." Evening has fallen for us to say, "Let my prayer be directed as incense in your sight, the raising of my hands an evening sacrifice." Why not morning? Give thought to this: we ought understand what we sing; David says, "Sing with understanding."[40] "The raising of my hands an evening sacrifice." Moses—or, rather, God—bade two sacrifices be offered, one in the morning, one in the evening.[41] The dawn one was in thanksgiving for the night; the person who was preserved through the night gives thanks in the day. The evening sacrifice was in thanks for the day; since you watched over me in the day, it meant, I give thanks to you for the whole day. The evening sacrifice does not include the one who sinned during the night—hence his saying, "The raising of my hands an evening sacrifice": go in at evening, stretch out your hands; if they make a confident appeal, let them be extended; if they made no unjust entries, if they did not rob the poor, if they did not oppress orphans, let them be uplifted as though representing a face.

"The raising of my hands"—in other words, See, Lord, my hands are clean; just as the one who has sinned, instead of being able to lift his face, is stooped under the weight of conscience, so too a defiled hand does not dare to face God directly. See; if hands are clear of iniquity, let them be extended. This is the reason that the patriarch Abraham declined to make a profit when the king of Sodom said to him, "Take everything, only release the women."[42] So as to be able to speak confidently, therefore, he took nothing; with clean hands he said, "I shall stretch out my hands to God, who made heaven and earth," and he stretched them out, since they were not defiled with unjust gain. "The raising of my hands." Paul commented on the phrase "the raising of my hands" thus: "I desire, then, that the men should pray in every place by raising holy hands without wrath or argument."[43] Evening requires of us the duties of evening: you raise your hands, the craftsman examines them. The morning time comes, and

---

[38]Pss 74:16; 104:19; Jn 1:3; Mk 4:39. [39]Ps 104:32; Nah 1:6. [40]Pss 119:105; 141:2; 47:7 LXX. Other Antiochenes like Chrysostom and Theodoret place importance on comprehension in recitation of the psalms, lamenting frequent lack of it. Severian's mention of a lamp and evening suggest a noneucharistic synaxis that has continued till late in the day, reminding us of Chrysostom's rebuke to his congregation in his Sermon Four on Genesis for being distracted by the lamplighter. [41]Cf. Ex 29:39. [42]Gen 14:21 loosely recalled. [43]1 Tim 2:8.

if you do not have a hand or mind that is clean, you do not presume to behold the morning time, either; experience is the teacher. Consider how when you continue to be clean, you enter with confidence as though treading your own halls; self-control during the night gives you confidence at the morning time. Hence David says, "If I remembered you on my bed, I meditated on you in the morning."[44]

I thank God when I remember that the word of God restored our fading voice, out of consideration not for our worthiness but for your desire. Let us therefore pray with truth of heart to enjoy peace, have confidence in the morning, shun heretical madness, adhere to orthodox faith and give glory to the Father, the Son and the Holy Spirit, now and always, for ages of ages. Amen.

Homily Four

On the fourth day of creation

The grace of God strengthened our fading voice on the last occasion,[1] thanks to your prayers and your desire. Using experience itself as a teacher, therefore, to the extent that desire and zeal in love of God allows, I come to the same task of exhortation, requiring you again to beg the same grace for your sake. Paul, a vessel of election, remember, having Christ within him to do the speaking and guided by the Holy Spirit, used the prayer of the listeners as a pledge, saying, "Brethren, pray for me so that a message may be given to me when I open up my mouth."[2] So how much more shall we, though lowly and as it were a nothing, beg your intercession so that the bond of our tongue may be loosed and a forthright message opened up, that divine grace may also maintain an unimpeded instrument and provide an abundant supply of ideas lest only the one uttering divine things be the better for it, and instead along with you he may draw heavenly riches.

So come now, let us pick up the sequence; it is fitting, in my view, that just as Moses the lawgiver accomplished the treatment of creation in orderly sequence, so it also behooves us to connect third to second stages while carefully distinguishing them and transmit to you an unconfused introduction to the account. Heaven was fixed in place, the firmament established, the sea portioned off, the earth cleared and supplied with a variety of crops, plants, trees, springs and in short everything needed to beautify it. The yield generated from it, in fact, far from lacking variety, was diverse and manifold: some things decorated the earth itself, some were made for the nourishment of human beings and brute beasts, others met the needs of the aforementioned people. Now is not the time, in fact, to review the different kinds of things growing from the earth, in case your ears are offended by the length of the treatment.[3]

Heaven was the beneficiary of its peculiar adornment. God then progressed to the waters and caused them to produce a living soul, the great and all-wise creator, who by his free will and holy word was responsible for everything. You know the truth of the facts from the very truth of the Word, when you hear him saying, *Let the waters be gathered together*, and immediately effect is given to the word. Likewise, *Let the earth put forth, Let the waters bring forth, Let lights be made*.[4] It would take a long time at this stage to review everything made by the Word; leaving behind the account of creation in the Old Testament, let us move to the account in the New of what was made by him through the Word alone. He it was, in fact, who created things of old and made new

---

[44]Ps 63:6.   **Homily Four** [1]Severian, still conceding his faltering, implies that he had spoken "yesterday." He will say so before the end of the homily.   [2]Eph 6:19.   [3]Probably a conventional disclaimer, especially since Severian has been unable to get sufficient mileage out of the text of each day of creation to sustain his homily on it.   [4]Gen 1:9, 11, 20, 14 (not quite in sequence).

things, according to John's account: "Everything was made by him, and without him not one thing was made."[5] What sort of account could describe this precisely?

Let us proceed with the sequence, however. This all-holy Creator, then, as we previously said, also adorned what he made first, and to what was made second he gave adornment in second place; likewise to third, fourth and all the rest in order of creation he also supplied ornamentation. Now, why did he make a point of this? Was he perhaps intending to teach us to respect even the limits of the elements themselves and acknowledge their order? He therefore first made the heaven above, second the earth, third the firmament, and fourth he separated the waters. What he made first he adorned first. How, then, some of the more inquisitive will ask, did he adorn the earth first when it was made second, their intention being to take issue with the account's being at odds with itself, as it were? The reply to them should be that nothing inconsistent was said by us in this case—instead, the account proves to be consistent: before this firmament, which was made after the heaven above and was established on the second day, the earth was adorned, there being need to observe the proper priority. When he had adorned the earth with plants and crops, when he had beautified heaven with sun and moon and the rest of the company of the stars, he proceeded to the waters.

What does the historian say? *And God said, Let the waters bring forth reptiles with living souls, and on the earth birds flying across the firmament of heaven.*[6] See the word of God putting words into effect and turning directions into actions; note God's syllables and words, brief but full of power. *Let the waters bring forth*: God's task is the word. In my view,

the works preceded the word, the power being swifter than the utterance; the word was not yet spoken, and the work was given its particular adornment. And what is remarkable is that God gave each of these elements double adornment; to the firmament he gave lights and dew, though the use of these lights was varied. This was made clear from the very words of Scripture, about which we discoursed the other day[7] in accord with our ability, if not worthily, when we outlined to you our treatment of them, on which it would be pointless to speak again at the moment.

To the earth he gave seeds and plants and to the waters creatures that swim and fly: *Let the waters bring forth reptiles with living souls, and birds that fly.* By *reptiles* he refers to fish, since they creep rather than walk; hence blessed David also says in keeping with the lawgiver, "This sea is vast and wide; creeping things are there that are beyond counting."[8] A remarkable fact, a remarkable design, remarkable the promise in this statement. How so? Because he is the maker of everything; he has before his eyes the past, the present and the future in a way not true of us even with things before our very eyes. Since he was on the point of providing the world with life in the first instance through water, he bids the waters in this first instance bring forth a life-giving nature so that you may learn whence comes the root of life. When I see the neophytes emerging from the holy waters after entering baptism with many vices like reptiles and emerging with eternal life, I see the lawgiver saying, Let the waters bring forth what was once a serpent but is now a living soul. What evidence is there of this for us? Those who approach the bath in their former sins bear the name serpents; many people went out for John's baptism, and he said to them as they came, "Serpents, brood of vi-

---

[5]Jn 1:3. Severian is inclined to leave the Old Testament text behind and face up to a range of New Testament heretics. [6]Gen 1:20. At the outset Severian had claimed that Moses was writing not as a mere historian (*historiographos*) but as an inspired author (*prophētēs*). [7]Severian treated the lights (Gen 1:14) in Homily Three: are we to take *prōēn* as strictly "the day before yesterday" or "the other day"? He will speak below of the third homily being given "yesterday." [8]Ps 104:25.

pers, who warned you to flee from the wrath to come?"[9] When a soul approaches baptism after living many years in evildoing and then setting it aside and escaping it, see whether in fact the Lord's command does not gain luster: *Let the waters bring forth reptiles with living souls, and birds that fly.* In other words, the person who is saved receives a double grace, bringing its soul to life and then gaining wings, attaining to the vaults of heaven and gaining a place in the ranks on high.

And on the earth birds flying across the firmament of heaven: on earth because of the body, in heaven because of the way of life.[10] It is not to indulge in allegory that we introduced this; rather, we found this spiritual interpretation in the facts. It is one thing to force an allegorical interpretation on the facts; it is another to retain the facts and arrive at a spiritual interpretation.[11] In order to show that by *birds flying* he refers to reptiles in the sea, he goes on, *God made the huge sea monsters and every single living reptile which the waters produced, and every winged bird.*[12] Is there, in fact, a bird that is not winged? Why say *every winged bird*? By flying here is meant extending one's hands; it is possible to fly with one's hands, as the prophet says, "I extended my hands all day long to a disbelieving and rebellious people," not that hands have wings but because the verb means "to extend."[13] What creeps is therefore said to be winged from its creeping and extending— hence David's saying, "creeping things and flying birds."[14]

God made the huge sea monsters, that is, the huge dragons in the sea; in fact, the other interpreters say, "God made the huge dragons," not the *sea monsters* but "dragons."[15] Nothing in the sea among the living creatures was made before a dragon; hence David says, "Praise the Lord from the earth, dragons and all deeps," and elsewhere, "This sea is vast and broad, creeping things are there that are beyond counting, small living things along with great, ships pass that way. This dragon which you formed to sport in it"; and elsewhere with the intention of showing that there is not a single dragon but many, he says, "You broke the heads of the dragons in the water."[16]

God made the huge sea monsters, then, *and God saw that they were all good.*[17] Why did he say *good* in the plural, and not in the singular for the multitude? When he made the stars and sun and moon, however, with many things made, he says, *God saw that it was good.* There were many stars, their vast number beyond counting, and he did not say, God saw that they were good, but it was good.[18] Why? Because even if there were many stars, they came from one light, and all met the same need, being assigned to providing light. In this case, however, since there was a great variety of creeping things, winged things and swimming things (there being a different basis to creeping, winged and swimming) and since there were many and varied species in each genus, he says, *God said that they were good.* There is commendation also for the variety of the works.

And God blessed them, saying, increase and

---

[9]Mt 3:7. Again a reference to his church's liturgy and life. [10]Phil 3:20. [11]Antiochene interpreters and congregations did not find allegory to their liking; an interpretation of Scripture based on the facts (*historia*) was preferable. Diodore had instructed his students to avoid it and allowed a spiritual interpretation (*theōria*) only on condition that it could be shown to be based on a literal interpretation. [12]Gen 1:21. [13]In the text of Is 65:2 the verb *exepetasthai* occurs, meaning "spread out [wings]." Again Severian has made a rod for his own back by being aggressively literalistic. [14]Ps 148:10. [15]Montfaucon notes that the different version does not appear in the Hexapla, where one might expect to find it. Neither Chrysostom nor Theodoret shows interest in identifying the sea creatures as dragons. [16]Pss 148:7; 104:25-26; 74:13. Severian's Old Testament scriptural documentation is largely from the Psalms. He shows signs of being familiar with Chrysostom's homilies on them. [17]Gen 1:21 LXX, "all" not in the text, despite Severian's argument. [18]Gen 1:18. There is no questioning Severian's precision (*akribeia*), a term for which "accuracy" is often offered as a mistranslation. What he is missing despite his eye for detail, however, is the significance of the author's repeated endorsement of the goodness of creation—a truth denied by vocal groups that seem to escape inclusion in his bevy of heretics.

multiply, and fill the waters, and let birds multiply. Why is it that when he made the stars, he did not bless them? Why is it that after making plants and trees, he did not bless them? Some things he blesses; others he does not bless. What was the basis of his determining the virtue of this group? Pay attention. Stars abide in the numbers that were made in the beginning, with no possibility of an increase in number or magnitude; being destined to preserve their identity of nature, they had no need of a blessing for their continuance. What was multiplied by propagation, by contrast, and was subject to increase in no other way was of necessity the recipient also of blessing.[19] I repeat the point so that the statement may be set fast in your mind; it is not the plant falling by accident into holes in the ground that has a permanent position, but the one placed in its depths with complete security. Winged and swimming creatures along with the human being require this blessing for the reason of propagation; where multiplying is possible in no other way there is room for blessing, whereas where multiplication is minimal, little blessing is received.

Since, then, we know the reason why these things were accorded blessing, there is need to devote ourselves also to the other verses of the Scriptures. *Increase,* since they were small, *multiply,* since they were few, *fill the waters,* since they had only partly done so. Now, we need on another occasion to ask the further question, Why he accorded the blessing only to the fish, the birds and the human being and did not give the others a share in it. For the time being, however, let us keep to the sequence as promised. *And God said, Let the earth bring forth a living being.*[20] God conferred on the earth a double honor: first, it generated seeds and plants, and after that living creatures, not without reason but because it was destined to

become a dwelling for the human being. And not only that: because the human being for its part would be nourished by it for its part, he honors it as nourisher and mother of this important being. Note here as well the sequence he followed: first he prepares what gives nourishment, then he brings in what receives the nourishment; as he did also in the case of the human being, first he outfitted the house and then brings in the occupant.

Let the earth bring forth a living being: by what means does the lifeless earth generate a living being? By what means did a roaring lion emerge, or a speeding horse, or a working bullock or an ass to bear burdens? By what means did the varieties of living beings emerge? By what means did such beings come from what was lifeless? Heretical savants are not embarrassed by the fact that the lifeless earth that does not have life produces it; but if they were to hear that it was God who generated from his own being, they would immediately set their tangled minds working and proceed to the conclusion, Therefore he was sundered, therefore he was divided, therefore he suffered, and all the things of this kind that they say. This is not the time, in fact, to refute what is said by them against the Only-begotten[21]—or, rather, against their salvation; God reaps no benefit from being praised, nor is he in any way harmed from being blasphemed, being already full of every good and in need of nothing, conferring riches on everyone and indebted to no one. After all, what could anyone give to the one who is the fountain of all good, on whose lovingkindness all things depend? As David says, "All things look to you; you open your hand and fill every living being with satisfaction."[22]

Let us, however, bring to a close the treatment in hand; this is our preference, and good order requires it. The land produces what it

---

[19]Even if Severian's astronomy is predictably deficient, he reasons his way through a problem of his own making in the interests of *akribeia.* [20]Gen 1:24. [21]In fact, Severian will now proceed to joust with the Arians again. [22]Ps 104:27-28.

does not have, in obedience to the command; does not the divine and unsullied nature generate what it has? Further, to prevent your taking the word *have* in too human a fashion and saying, Do you see how the teacher himself conceded that the Father has priority over the Son? instead of making allowance for the expression, since we are human and have a tongue of clay, delivering to human beings a treatment of the divine nature that beggars description; being human, we are taught to speak like human beings. What the wretches fail to realize, in fact, is that it is God they are talking about, uttering remarks that are not appropriately applied to God. Note the knavery: when they raise questions, they speak on the basis of human reasoning, as in saying, Everything generated has a beginning to its existence. How so? Their response is immediate: When you were born, did you not have a beginning? your father? your grandfather? If you present them with a different argument that is based on their own arguments and capable of overturning their folly, they immediately mince words, The discussion is about God, and are you presenting me with human arguments? On the one hand, they develop the root of the problem from common reasoning, and on the other, they refuse to accept the demolition of the problem on the basis of the same reasoning.

They often ask, Who is able to be and to be born? So if I quote Scripture introducing such a thing not only in the case of God but also in the case of mortals, what do you do? Scripture speaks of blessed Abraham's children being born, not as though they did not exist but as though they existed before: Abraham begot Isaac; Isaac begot Jacob, Jacob Levi, from whom came the priestly tribe. So when he met Melchizedek—Abraham, I mean—Paul the apostle gives the story a theological interpretation in the words, "Now, Melchizedek met Abraham and blessed him," and immediately went on, "One might even say that Levi himself, who receives tithes, paid tithes through Abraham, for he was still in the loins of his ancestor Abraham."[23] He was a mortal man before he was born. Since the root was fully alive, he produced fruit with the living root. In this case, where there was no suffering, no form of succession, no fruitful womb, no series of human passions, they are not willing to admit that what existed was generated from what existed, though abiding eternally.

But they object, If he had been generated, how could he have always existed?[24] Everyone who has been generated has a beginning. His father's name? Among us it has had lengthy circulation. Take an example. Suppose a young man is desirous of marrying. First he becomes a suitor, then a fiancé, then a husband; if there are children, he is then called father; but if no children accrue to his name, despite his living countless years with his wife, he is not called father. Likewise with the mother: first a maiden, then a fiancée, then a bride, then a wife; she becomes pregnant, she carries the fruit, but if things do not take this course, she is not called mother. God in his wisdom did this lest fathers boast of their children and a father say to his child, I conferred life on you, it was on account of that you were born, you were brought into existence through me. Instead, the intention is that, even if they say this, they would immediately be told, It was on account of you that I was born, and it was on account of me that you are a father. Similarly, too, in the case of the mother: You conferred sonship on me, I conferred motherhood on you. With us there is a gift and a reward. Likewise, too, the son is not immediately a son: he

---

[23]Heb 7:1, 9-10. The anti-Arian polemic again leaves the text of Genesis well behind.   [24]This is the major tenet of the Arians and Eunomians that Severian sees arising from the Genesis account, and he sets about refuting it. We would seem to be a couple of decades after the Constantinople creed of 381, and much longer from Nicaea, but subordinationism was alive and well.

is first a seed, then a fetus, and it is when he is born that he is a son.

This involves subjection to the necessities of time; it is a victim of passions, it depends on bodily condition. But where the nature that generates is incorporeal, where the fruit that is generated is incorporeal, what reason lies behind the claim, There was a time when he did not exist and later was brought into being? Our response is as follows: If God is always like this, if nothing ever accrues to him, he has also always been a father; and if he has always been a father, he has always had a son, the Son assuredly being coeternal with the Father. While we claim that the Son was generated without passion, we are not in a position to explain the manner of the generation; this is true knowledge, admitting not to know what surpasses our nature. So while we bow down before what was generated, we do not pry into nature. If the one generating were human, therefore, he would be responsible also for a human generation; if he had a body, it would be as a body that he generated. If, however, he is not burdened with a body, do not ascribe bodily passions to the incorporeal one. But he generated from what is his, they claim, he generated in passion, by cutting, by flowing. I shall convince them on the basis of earthly things: a vine generates, an olive tree generates, water also generates, not in accordance with our nature but in keeping with its own process. Every woman, on receiving from God the gift of motherhood, conceives and swells up; but on delivering the fruit she trims down. In the case of trees, by contrast, you find the opposite: before giving birth there is no swelling, whereas when they give birth, it is then they thicken up, the fruit grows, the root is multiplied, with no reduction to the root that gave birth or lessening of what is produced. The vine does not generate like us. If you hear that God generates, do you apply human passions to one who

surpasses human nature?

And God said, Let the earth bring forth living beings in their various kinds, four-footed creatures, reptiles, wild beasts. The *four-footed creatures* are the cattle, the *reptiles* and *wild beasts* are snakes and dragons, and by *wild beasts* there is reference not only to yoked cattle but also to beasts of burden. Every grass-eating animal, whether ox or sheep, is called *cattle*, being an acquisition of human beings. The fact that sheep and oxen are called cattle Scripture confirms: "He had possession of flocks of sheep and herds of oxen."[25] The land was filled, it was bedecked with crops, it produced animals; all that was missing now was a master of the house. The heaven was beautified, the earth given variety, the sea filled, the sky adorned with a multitude of birds. Everything was complete; only the human being was missing. Now, there was no insult in being left until last—rather, esteem: the house was made ready and the master of the house introduced; God does nothing in untimely fashion, nothing intemperately, everything being done in response to need. Note the order: first God made plants and grasses and then the wild animals feeding off them. If they had not been for food, the creation of the animals would have been untimely, handicapped by the need for crops. He made the foodstuffs and then prepared what fed off them: first the necessities of life and then the introduction of what partook of the necessities.

The Scriptures announcing him preceded Christ, and then came the one to whom they gave witness; first the witnesses, so that the one to whom they gave witness might be believed. The Law came first so as to announce the lawgiver; the biblical authors came first so as to interpret the one of whom they wrote. Note God's wisdom: the writings of the biblical authors he made available not only in the church but also for Jews; for them to be con-

---

[25]Gen 26:14, where *ktēnē* (which, as Severian says above, derives from the verb "to acquire"), is associated with both sheep and oxen.

victed, he made them available even to Jews, unworthy though they were, hostile to God, foes of Christ. So why did he do this instead of removing them from them? The reason is obvious, requiring no great unraveling. So that my preaching might be above suspicion; if I alone had had the biblical authors, it would have been possible for the unbeliever to gainsay me.[26] Would I not have presumed to say, Moses said, or Isaiah said, or the remaining band of authors said about Christ and about what would happen at the time of his coming? It would have been possible for the one wanting to gainsay me also to reply, How do we know that Moses was a biblical author and said this or preached it, as you Christians wanted to maintain in support of your teachings and come up with these names? Do we have to put up with this kind of prejudice? As it is, however, every pretext is forfeited by the one wanting to gainsay me, no matter the length of his justification, since these testimonies that we cite in support of our teachings are in their possession; how would it not be possible to refute their facile arguments?

To avoid these claims being made, then, he allowed the books of the Scriptures to be found among them so that even if as one who distorted them for the sake of my own teachings I would not be believed for reasons of similarity, they might believe on the grounds of dissimilarity. If you were to ask a Jew (I don't mean one of the prolific rabble and unruly mob but one capable of speaking on the Law),[27] Does Christ exist? and he replies not with No, but by admitting, He does, but instead of the one you claim, he is someone else, for the time being he has not dismissed the matter, only questioned the identification. It is one thing to deny the fact, another the identification; for instance, if someone presses you to pay a loan, it is one thing to say, I owe no debt, and it would be another thing so say, I owe no debt to you, only to someone else; for the time being the debt is admitted. So whereas they admit that Christ exists, they are noncommittal as to whether he is the one preached by us, and they wait for one who does not exist since they deny the one who does. Take note of the lawgiver Moses introducing the Son and his knowledge in the formation of the human being. He said, *Let a firmament be made*, he said, *Let the earth put forth*, he said, *Let the waters bring forth*. When he came to the human being, he said, *And God said, Let us make a human being.*[28] I ask a Jew: If he is one, and with him there is no Son whom we preach, if there is no Holy Spirit whom we adore, to whom does he say, *Let us make a human being?* By a single command he makes heaven, earth and likewise the rest; when he creates the human being, in his wish to give a glimpse of the divinity of the Son through the window, as it were, he says, *Let us make a human being*, his purpose being to present him as his associate also in the former instances.

Under pressure, then, and unable to distort the obvious sense of the passage, the Jews say that he spoke to the angels; since they could not openly deny the nature of the expression, they come up with a denial in some other way. To whom, then, did he say, *Let us make?* Angels, they say. My question is, Who is the greater, the angels or the human beings? Definitely the angels; whenever we attain to a modicum of virtue, we then do not surpass them, only equal them. As it is, however, we are far inferior to their nature and of a lower status than the incorporeal nature of the angels. Listen to David testifying about him: "What is a human being that you are mindful of him, or son of a human being that you

---

[26]The creation account left to one side, Severian demonstrates God's wisdom in leaving the Jews with the Jewish Scriptures—a rather otiose exercise, one would think, whereas Chrysostom concedes that "the books are theirs." Severian has shown his animosity toward the Jews of his day. [27]Severian slightingly alludes to the jibe found in Clement of Alexandria about Jews, *Ioudaioi*, as *chydaioi* ("prolific" or "vulgar"). [28]Gen 1:26.

think of him? You have fashioned him as little less than angels."[29] For the time being we are less than angels: we are less, the angels are greater. In making the human being, who is less, you had need of the angels as advisers and helpers. When he made the greater—not a single angel but those countless myriads together: just as he made all the lights together, so angels and archangels together, and Daniel cries aloud, "Ten thousand times ten thousand served him, and a thousand thousands attended on him"[30]—he made ten thousand times ten thousand angels and a thousand thousands of archangels, with no need of adviser or helper. And yet in making a single human being out of clay, does he take counsel, introduce a word, accept advice? "What is a human being?" Is he not "of the earth, earthy," dust and ashes? Even Abraham cries aloud in proclaiming his own insignificance, "I am dust and ashes." What are angels? Are they not spirit? Are they not fire? Listen also to David crying aloud, "He makes the angels his spirits, and his ministers fiery flame."[31] In making the nature of fire, the spiritual and incorporeal spirits, he has no need of adviser, no helper, no one else to aid in the making, whereas in creating this being from the earth, this piteous, insignificant, tiny being that would later not exist, dissolving in a grave, consumed by time, does he looks for advice, does he give consideration?

Yes, they answer, it becomes the Lord in his great goodness to say to the slaves attending on him, What is to be done? What are we to do? I concede this as well, and after such a contest I allow that the phrase *let us make* is said to angels. After hearing *let us make*, did you not see *in our image and likeness*? With this phrase, in fact, I ought stop the mouths of both Jews and heretics; the Jew is not in truth the same Jew, nor likewise the heretic—rather,

he is even worse. The former, you see, crucified the visible body; the latter assail the invisible divinity—or, rather, their own salvation; yet the former as well were convicted of venturing on impossible exploits. Hence in the present age as well they have paid the penalty in part for this presumption, seeing their own race scattered throughout the world; later the ultimate penalty will be imposed on them when the general judgment is destined to be held, and at the due time the appropriate account will be required of them.

What is the reason, then, for my proposing all these issues to you? My intention, in fact, has been for the sequence to be followed again. Neither the heretic nor the Jew presumes to claim that there is a single image and likeness for God and angels: surely the angels, who were made, were not assistants with God? Only ministers, singing praise, giving thanks, aware that they were made, that before this they did not exist and were made by the spirit of goodness. They also acted as witnesses, observing what was made after them; they observed heaven being made from what did not exist and were astonished; the sea being set within limits and were amazed; they observed the earth adorned and were startled. The fact that angels were not assistants but admirers God tells Job, "When I made stars, all the angels sang my praises."[32]

Let us make a human being. The sentence suggests both the speaker and the listener. Note the beam of orthodox faith ever resplendent; the sun in its shining joined its own beam. *Let us make a human being in our image and likeness.* He retained the order of the persons[33] and the unity of being. *Let us make a human being in image*, not in images: it is not the case that the Father has one image, the Son another. *Let us make* (the purpose being to bring out the plurality of persons) *in*

---

[29]Ps 8:4-5. Chrysostom in his Homily Eight also represents the Jews proposing the angels as associate subject of the verb "let us make." [30]Dan 7:10. [31]1 Cor 15:47; Gen 18:27; Ps 104:4. [32]Job 38:7 loosely recalled. [33]Severian speaks of *hypostases*.

our image (to explain the oneness of being).[34] Who is an associate in this marvelous address and remarkable creation? Jews voice opposition and are embarrassed to be reduced to silence; heretics indulge in frenzy, truth opposes them, the cause of religion delivers an unassailable confession.

How, then, shall we bring out who it is to whom he said, *Let us make a human being?* or who is his counselor? The phrase *let us make* presumes the presence of a counselor. Accordingly, blessed Isaiah says of the only Son of God, who for us has come in a form like ours, "A child was born for us, a son and youngster was given":[35] the child that did not exist was born, the Son that did was given. "And he will be called messenger of great counsel": Son on account of his divinity, child on account of his humanity. "Messenger of great counsel, marvelous counselor": if you call the counselor to whom you said, *Let us make a human being in our image and likeness,* "messenger of great counsel," O prophet, you have not yet mentioned the status of the counselor proclaimed by you. After all, Moses also was a counselor; he was obviously giving advice in saying, "Do not kill them, lest the nations say, It was on account of their not being able to have children that he killed them."[36] Do not limit your wonder to the counselor, however, do not use it as a common name; there may be many counselors, but do not insult this particular one.

You have not yet considered, however, the status of the one who is announced; listen to what is said about the marvelous counselor, for Isaiah gives a comment following on the preceding one. "Marvelous counselor, mighty God." He did well to add the word *mighty* to God. Why? Just as there was no need for the status of the single counselor to be undermined for reason of there being many counselors, so although there were many gods

(Scripture says, "I said, You are gods and all children of the Most High," and again God said to Moses, "Lo, I have made you like God to Pharaoh"[37]), this one who is announced should not be insulted. And in case you might think that he is God in the sense of Moses or the apostles, he added "mighty God"; Moses was God, not mighty but given strength. It is one thing to be given strength, another to be mighty; one thing to confer grace, another to receive it. "Mighty God": Moses was God only when given strength; even if he was a worker of wonders, he still received grace. Whereas the apostles were under authority, the Savior had the authority and gave it.

"Mighty God": far from this being enough, he adds "invested with authority" to teach both us and heretics not to say that the ruler with authority is subject to authority; it is one thing to be subject to authority, another to have authority. Do you want to learn the difference between having authority and being subject to authority? The apostles were subject to authority; the Savior has authority. In Macedonia Paul saw a servant girl possessed by a spirit of divination and saying to everyone, "These people are slaves of the Most High God. Very annoyed, Paul turned and said to the spirit"— not to the one under the influence but to the one exercising influence—"I bid you in the name of the Lord Jesus Christ to leave her."[38] He uses the term "Lord" to show that he was his servant. Since the miracle of demons obeying people was beyond the power of a human being, he said in order to prevent his words being misinterpreted, "I bid you in the name of the Lord." It is for a slave to give orders; it is for a master to exercise authority.

You saw a servant giving orders; observe a master commanding. A possessed person who was deaf and dumb was brought to the Lord. The Lord did not say, I bid you, deaf and

---

[34]The term is *homoousion.* [35]Is 9:6, a text Chrysostom also cites here to make this point. Does Severian have him at hand, or are both drawing on common stock? [36]Does Severian have Num 14:15-16 in mind here? [37]Ps 82:6; Ex 7:1. [38]Acts 16:17-18.

dumb spirit, but "I command you"; bidding is for Paul, commanding for the one with authority. "I command you, leave him, and do not enter him again." The demon obeyed, recognizing his authority. Let the words of blessed Ezekiel to the heretical synagogue be cited, "As I live, says the Lord, your sister Sodom is more in the right than you."[39] What does he mean? Unless you understand what he means, you will not be able to advance to a grasp of the spiritual meaning.[40] Devoid of all hope through lives of lawlessness, the Sodomites were consumed by fire sent from heaven, and despite their destruction and the burning of their city, Jerusalem many generations later visibly flourished but became guilty of worse vices. So since they surpassed the vices of the Sodomites, God swore through Ezekiel in these words, "As I Adonai live, says the Lord, tell the faithless daughter Jerusalem, Your sister Sodom did not commit half your sins, and Sodom is more in the right than you," that is, by comparison with you Sodom is righteous. It would be like saying to heretics, Even Jews were in the right by comparison with the heretics' frenzy, demons were in the right, because the latter call him Son whereas the former call him a creature. "Sodom is more in the right than you."

My question in passing is, What was the reason why those who committed Sodomite crimes did not perish like Sodomites—or, rather, if they committed double the crimes, why were they not left desolate like them? God, then, had regard for not only the egregious impiety of the Jews but also the piety of the faithful later. He foreknew that the holy virgin mother of God was destined to come from Judea,[41] he foresaw the band of the apostles, he had prior vision of the ranks of the confessors, the countless numbers of the Jews destined to come to faith. When Paul went up to Jerusalem, remember, his fellow apostles said, "You see, brother Paul, the countless numbers of Jewish believers there are."[42] It was through foreseeing the believers, then, that he spared the unbelievers—not for their sake but on account of the fruit due to be born of them. This is confirmed by Isaiah: "If the Lord of hosts had not left us a seed, we would have been like Sodom and would have become like Gomorrah." Surely we are not for our part doing violence to the text, Isaiah speaking of someone else? Listen instead to Paul, brother and interpreter of the prophets, saying this: "At the present time there is a remnant chosen by grace in order that the remnant may be saved. As Isaiah said, If the Lord of hosts had not left us a seed, we would have been like Sodom."[43] In other words, God foresaw everything; it is not through experience that God learns, as we for our part come to learn of developments in time.

Further, as I said before, he had in sight the ends of the ages: he saw Adam sinning, he foresaw also the righteous ones due to come from him, he observed him being expelled from paradise, yet he also foresaw that a kingdom has been prepared for him. What is surprising, however, is that the kingdom was made before paradise: are you surprised that Adam was expelled from paradise? Be surprised that the kingdom of heaven was prepared for him before paradise; the Savior says, "Come, you who are blessed by my Father, inherit the kingdom prepared for you before the foundation of the world."[44] Let heretics be confounded to learn what was prepared for the saints before the foundation of the world, and yet they claim that there was a time when the

---

[39]Mk 9:24; Ezek 16:52. [40]Again Severian shows a readiness to proceed to another, spiritual meaning (*theōria*), admittedly related to the historical. [41]The term *theotokos* would not remain common parlance for long in Constantinople once Nestorius became bishop two decades later. Severian uses *kyriotokos* in Homily Six. [42]Acts 21:20. Severian digresses to "a question in passing," namely, the respective fates of Sodomites and Jews (further, that is, from the text of the day). [43]Is 1:9; Rom 9:27, 29; 11:5. [44]Mt 25:34. Almost by accident the digression finally brings Severian back not to the text of the day but to the christological polemic.

Son did not exist. They give the appearance of confessing the Only-begotten since they cannot cancel the text; they concede the statement but undermine the fact. If we say only-begotten Son, they immediately reply, Scripture says also "firstborn of all the world";[45] according to the heretics, therefore, the two are not consistent: if he is firstborn, he is not only-begotten. That is to say, the firstborn, when he has brothers, is called firstborn, whereas the Only-begotten, if he has brothers, is not called only-begotten, for an only-begotten is the only son born to anyone, as Scripture also confirms in saying to Abraham, "Take your son, your only son."[46] The one who has brothers is firstborn; he gains precedence by being born first. An only-begotten, by contrast, is the only son born to someone, not the only one made, which is the facile claim of heretics. If only-begotten meant being the only one made such, Elijah would also therefore be only-begotten in being the only one of that kind, which makes no sense. Scripture normally applies the term "only-begotten," however, to the only one born to someone, as was previously explained.

Pay attention. The firstborn, if he has no brothers, is only-begotten. I find not one, not two, not three, but many firstborn. A strange fact. How is it that there are many firstborn? There should be one. I have prolonged my treatment of "firstborn" and "only-begotten"; let us solve the problem. God calls the first believer in his particular generation firstborn, not that he has precedence over other believers, but he was the first to appear in his particular time. For example, when the people were in Egypt, God said through Moses, "Israel is my firstborn son. I said, Send me my people." See a firstborn people, since at that time it was the first people to acknowledge God. It was later

that David emerged, after the Law, after many generations, and God promises to raise up the Christ from his progeny, putting it like this: "I found David my servant, I anointed him with holy oil, he will call upon me, You are my father, and I shall make him firstborn."[47] Now, if David was firstborn, the people were also firstborn. Adam was firstborn in his generation, Noah, Shem firstborn, Abraham firstborn in his generation, Moses, Isaiah, since in their times they made initial steps toward true religion. From these many firstborn a great church was assembled, and it is in heaven; Paul confirms this: "You have come to Mount Sion and to the city of the living God, Jerusalem, and to innumerable angels in festive gathering, and to the church of the firstborn who are enrolled in heaven." Of those firstborn there is one, Christ according to the flesh, only-begotten according to his divinity; when he draws to him those who have precedence in each generation, he is also said to be firstborn along with them all. Hence Paul says "firstborn among many brethren."[48]

Much could be said about the human being; but the account will keep for what follows on the sixth day when he is formed, the purpose being that with the help of God's grace the treatment may be made perfectly clear to the best of our ability—not from our own reasoning but from what we have been taught. There is a common source, in fact, and all the gifts are set before us in common,[49] provided we are willing to make the effort with complete enthusiasm. Let us, however, direct the homily to moral considerations. Yesterday[50] it was shown how those who openly display their piety should raise their hands; let the one who gives to the poor say, "a raising of my hands"; let the one who raises the fallen say, "a rais-

---

[45]Severian is probably thinking of one of the Arians' key texts, Kelly informs us, Col 1:15, "firstborn of all creation." He first explicates their argument before refuting it. [46]Gen 22:2. [47]Ex 4:22-23; Ps 89:20, 26-27. [48]Heb 12:22-23; Rom 8:29. [49]Is this a nice way of admitting that Severian has drawn on the works of his predecessors (as we have noted resemblances with Chrysostom's commentary on Genesis in these homilies)? [50]Earlier in the homily he had spoken of the third homily as given "the other day" (*proēn*). With christological development and digression complete, Severian moves not back to the text of Gen 1:26 but to a parenetic conclusion.

ing of my hands." We need, however, to look at the beginning of the psalm, since there is a definite obligation to understand what we sing. Why do we say, "Let my prayer be directed as incense before you"?[51] All incense, in fact, is directed;[52] God does not take satisfaction in the fragrance of spices—so why, "Let my prayer be directed"? The article is missing, giving the text in this form, "Let my prayer be directed as incense before you." What sort of incense? There were two altars in the tabernacle, one in the court outside in the open, the other in the holy place under cover. The inside altar was only for incense, not for shedding of blood, whereas the outside altar was for animals being sacrificed, offerings of bread and some other things. God bade Moses erect the outside altar from uncut stones and the inside one in the tabernacle from polished gold.[53]

What the grace of God is referring to in this we must find out. It has reference to two peoples serving God's glory, one untutored, the other tutored. The one that is rough and unintelligible in speech delivers words like uncut stones; in turn the precious stone is spoken of as polished gold. The latter is not exalted or the former rejected. Now, the spices comprised four kinds: stacte, onyx, galbane and frankincense. So since the spices are composed of different elements, and virtue of different elements, he is saying, "Let my incense be directed as incense before you," in being composed of many elements but producing a single fragrance. His meaning is that when someone enters prayerfully, practicing fasting, almsgiving and faith, the fourfold virtue can be compared with that incense that is directed in your sight. Blessed David also speaks in similar terms somewhere: "Lo, how good, how

pleasing for kindred to live together in unity! It is like spices on the head that flow down on the beard, the beard of Aaron." He compares love with priestly spices, prayer with priestly incense.[54]

Do you possess self-control? You are closely related to a priest. Priesthood I may not possess, so to say, but self-control I do possess; my self-control is a close relation of your priesthood. How is this so? The one who acts as a priest must be chaste, and I who worship must be chaste. If I possess self-control, I am adopting priesthood. How is this so? In fleeing from Saul, David came to Abiathar the high priest and said to him, "Give me loaves," since I was suddenly dismissed by the king and have no rations. The high priest, who was learned in the Law, replied, "We only have holy bread, which a priest alone is allowed to eat." Since he saw the need, then, though reluctant to make available the loaves of proposition, he inquired about the purity of those who were not priests, "If the young men with you are purified of contact with women, take them,"[55] considering self-control to be closely related to priesthood. And in case anyone should understand the giving of the loaves to those who were not priests to be a criticism of the priest, listen to how favorably the Savior recalled its happening. Jews at one time reproached the apostles for picking grain, rubbing it with their hands and eating it; the Savior said to them, "Have you not read what David did when he was hungry, eating the loaves of presence, which it was not lawful for him and those with him to eat, but only the priests?"[56] Do you see self-control closely related to priesthood? Do you see how God, far from being a respecter of persons, focuses on the reality?

---

[51]Ps 141:2. We have noted Severian's accent on comprehension in recitation/singing of the Psalms in the liturgy, a reminder found in Chrysostom and Theodoret and characteristically in all the Antiochenes. [52]While Montfaucon retains the text in this form, he admits that Savile had suggested, "How is incense directed?" [53]Ex 30:1-6; 40:1-6. Chrysostom in his homily on Ps 141 had likewise seen a parallel with the altar of incense "in olden times" but without the mention of the absence of an article with "incense" and without proceeding to allegory. [54]Ps 133:1-2. [55]1 Sam 21:3-4. Montfaucon chides Severian for a lapse of memory in citing Abiathar instead of his father, Ahimelech, but the error derives first from the Markan account of the incident (Mk 2:26). [56]Lk 6:3-4.

Let us gird ourselves, then, for good works, for righteousness, so that fasting may take wings: just as a bird, unless it has the cooperation of its wings, cannot fly, so too fasting has two wings, prayer and almsgiving, without which it cannot rise on high. Note Cornelius possessing these wings along with fasting; hence he also heard a voice coming from heaven: "Cornelius, your prayers and your alms have ascended to God." Imagine fasting to be a living being, dearly beloved, and likewise its wings to be almsgiving and prayer, without which it cannot rise on high. Such a thing, even if it does not speak, bellows what is righteous with a loud voice, virtue being a great supporter of righteousness—hence the saying, "Hearken, Lord, to my righteousness."[57] While first, then, the highest good consists of prayer, almsgiving and righteous behavior, what is secure, unshakeable and the root of everything is the knowledge of God, worship of the Only-begotten and confession of the Holy Spirit—one faith, undivided, secure, total and integral.

What I am about to say has been said, but I shall still say it. God in his wisdom has allowed heresies to get a name for their teachings from their originators so that it may be clear that what is decreed by them is not God's teaching but human invention—Macedonians from Macedonius,[58] Arians from Arius, Eunomians from Eunomius, and likewise the other heresies. But wishing to preserve the faith of the apostles intact, he did not allow them to be named after a man; even if they call us Homoousiasts, they are not referring to a man but proclaiming the faith. The fact that being called after people is the mark not of the faithful but of heretics Paul states in reproaching the Corinthians: "I

hear there are divisions among you; one says, I belong to Paul, I belong to Apollos, I belong to Cephas."[59] Do you see that being called after people arises from schisms? Is not Peter more deserving of credence than Macedonius? Do not the names of the apostles give way to the glory of Christ? Are you not scorning the faith, the undivided kingdom, the integral glory? Enough for the time being: we have the lamp and the light, "the Law being a lamp for my feet and a light for my paths."[60] Why a lamp? Why a light? A lamp for the catechumens, a light for the initiated.

I beg you, dearly beloved, to maintain your fasting undiluted, uncontaminated, free of injustice, free of oppression. Consider the futility of those who devote themselves to abstinence from food and pay no heed to abstinence from sins. I do not drink wine, they say, I do not take oil, I do not eat meat. Well and good if done for God's sake, well done—but let us examine the facts. Bread, water, wine, meat, oil: all these are God's creations; oppression, injustice and impiety are the devil's works. You abstain from the works of God for the sake of fasting; do you not abstain from the works of the devil for the sake of fasting? Bread and wine and oil and all the rest are works of God, totally good, even very good; Paul says, "Everything created by God is good, and nothing is to be rejected, provided it is received with thanksgiving, for it is sanctified by God's word and by prayer."[61] If it is blessed, then, if it is sanctified, why do we abstain? But injustice, oppression and such things are works of the devil. You abstain from the works of God for the sake of fasting, and do you not abjure the works of the devil for the sake of piety? In fact,

---

[57]Acts 10:4; Ps 16:1. [58]Macedonius was a fourth-century homoeousian bishop of Constantinople who actively campaigned against Arians. He, like other homoeousians, denied the divinity of the Holy Spirit. The name Macedonians originally applied to homoeousian groups associated with Macedonius in and near Constantinople, but after 380 the term expanded to cover all non-Arian groups who would not affirm the divinity of the Holy Spirit. Severian appears in many ways to be similar to Macedonius. Both are anti-Arian and support ascetical ideals, such as fasting, yet they differ in their confession of the Holy Spirit as divine. Yet, as Severian states, the foundation of all beneficial spiritual action is knowledge of God, which includes the confession of the divinity of the Holy Spirit. [59]1 Cor 1:11-12. [60]Ps 119:105. In the homilies Severian refers (as here to catechumens and initiated) to details of liturgy and life in his church. [61]1 Tim 4:4-5. It is this accent on the goodness of creation that was found wanting above.

judgment is not passed on the one who does not fast, whereas on the one guilty of injustice God has threatened retribution. We shun what is inculpable; do we not flee what is culpable? Almsgiving is a good practice; while in appearance it involves outlay, in reality it results in profit; just as a farmer invests in the soil, and from it he receives seed, so alms appear to be given to others, yet in reality profit accrues to the giver. "He has outlaid," David says, "he has given to the poor, and his righteousness abides forever."[62] Likewise let us fast, likewise let us worship, likewise let us believe, glorifying the Father, singing praise to the Son, worshiping the Holy Spirit, because to him be the glory for ages. Amen.

Homily Five

On the fifth day of creation

While what has been given to human beings by the loving God is wonderfully manifold, the first and greatest of all his gifts is the teaching of the Scriptures. Sun and moon, in fact, all the company of the stars, rivers and springs and lakes have been made for the benefit of our bodies, whereas the holy Scriptures were given for the improvement of our souls; the more the soul is superior to bodies, the greater the superiority of the divine Scriptures to the other gifts. Hence the Savior says, "Study the Scriptures, because you think that in them you have eternal life."[1] Let us therefore study the treasures of the Scriptures, lay hold of what is promised and endeavor to explain the creation of the human being to the best of our ability.

Let no one in turn, however, find fault with what is being examined with precision; it is typical of people in the habit of talking

nonsense to find fault with God's arrangements and call into question what is said with precision. I heard some people's fault finding, What use is it to mention fire and water and the fact that fire screams when water is thrown on it? It is not natural science we are anxious to learn, they say, but the true doctrine of God.[2] There is need to recognize, however, that such words proceed from laziness and indifference; after the true doctrine of God, natural science lays a basis for religion, and if they reject natural science, they would fault the Old Testament authors, they would call in question the New Testament authors. The apostle concerns himself with natural science: "Not all flesh is alike; rather, there is one flesh for human beings, another flesh for animals, another for fish, another for birds. There are both heavenly bodies and earthly bodies." Why does Paul concern himself with natural science and take the example of musical instruments: "There are doubtless many kinds of sounds in the world, and nothing is without sound. If the trumpet sounds an uncertain note, who will get ready for battle? If the flute or harp does not give distinct notes, how will it be known what is being played on flute or harp?"[3] What does Paul's tongue have in common with flute or harp? He involves himself with natural science on the basis of what is invisible, however, so as to present what is spiritual.

What was the use of such matters of natural science being raised in the book of Job? "A lion's strength, a lion's roar, the audacity of dragons was snuffed out, the monster perished for lack of food, the vultures' young fly high." Why did another Old Testament author say, "Like a lion choosing and seizing its prey, and growling over it, and the mountains are filled with its roar"?[4] The Savior also concerns

---

[62]Ps 112:9. It has been Severian's longest homily to date, though perhaps with less on the text of the creation account. **Homily Five** [1]Jn 5:39. Severian is obviously not taking this dominical saying as a reproach to the unresponsive Jews Jesus is here addressing, and so he would seem to be reading the verb "study" as an imperative, as did Origen and the Vulgate. Raymond Brown believes that "the indicative suits the argument better." [2]Is Severian reflecting reaction to his homilies, a preference of *theologia* to *physiologia*, or is it a preacher's conventional gambit to further such commentary? [3]1 Cor 15:39-40; 14:10, 8, 7. [4]Job 4:10-11; Is 31:4.

himself with natural science: "The kingdom of heaven is like a mustard seed, which is smaller than the other seeds, but when fully grown is bigger than all the shrubs," and again, "The kingdom of heaven is like someone sowing seed: it germinates and grows when he is unaware of it; the earth produces of itself, first the stalk, then the head, then the full grain in the head." The Savior invokes natural science of the sky: "If the sky at evening is red, you say, Fair weather, the sky is red; and in the morning, There will be a storm today, the sky is red and threatening."[5] So what is the value in this? I mention these things on account of those anxious in their ignorance to find fault. The homily deals with God, and yet you avoid giving close attention to the teachings?

Since the task, then, is with God's grace to speak on the creation of the human being, if not in a manner worthy of the subject, at least to the extent of our ability, of necessity let us develop our theme. The heaven was adorned, the earth was wreathed in crops, the waters of the sea were marked off, plants sprouted, the brute beasts came forth, the world was filled, the house was adorned, only a master of the house was missing from all the things made. *God said, Let us make a human being in our image and likeness.* Last day[6] it was shown what was the force of *let us make*, to whom it referred and to whom the remark was addressed—that is, who was the counselor and with whom the deliberation was shared. Since, however, on the basis of the Scriptures we presented the Son as the source of the ancient counsel and kept silence about the Holy Spirit in case among our healthy congregation some who are ailing might take exception, there is need to acknowledge that to Father, Son and Holy Spirit belongs one glory, one knowledge and one activating word. In this place it is said

that the Son is the counselor; elsewhere it is said that no one knows the knowledge of God except the Holy Spirit. Paul says, "No human being knows what is truly human except the spirit of the human being that is within him; likewise no one knows what is God's except the Spirit of God."[7] If the spirit in you is at odds with your being, the Spirit in God is at odds with God's being.

Is something willed by the Father? It is the same as is willed by the Son and the Holy Spirit. Is something willed by the Son? It is the same as is willed by Father and Spirit. Is something willed by the Spirit? It is the same as is willed by Father and Son. Does the Father raise the dead? The Son also does; the Savior said, "As the Father raises the dead and gives them life, so too the Son gives life to whomever he wishes." See the conjunction of the will. So where is the will of the Spirit? Listen: "All these are activated by one and the same Spirit, who allots to each one individually just as he chooses."[8] There is one kingdom belonging to Father, Son and Holy Spirit. God blames those also who try to do something without God's knowledge, saying through the prophet, "Woe to you, rebellious children, says the Lord. You did your own will, not mine; you made a treaty, but not with my Spirit." In a clear demonstration of the Trinity the prophet Zechariah said, "Let the hands of Zerubbabel be strengthened, says the Lord, let the hands of Jehozadak the priest be strengthened, and the hands of the people, because I am with you, says the Lord, and my word is dependable. My Spirit is in your midst."[9]

Furthermore, our rebirth testifies to creation: unless the Spirit was associated with the Father and the Spirit in creation, he would not have shared in the rebirth. How are we baptized? "In the name of the Father and of

---

[5]Mt 13:31-32; Mk 4:26-28; Mt 16:2-3. While some of his listeners could reasonably be wearied of Severian's literalistic response to the creation story, he assures them that there is a theological pattern behind details of the text. [6]Gen 1:26. Homily Five follows with only a day's interlude. [7]1 Cor 2:11. [8]Jn 5:21; 1 Cor 12:11. [9]Is 30:1; not Zechariah but Hag 2:5-6 loosely recalled. Severian replaces Joshua with his father, Jehozadak.

the Son and of the Holy Spirit."[10] Which is the greater birth, creation or initiation? In the former case, a beginning is made with life, and we proceed to death; in the latter, a beginning is made with death, and we proceed to life.[11] How could it be, then, that while in the greater sharing the Holy Spirit is admitted with Father and Son, in the case of bodily creation he is excluded from sharing the honor? We would not have been created unless we had been given form by the Holy Spirit; and since in the first creation he was associated with Father and Son, likewise also in baptism he is associate and cooperator. Likewise with the resurrection, it would not be possible for us to be raised unless the Father wished, the Son cooperated and the Holy Spirit made it possible. Listen to the words of the Lord—I used the word *Lord* advisedly: if they are also Paul's words, they are still the Lord's words— you can listen to him: "If you desire proof that Christ is speaking in me." So the one speaking in Paul says, "But you are not in the flesh; you are in the Spirit, since the Spirit of God dwells in you. Anyone who does not have the Spirit of God does not belong to him. But if Christ is in you, though the body is dead because of sin, the Spirit is life because of righteousness. Now, if the Spirit of him who raised Christ from the dead dwells in you, he who raised Christ from the dead will also give life to your mortal bodies through his Spirit that dwells in you."[12] The first creation was not independent of Father and Son and Holy Spirit, nor the second birth nor the final resurrection. *Let us make a human being.*

At this point I give an assurance to the fault finders. The word for "human being" in Hebrew means "fire." Pay attention, I beg you; while the person who listens with sincerity as a friend and companion of truth is sound, the persons who give ear with hostility do not seek what is to their benefit but what is to their harm, do not seek something to gain but something to criticize. "Human being" in Hebrew means "fire." It was not by chance that this name was given to Adam; there are four elements in the world—again I invoke natural sciences, even if they disapprove—earth, water, air, fire.[13] Each of the other elements remains as it is—for example, if you take a sod of earth, you cannot add to it from what is being held; so if you take a sod of earth, it remains what it is. Likewise, if you take water in a measure, it remains the same water; it is not ready to be added to. If you fill a flask with air, you cannot fill another flask from it. Fire, by contrast, does not remain as it is: a small lamp is lit, and from it you light countless wicks, a whole furnace, a great flame, and instead of retaining its original appearance, it multiplies to the extent of the available material. Since God foreknew, then, that from one human body the ends of the earth are filled (one lamp lights so many wicks, west and east, north and south), he imposed a name suited to the reality. Hence he gave it the name *Adam* as a pledge for the world; intending to fill the four quarters from him, he imposes the name *Adam: A* for east (*anatolē*), *D* for west (*dysis*), *A* for north (*arktos*), *M* for south (*mesēmbria*). The name with its four letters confirms the human being's destiny of filling the world.[14] Hence its Hebrew name "fire."

---

[10]Mt 28:19. [11]Even if (of necessity, considering the speaker's difficulty in finding sufficient material in his text?) we see Severian getting further theological mileage from the opening phrase to Gen 1:26, again we are given insights into the liturgy of his church—in this case baptism (perhaps the references to death and life reflecting the ritual of immersion). Also, as the *homoousion* of the Son had received ample attention in the previous homily, so the *homoousion* of the Spirit here. [12]2 Cor 13:3; Rom 8:9-11. [13]One hopes none of Severian's critics were aware that his further foray into *physiologia* is based on an erroneous relationship between the two different if not totally dissimilar Hebrew words. [14]The commentator's naiveté is disarming or, to Montfaucon, damning. It is as well he did not involve himself in the Hebrew meaning of not the *'iššâ* he had cited above, from Gen 2:23, but *'ādām* ("man") and *'ādāmâ* ("soil"), on which there is a play on words in Gen 2:5, and the difference between the defined form of "man" (*hā'ādām*) and the undefined personal name Adam (*'ādām*, Gen 2:22).

So since it has the name "fire," Scripture does not hesitate to call the angels human beings; when those in Mary's company came to the tomb, remember, it says, "Lo, two men stood beside them." They were angels, and angels are called fire: "He makes the angels his spirits, and his servants flaming fire."[15] It calls them men because they share intellect with the human being. Why are you surprised? God himself is called fire, he is called a human being; the Savior says of his own Father, "There was a certain person, a landowner, who planted a vineyard. He sent his servants, and his servants were killed." And to make it brief, "That person said, I still have one son; I shall send him in the hope that they will respect him."[16] What is the meaning of "person" in connection with the divine name? He did not speak of it as a parable, note; he did not say, "It is like," but "There was a certain person." Hence Moses said, "God is a consuming fire," and the Savior said of his coming, "I have come to cast fire on the earth."[17] So he adopts a term suited to the reality: Since the fire, as I said before, becomes big after being small, and a human being filled the ends of the earth after being small, the human being was called fire, which was due to the phrase *let us make the human being* having the meaning in the Hebrew *let us make fire.*

Let us make a human being in our image. Many people who were simple and uninstructed in spiritual matters had the idea that the human being was made in God's image in the sense that God has a nose, eyes of the same kind, ears of the same kind, a mouth of the same kind. This notion, however, is flawed and inappropriate. Even to this day there has been a heresy claiming that the divinity has a human form; since they heard, "The eyes of the Lord," "The ears

of the Lord," "The Lord smelled," "The mouth of the Lord said," "The hand of the Lord did," "The feet of the Lord stood,"[18] they depicted what is incorporeal with limbs, not realizing the inappropriateness of the notion. God says this for you to learn that a human being bears no resemblance to God as far as bodily appearance goes; I do not cancel the statement that says, *Let us make a human being in our image.* Instead, he shows what *in our image* means. "I shall fill heaven and earth, says the Lord"; and again, "Heaven is my throne and earth a footstool for my feet."[19]

Are we to follow the text? Are we to adhere slavishly to the expression? On the contrary, the movement of thought forbids me. How am I to understand heaven as a throne? The throne contains the person seated, whereas God is not contained. Nothing contains God; instead, he encircles and surrounds everything. So if he has heaven as a throne, how will he hold heaven in the palm of his hand? "Heaven is my throne and earth a footstool for my feet." Where is he seated? on what is visible? Stars under the firmament, water above: if he sits above, he is not above the heavens, only the upper heaven. If he is definitely seated, his feet rest on the earth. Is that the kind of posture you ascribe to the one who is without posture? Is it not irreverent also to think in those terms? Further, if his feet tread the earth, how do we sow, how do we reap, how do we travel without tramping on his feet? How did he hold heaven in the palm of his hand? How did he have large fingers that were commensurate with divinity?[20] And with fingers like that, how did he write on small tablets, not with many? We write using three fingers, with assistance from the others, God wrote on tablets

---

[15]Lk 24:4, where it is not "human being" (*anthrōpos*) that occurs but "male" (*anēr*); Ps 104:4. [16]The parable Mt 21:33-41 is indeed abbreviated; this time the term *anthrōpos* occurs. [17]Deut 4:24; Lk 12:49. Severian's literalism, like his naiveté, appears in his insistence that the parable in Mt 21 does not qualify as a parable because Jesus did not begin in a fashion Severian postulates for parables. (Is God also a sower?) [18]Ps 34:15; Gen 8:21; Is 1:20; Job 12:9; Ps 132:7. [19]Jer 23:24; Is 66:1. [20]Like Antiochene predecessors, Severian is concerned about anthropomorphic thinking, a "slavish adherence" to expressions in the text, but—typically—he tends to out-Herod Herod in listing all such possible excesses.

with one: have you seen anyone writing with one finger? These are figments of the imagination rather than actual words.

Let us make a human being in our image. God wants us to be imitators of him in virtue. What is the meaning of *in our image?* God is holy: if we were holy, we would be in the image of God; Scripture says, "Be holy because I am holy." God is righteous: if we had a share in righteousness, we would be an image of God; Scripture says, "The Lord is righteous and loves righteousness."[21] If we were kind and merciful, we would be an image of God; the Savior says, "Be merciful as your Father is merciful." Do you see where the image lies? Paul also brings out the meaning of image in saying, "Put off the old self and put on the new, created according to God in knowledge of truth, in the image of its creator."[22] Do you see that the expression *in our image* refers to the virtues? In what consists the image? Likewise in authority: *Let them have control of the fish of the sea and the birds of heaven, the wild beasts, the reptiles, the cattle and all the earth.* What marvelous sequence on God's part! What precision in narrative! Why does he begin by saying, *Let them have control of the fish of the sea?* The order of governance follows the order of creation. Since fish from the sea were the first ones made, and birds, and only after them the four-footed creatures from the land and the other animals, he therefore makes a beginning with the first ones made. *Let them have control of the fish of the sea and the birds of heaven, the wild beasts, the reptiles, and the cattle.* Hence the three youngsters in their hymn of praise in the furnace also observe the order: "Bless the Lord, seas and rivers. Bless the Lord, sea creatures and everything moving in the waters. Bless the Lord, all the birds of heaven. Bless him, wild beasts and cattle. Bless him, sons of men."[23]

There were also other examples to take account of—but let us return to the text. *God formed the human being.*[24] He did not simply say "he made" but *he formed.* We use "form" in the case of comeliness, as when you see a handsome face and comment on its beautiful formation. Far from making anything that was bodily unattractive, he had a view to comeliness and usefulness. For example, the eye has both characteristics, usefulness and comeliness: it gives sight, brightens the face, adorns the features and sees everything. The ear has usefulness, it has appearance; the earpiece attached to it is an adornment for the creature. Similarly, the nose provides the necessary sense of smell; but unlike the other creatures, it acts as a bridge and ensures comeliness, as is the case with the human being, the other animals not having nostrils, only a single organ. This was also the reason why God *formed* it—hence David's saying, "He who planted the ear, does he not hear? He who formed the eye, does he not perceive?"[25] This was also the way he made the earth, with a view to comeliness, with a view to usefulness. To avoid highlighting to you many comely things, I shall pass on after mentioning one. God gave the human being—I refer to the man—along with the other creatures also duality of breasts. Why does a man have a breast? For comeliness; granted that a woman has them for natural requirements, to supply milk—but why does a man have breasts? For comeliness, for proper adornment; just as with builders some things are done out of necessity, others for comeliness, so too God both adorned the human being and equipped him for meeting needs.[26]

He formed him by taking dust from the

---

[21]Lev 19:2; Ps 11:7. [22]Lk 6:36; Col 3:9-10. [23]Pr Azar 56-60. While Chrysostom in his ninth homily and second sermon had also taken "image" to imply governance and had also warned against anthropomorphic thinking, the idea of imitation of divine virtue does not occur there. [24]Gen 1:27. [25]Ps 94:9. Could Severian here be benefiting from the discussion by Didymus of the appropriateness of the word *form* in the creation of the human being in commentary on Zech 12:1? Chrysostom, admittedly, had likewise waxed eloquent on this choice of words. [26]Severian, in his attachment to detail in the text, can sometimes gild the lily, as he does here with his quaint example of God's forming us for use and charm.

earth. Blessed are the hopes of us Christians if we understand what we hear. Why did he not say, He took a sod from the earth? He formed a body of those proportions: did he not have need of a sod, taking dust instead? God foresaw what was going to happen as though actually present; in his foreknowledge that the living being would eventually die and turn into dust, by taking it for use initially in creation he demonstrated the hope of resurrection. He takes dust from the earth, so that when you see dust in a grave, you may know that he who formed that being also raises it. *God formed the human being by taking dust from the earth, and breathed into his face a breath of life.*[27] Note the difference between human beings and brute beasts. In making all the others, God produced everything at the one time, the soul along with the body. Pay attention, I beg you. In the case of the creatures that swim he made body and soul together. *Let the earth bring forth living beings:*[28] the soul emerged at the same time as the bodies. In the case of the human being he first makes the body, then the soul. What kind of hope does he have in mind? Their dissolution will be of the same kind as their formation; animals enjoy no resurrection for the reason that the way they were made is the way they also die, body and soul disappearing together. He took the body of the human being from the earth, whereas in creating him he personally gives the soul, creating it, not emitting it from his own being; his purpose was that when the body dies—or the person—we should not despair of the soul. After all, what is involved in the body's being buried in a grave? Do not expect that the soul is there; it was not taken from earth, nor does it return to earth. So he gave the basis for hope. Hence also in Ezekiel

he prophesies the resurrection in these terms: "A body was formed from the dead bones." It goes on, "Let the breath come from the four winds and enter these corpses, and let them live." In similar terms David also cries out, "You will remove their breath, they will fail and return to their dust. You will send your spirit, they will be created and renew the face of the earth." Do you see the creative Spirit? Do you see it cooperating with God?[29]

Let us, however, return to the text. *He breathed.*[30] By using the term *he breathed* he brought out the simplicity of the soul, accordingly not ringing the changes on it. Pay attention at this point. When creation had lost its original vigor, Christ renewed it at the incarnation. Adam was formed from the earth, Christ formed the eyes of the blind from mud so that you might come to recognize the one who took dust from the earth and formed you. God breathed a breath of life into the face of Adam; Christ breathed on the face of the apostles and said, "Receive a Holy Spirit."[31] The breath Adam lost Christ here restored, and the human being once again became a living soul. Pay attention: this is the movement of thought; even if my voice is failing, I still press on with my customary expectations and anticipate the entreaties of the brethren, trusting speech to be given me, not because of any worthiness of mine but because of the eagerness of the listeners. Even if we cannot match the merits of the saints, nevertheless they also suffered this trial and were handicapped by physical weakness. David confirms this in the words, "I am weary from crying, my throat is parched." It is better for a parched speaker to say something sound, however, than for someone with a sound voice to have a soul that is unsound.[32]

---

[27]Gen 2:7. [28]Cf. Gen 1:24. [29]Ezek 37:9 loosely cited; Ps 104:29-30. [30]"The text" to which Severian "returns" is that of Gen 2:7; he is once more finding the six days of creation in Gen 1 not fertile enough to prompt his thinking, and so he moves as well to a spiritual level. He is thus opting not to deal with the seventh day, the basis of the sabbath and the Priestly author's principal concern, as Chrysostom had likewise passed over Gen 2:1-4 rapidly; early commentators tended to focus on the Hexameron, the six days of creation. [31]Jn 20:22. [32]Ps 69:3. Again Severian admits his physical limitations as a preacher—or, according to Carter, his hoarseness resulting from having to preach twice daily.

God planted a garden in Eden in the east.[33] Why was Eden not in another quarter but in the east? The beginning of the existence of human beings was also the beginning of the course of the lights. God gives a premonition of what was to come: he sets the human being in the garden in the east so as to make clear that just as these lights rise, travel to the west and set, so too he must travel from life to death and set, on the model of the lights, likewise having a different rising in the resurrection of the dead. Adam traveled to the west and set in a grave; things of earth followed him and were buried with him as he set. Christ came and caused the one who had set to rise. Hence the prophet says of him, "Here is a man, his name is Dawn, and it will dawn beneath him," that is, from the grave. In Adam the human being set, in Christ it rose; Paul confirms this: "For just as all die in Adam, so too all will be made alive in Christ."[34]

God took the human being he had made, and set him in the garden. He brought him into a house that had been prepared: just as when you invite someone to a meal, you first prepare the house and then bring in the guest, so too in this case he prepared the garden as a worthy dwelling and then brought in the guest. Where was he formed? On the earth, outside the garden; just as the lights were made elsewhere and set in heaven, so Adam was formed outside in another part of the earth and then introduced into the garden. Where was it? Scripture says at the end when Adam was expelled, *God banished Adam from the garden of delight to till the earth from which he was taken.*[35]

He set him in the garden of delight to till and keep the garden.[36] To till: what was missing from the garden? If there was also need of a

tiller, whence did the plow come? Whence the other farming implements? To till and keep the commandment of God and believe the commandment was God's work; the Savior says, "This is the work of God, that you believe in him whom he has sent."[37] So just as believing in Christ is a work, so too believing in the commandment, that if he touched the tree, he would die, and if he did not touch it, he would live. Observance of spiritual teachings is a work. What was Paul's work? Surely Paul was not a farmer? Surely he did not have another occupation? Was not teaching his whole work? Was it not preaching? He says to the disciples, "You are my work in the Lord."[38] *To till and keep it,* the text says. From what? There was no robber, no vagrant, no one scheming—so keep it from what? To keep it for himself, lest he transgress and lose it, and on the other hand keep the garden for himself by keeping the commandment.

My thinking deteriorates with my voice, but let us keep the ideas coming.[39] *He set him in the garden.* Scripture now proceeds to sketch the future from what had preceded. *A river flows out of Eden to water the garden.* Learn from this that the garden was not a plantation, since its dimensions were small. In releasing water the river was so large that four rivers were formed from its overflow. *A river flows out of Eden to water the garden.* From that source, after providing water, it divided into four major waterways: the Tigris, the Nile, the Euphrates and the one called in Scripture Pishon, which they now call the Danube. Note the magnitude of a river that divides into four, and it is such a one that waters the garden. Why was it of that kind? Adam was the only person there: what need had he of

---

[33]Gen 2:8. [34]Zech 6:12, where the LXX reads Hebrew "shoot," in reference to Zerubbabel ("shoot of Babylon") as "dawn"; 1 Cor 15:22. Severian further develops the typology. [35]Gen 3:23. We have seen Severian putting to the text all these questions of doubtful relevance, some of them landing him in hot water. [36]Gen 2:15. [37]Jn 6:29. [38]1 Cor 9:1. [39]Again Severian pleads a failing voice. It is interesting, however, that in his homilies on this place Chrysostom had strangely little to say about the two significant trees, the tree of life and the tree of the knowledge of good and evil (Gen 2:9), and had passed over the verses on the four rivers (Gen 2:10-14), which are somewhat obscure in the Hebrew. Severian, typically, will not give them a wide berth.

such a river? It was not for him alone, however; rather, it was for the ends of the world. It was made ready for patriarchs, prophets, apostles, evangelists, martyrs, confessors, saints, faithful, true believers, people of pious life, all the righteous. After all, if the Savior promised paradise to the brigand who made his profession in a single moment, "Today you will be with me in paradise," the one who had labored from his youth, Abraham, Isaac, Jacob and the patriarchs stemming from him . . ."[40] And before all them it is the brigand who succeeds to paradise. So God does the works not in accord with what is immediately obvious but to leave us something to look forward to. Why did he make such a wide expanse of earth—for Adam, or for those who live in it now? *From there it parts into four major waterways;* he did not say four stretches but *waterways,* that is, springs.[41] Pishon is the name we have until recently given one, then Gihon; it is the Nile, Gihon being its former name. Jeremiah confirms that: "What reason have you to go to Egypt to drink the water of Gihon?"[42]

Pay attention here. Imagine the garden; this is something better done in imagination than in description. A large river in flood emerges and waters the garden. From there it moves into a subterranean cave and makes its way beyond the bounds of earth, known only to the Lord, who determined its path. Its flow is largely hidden from sight, and it spreads to different places, one being found in Ethiopia, another in the west, another in the east, according as God attracts its flow underground and gives rise to fresh springs from the original

river. Why is it like this? To prevent people following traces of the rivers and finding the garden, lest it be overtaken by human beings; after all, if it were accessible, the rich would be the first to find the garden, whereas God closed it to both poor and rich, so that they might find it only by virtue. What great efforts were made by patriarchs, prophets, saints, who searched for the garden without finding it! The brigand did not know the way, but he believed and truly found the way in the person of the one who said, "I am the way."[43] He found the garden that disobedience had closed to the first human being.

Now, I am looking for the reason why the historian in mentioning the first river said, *Fine gold is there, antimony and lapis lazuli.*[44] If he were making a complete map of the world, he should have mentioned the fine things to be found in every place, emeralds, sapphires, where topaz is to be found and the different kinds of material. Instead, he chose gold and two precious stones, the privilege of priesthood, since the priest wore a gold leaf on which was inscribed God's name. There were twelve stones on the priest's breast: cornelian, topaz, emerald, antimony, sapphire, jasper, jacinth, agate, amethyst, chrysolite, beryl, onyx.[45] From these twelve stones lapis lazuli was assigned to the priestly tribe and antimony to the royal tribe. Why? Because burning and giving light are characteristic of fire, and administering benefits and punishments characteristic of a king. He indicated the primacy of the tribe of Reuben with cornelian, Symeon with topaz, Levi with lapis lazuli, and with the redness[46] of

---

[40]Lk 23:43. A lacuna has developed at this point. It is interesting that Chrysostom also, in his seventh sermon, spends much time on the Lukan incident of the promise of paradise to the brigand on the very day of his sudden conversion. The LXX offers the Persian loan word *paradeisos* for "garden," susceptible of ambiguity. [41]Severian is not going to leave these verses unexplored, despite the obscurity. Of the Hebrew term read as "head" (*archē* in the LXX), Speiser, who renders it "upper course," says it "can have nothing to do with streams into which the river breaks up after it leaves Eden, but designates instead four branches which have merged within Eden. There is thus no basis for detouring the Gihon to Ethiopia, not to mention the search for the Pishon in various remote regions of the world." Severian could not be expected to heed this monitum. [42]Jer 2:18. [43]Jn 14:6. [44]Gen 2:12. Though at the beginning Severian was insistent that Moses as author of the creation account was not a mere *historiographos* but a fully inspired *prophētēs,* here and in Homily Four he has been prepared to use the former term. He casts the author in his own image, one who leaves no detail unexplained. [45]Ex 28:17-20. [46]Or, in a different reading, "the fire."

---

antimony Judah, from which is descended the Christ. Of course, Isaiah a long time later says to Jerusalem, "I have inscribed your walls on my hands, and you are continually before me. Lo, I am preparing antimony as your precious stone [meaning the Savior]. Lo, I am laying a foundation stone in Sion, chosen, precious, and whoever believes in it will not be confounded." Hence antimony was assigned to the royal tribe and lapis lazuli to the priestly tribe, since performance is quite proper to priesthood.[47]

To that river are attributed four river sources. So why is the water from them not equal in volume? It is, in fact, a question to be explored by the scholars, why they all do not have equal volume if they spring from one river or one source. What is the reason, then?[48] They are affected by the terrain and the nature of the places through which they flow: just as water itself is naturally of the same quality, but its quality if it is tainted with absinthe differs from its quality if tainted with dill or with rue, there being one nature but a change caused by the additives, so too in the case of rivers. Since they travel through strange places, one through a place with one quality, another through another, they are affected by the places.

Now, since he determined the quality of the rivers by their location, he now makes in the garden *every tree fair to behold and pleasing as food*.[49] In advance he removed any excuse from the transgressor; since it said in reference to the woman, *The woman saw that the tree was fair to behold and pleasing as food*,[50] to prevent anyone thinking that that one alone was more charming than the other trees he confirmed that they all had this attribute in being pleasing and fair to behold, for you to learn that,

far from transgressing out of need, he[51] went astray despite enjoying an abundance. The text goes on, *There was also the tree of life in the middle of the garden, and the tree for knowing good and evil.* There were three differences in the trees: some were given to him for living, some for living well and some for living always. So he could live by accessing the trees by which God nourished him, but he was forbidden access to the trees by which he could live well; living well was possible by accessing the trees that God had not forbidden and not accessing the trees he had forbidden. Living well is obeying God. That tree of life was *in the middle* like a prize, the tree of knowledge like a contest, like a ring; by keeping the commandment regarding this tree you win the prize. Notice what is remarkable: all the trees around the garden were evergreen, all in fruit; only two in the middle were a ring, a stadium, whereas those around them were there for nourishment.

Let the account of the transgression and the tree keep for another time; the text in hand awaits. God brings all the animals to Adam. Let the heretics give heed, and do not be surprised if the text is directed to the heretics in every verse and in every word; those who rear up against the glorious kingdom are condemned on every score. "A stone cries out from the wall." It is not I that says so, but a verse from Scripture; "not one jot, not one tittle"[52] leaves the heretics blameless, at all points those denying the Lord of all are condemned. So pay attention. It was a remarkable thing to behold, Adam standing there and God like a servant bringing them to Adam; *God brought the animals*, the text says.[53] Pay attention to this,

---

[47]Is 49:16; 54:11; 28:16 (naturally, for Severian the Genesis account predates Isaiah of Jerusalem). The six days of creation left well behind, Severian is busy chasing up other details of Gen 2, here wanting to relate the Greek term (for lapis lazuli?) *prasinos* to the verb *prassō*. [48]Having left to the *philomatheis* a detail that is of no interest to the text, Severian typically cannot resist chasing it up himself. [49]Gen 2:9. [50]Gen 3:6. [51]Or "she." To this point at least, Severian has not directed strictures against the woman as the source of the transgression as Chrysostom had in Homily Sixteen. He is known to have had had better relations with the women of the court at Constantinople, including the empress Eudoxia. [52]Hab 2:11; Mt 5:18. [53]Gen 2:19. Severian likes to dramatize a biblical scene, which probably has the effect of entrenching literalist understanding.

not to the text but to the notion. Imagine God standing there and Adam assessing them; God parades them all and says to Adam, Come now, say what you think this one should be called. Let its name be lion; God so determined, the text says. Next, this one: Let its name be bull. Good choice. In a similar fashion God confirmed each of the names, Scripture saying, *He brought them to Adam to see what they were to be called; and whatever Adam called them, that was their name.*[54] Take note: since he had made him in his image, he wanted to promote him to public importance and show in truth that he bore the image of wisdom. Note the remarkable feature: God in turn confirmed the names, wanting a sign to be given through this example that Adam's decisions were in harmony with God's wishes. Of course, in its desire to show that God had predetermined the names he imposed, Scripture says, *And whatever Adam called them, that was their name*—in other words, It was predetermined, God decreed it.

Let us return, however, to the text in hand. Adam stood there, God presented the animals to him, and the master was not insulted by presenting them to the servant. If the heretics were to hear that Christ presents us to the Father, they would immediately say, Do you see that he is a servant? *He brought them to Adam.* The servant stood there making decisions, and the master presented them. God was not insulted by presenting them to Adam, whereas if they were to hear of Christ presenting us to the Father, they would reduce him to the level of a servant. If the Savior says, "No one comes to the Father except through me," immediately the heretics prick their ears, or rather strain them. In presenting the animals to Adam, God is not his attendant; if God presents a

human being to God, does he take the role of an attendant? But in case ignorance of the text fosters the ailment in you: I am aware that the Son presents to the Father and the Father to the Son; he said, "No one comes to the Father except through me," and he likewise said, "No one comes to me unless the heavenly Father draws him."[55] I know I said this before,[56] but the statement is relevant to the argument; at that time it happened to go unheeded, whereas now I am saying it.

Think of the great number of four-footed animals; think of the tame ones, the wild ones, those on the mountains, those on the plains, those in Gaul, those in India, those in all the regions of the world. Likewise serpents, genera and species, all the birds, the swimming creatures, all those in the sea, those in marshes, those in rivers—all these he brought, and Adam gave each one a name, and instead of demurring God concurred. Countless names, and God acquiesced, whereas God mentions a single name in testimony from heaven—"This is my Son"[57]—and the heretics challenge the voice testifying to the single name, that holy voice which accepted countless names without canceling any. The animals were brought and named. He now stands there as king. Just as when men join the army, they are given the royal seal as a distinguishing sign, so when he was on the point of consigning lordship to him, he has him give names as lord, only the Lord and Father giving names. Pay attention. God gave some of the names, Adam others. God gave names to heaven, earth, sea, firmament, day, light, night, fruit, plant, grass, trees, whereas Adam named the cattle and the birds—peacock, eagle, calf, sheep; the latter gives names to species, the former to genera, lest the maker's word be frustrated,

---

[54]Gen 2:19. Severian does not add the naive comment of Chrysostom, "The names he imposed on them remain up to the present time." [55]Jn 14:6; 6:44. The attraction of Adam's naming the animals, in preference to development of the Fall pericope, lies in its use by Arians to promote their subordinationist views. [56]R. E. Carter, "The Chronology of Twenty Homilies of Severian of Gabala," 11, points out that this is a reference to a sermon, now entitled *De Sigillis Sermo*, the first in a series of christological homilies, recently given in Constantinople in January 401, where the two Johannine citations also occur. [57]Mt 5:17.

Let us make a human being in our image. God gave names to the lights—the Bear, Orion, the Pleiades, the evening star, the morning star—all these God named; David confirms this in saying, "He counts the great number of stars and gives names to them all."[58] God gives names to what is on high, Adam to what is on earth; God names heaven, earth, everything else, Adam names fire, human beings.

What does Adam name? He names cattle, birds, serpents, wild beasts. Adam gives a further name, bone, flesh, saying of the woman, *This is now bone of my bones and flesh of my flesh.*[59] When he formed him, remember, he did not say that he formed him from bones and flesh; likewise, God said *male,* he says *man,* God said *female,* he says *woman.*[60] And what is remarkable is that he was filled with the Holy Spirit; not yet the wretched transgressor, he was full of grace, enjoying in himself the fullness of inspiration, which a few days ago I clarified in the case of your good selves. That is to say, he knew the past, he knew the present, he knew the future. In what way did he have knowledge of the present? Bone is in the body and not visible from outside; but since he had the Spirit, he said, *This is now bone of my bones.* How could he have known it unless the Holy Spirit had revealed it? Why, then, bone first and flesh next? Because he had first taken a rib from him: *This one will be called Woman because out of Man this one was taken.*[61] In inspired fashion he mentions the past, refers to the present, tells the future: *For this reason a man will leave his father and mother.* There was no married life yet, and from where came father and mother? Again let heretics give heed. God wanted to make a wife for Adam. *God caused a spell to come upon Adam, and he fell asleep.* Every word of God of old has proved a norm for nature; from the outset he taught how the new creature is detached from the person. *God caused Adam to fall asleep.* What a remarkable thing: he mentions the time when marital intercourse occurs. Sleep is called a spell because a person is, so to say, outside himself.[62] The soul is inside and is not inside: it does not feel, it does not understand, it hears without hearing. As we say these days, He was in a spell, being out of touch with reality; this is what the soul is like when it is out of touch with the senses, it is in a spell.

He fell asleep, and God took one of his ribs. Let the heretics pose the following questions: How did God take it? How was it that Adam did not feel pain? How did he not suffer? A single hair is pulled from the body, and we suffer; even if someone is fast asleep, the sleeper is woken by the pain; so with the removal of such a large member, the excision of a complete rib, did the sleeper not wake up?[63] He did not pluck it out violently so that he would awaken, he did not excise it; rather, Scripture intends to show the rapidity of the craftsman and so says, *He took.* The ligaments were loosened, and he did not feel it? He took the rib just as he took the dust. If one person had done the binding and another had done the loosing, it would have been a struggle; but if it was the binder who loosened, how painlessly he did the loosing. *He took the rib, and closed up the flesh in its place.* How did he close it up? Did he pull some of the other flesh? Everybody that is pulled on becomes more fragile. How did he close it up? We talk about a body and fail to understand; we talk about God, and do we meddle? *The Lord fashioned the rib he had taken from Adam into a woman.*[64] How were eyes fastened in place from a rib? how a heart for thinking? how a tongue for speaking? how

---

[58]Ps 147:4. [59]Gen 2:23. [60]Cf. Gen 1:27. Chrysostom also proceeds to attribute the gift of inspiration to Adam. [61]Gen 2:23. [62]Severian is playing upon the roots of the word "spell," *ekstasis.* [63]Chrysostom, too, was aware that literalistic listeners had raised these questions but warned them not to "meddle." Severian, we have often seen, is all for meddling. [64]Gen 2:22. Despite Severian's disclaimer about "meddling" and "prying," he is treating the verses about the formation of woman as a surgical textbook. He will go into even further anatomical detail in Homily Seven in repeating his comments on this incident.

were the intestines unfolded from a rib? how was a liver made from a rib? You are incapable of grasping how these things were done, and yet you pry into the craftsman?

Instead, see the figure of Christ at every point. God did not take the rib from Adam before he put him to sleep. Why? It was through a rib that the sin was destined to be committed which entered through the woman. The Savior came from a rib, bearing water and blood[65]—water that washed away sins and blood that provided us with the Eucharist. Note the type: when Adam was put to sleep, a rib was taken; when sleep came upon the body of Christ, his side was opened so that he might win back the tragedy of old by the new story—I mean the sleep coming through crucifixion.

He fashioned the rib into a woman, and brought her to Adam. What great lovingkindness on the part of the Lord! What marvelous things he makes, forms, confers! He produces living beings, he acts as a matchmaker; since Adam was an orphan and Eve a maiden without father or mother to discharge that role, as it were, God fills the role of father and mother. Note the law: every statement by God in olden times is a norm for nature. *God brought the woman to Adam*, and this remained the law to this day, the woman being for the man; he does not escort the man to the woman.[66]

They were naked, and were not ashamed. The norm abides, the law cries aloud: a man is ashamed with everyone except his own wife; a woman is embarrassed by everyone except her own husband. While I said this in keeping with the law, the reason for their not being ashamed of nakedness was that they were clad in immortality, vested with glory; the glory did not allow them to be seen as naked, since

it covered their nakedness. Where else could you see someone naked and not ashamed? You would find it in Christ. Peter, John and James went to the tomb in search of the body but did not find it; instead, they found his garments folded,[67] the purpose being a demonstration that after the resurrection of Christ the appearance of Adam in olden times might be preserved in him; he was undressed, not naked but clad. Christ rose, and he laid aside the garments that Adam had put on, he was naked but not seen as naked. After the resurrection, women saw the garments laid aside. Martha and Mary saw him, recognized him, prostrated themselves but did not see him as naked.[68] Whence came the garments he put on? He had cast them aside in the tomb, remember; soldiers had divided his outer garments. From where came the garments he wore in this way? How was the naked one not naked?

And I have another inquiry: why did they see the garments and the shroud by themselves, and by itself the cloth in which the saving head had been bound?[69] To demonstrate the holy grace, the occurrence of the resurrection without tumult. Since the Jews were bent on claiming that he had been spirited away by the disciples,[70] he leaves his garments in the tomb; body snatchers snatch body and clothes together. Now, it would have been possible to see the Savior emerging from the tomb in the way Joseph did from the house of the Egyptian woman.[71] Note the difference: after the resurrection, Christ appeared to them naked, and Peter was naked; but while the former possessed immortality, the latter was still mortal. Jesus stood on the shore, and vested in glory he said, "Children, surely you have something to eat?" No, they replied, we do not (not recog-

---

[65]Cf. Jn 19:34, where also a modern commentator like A. Feuillet will see in the use of *pleura* ("rib, side") an echo of its occurrence in the Genesis account. The play upon the two meanings occurs also at the end of the seventh homily (Savile 5:652). Again Severian shows his readiness to move to another level of meaning.   [66]It would seem an unsafe principle to cite statements from ancient texts that are not meant prescriptively as having normative effect in later ages. Literalism does not make allowance for genre.   [67]Jn 20:3-7, where James is not included.   [68]Various Gospel accounts are harmonized here by Severian, who takes the Mary (Magdalene) at the tomb to be the sister of Martha (not included in those accounts).   [69]Jn 20:7.   [70]Mt 27:64.   [71]Gen 39:12.

nizing him). He then said, "Cast your net on the right side of the boat." They cast and netted a great number. John recognized him and said to Peter, "It is the Lord." How remarkable: it was not from his voice he recognized him but from his deeds. "Peter put on his upper garment, for he was naked." He was ashamed of his mortal body; he was not embarrassed by the immortal one.[72]

Let us, by contrast, bow down to the one who invests us with glory, who invests the world with immortality; let us beseech him to invest us with faith, hope of salvation, glory in Christ. Because to the Father, with the only Son and the Holy Spirit, be the glory, now and forever, for ages of ages. Amen.

Homily Six

> On the sixth day of creation, on the first-
>   formed,
> on the serpent, on the tree of knowledge,
> on life in the garden and God's converse
>   with Adam

Come now, let us once more take up our promise and bring to an end our treatment of the garden.[1] After all, if Adam's expulsion from the garden proved an insufferable misfortune, much more would our expulsion from the mention of the garden also be a misfortune. Now, let us address our theme, not by conducting the study in ordinary terms but by finding the solution to problems in holy Scripture itself. After all, the person who thinks and judges in the way he wishes deceives himself, whereas the one who finds a solution to problems in Scripture has truth itself to guide him to it. Since many even of the faithful have problems in reading it,[2] then, and many unbelievers blaspheme it in their ignorance, with the inten-

tion of giving encouragement to the saints and a rebuke to the unbelievers let us begin, to the best of our ability, begging God to supply us with an abundance of truth.

On the one hand, then, how the human being was formed, how he received bodily form, how his soul was created by God and incorporated in his body, how he had the garden as his dwelling has been sufficiently explained, if not worthily, at least to the extent of our ability. At this point, on the other hand, let us direct our attention to the text. While all the earth was given to Adam, the garden was his special dwelling. Now, he was allowed also to move beyond the garden; but what was beyond the garden was assigned as the dwelling not of the human being but of the brute beasts, the cattle, the four-footed animals, the wild animals, the reptiles. The garden, however, was a royal and lordly manor for him. God also brought the animals to Adam for the reason of their difference from him; subjects are presented to the master only when there is need of them. The animals were named and immediately banished, whereas Adam remained in the garden.

At this point let us focus on the precise meaning. The brute beasts were instructed to approach Adam, bow down and cringe before him. For example, it was like the three different kinds of trees: there were trees that provided him with food for living, trees that equipped him for living well and a tree that kept him living forever. Likewise, he was given three different kinds of brute beasts: one for food—assigned not for himself alone but for the human race in general—another for service, another for consolation. For example, for food were those that are now slaughtered, for service were horses, camels, asses, oxen and the other working animals, and for consolation the

---

[72]Jn 21:4-8. We have come some distance from the days of creation. Lenten themes are also going without mention.   **Homily Six**
[1]As noted above, the precise sense in each use of *paradeisos*, whether "garden" or "paradise," is unclear. Either way, the commentator has strayed from the six days.   [2]Severian will proceed to nominate a spiritual approach to paradise as one of the errors.

animals that mimic, the joyful cries of birds in flight, which also charm the ear. In other words, just as a body after hard work does not take on further labor unless if divests itself of that labor, so too the soul that undergoes the labor of virtue does not measure up to the demands of virtue unless consoled by pleasant sights.

When God sees a soul that is weary, he consoles it with what is pleasant, as also happens in our case. Often on returning from the market place a person is stressed in mind with countless worries, often experiencing depressing sights and encountering unbearable misfortunes and losses; but on reaching home he derives consolation from his child, and the tender thoughts alleviate the harshness of work. You see, when his wife does not approach him in his discouragement by way of comfort since her consolation would be untimely, and no servant presumes to offer encouragement, God introduces the simplicity of nature to offer pardon for what it is unaware of and by this means soothes the soul wearied by labor. If a servant laughs, he is thought to be mocking the master's moods; if the wife jokes, she is thought to be insensitive to the misfortune; the child is not suspected of flattery in its natural guilelessness. It often happens that what friends did not manage with their advice or sages with their suggestions, a child by merely giggling succeeds completely in solving the problem. At this point, at the very climax of distress, on seeing the child he spurns its advances and rebuffs its consolation as untimely; but by its persistence he is won over, and to its frequent glances his mind capitulates. He then picks up the child, dismisses his distress and says, God gives me only this, and I have no concern for anything else.[3]

Do you see how even from chance events God prompts comfort for the soul? Since Adam was by himself in the garden, therefore, with no friend, no neighbor, no kith and kin, God presented him with the animals for his consolation—for example, as is the case today, the animals that mimic, some imitating gestures, some sounds: a monkey mimics people's gestures and the like, a parrot and other birds his voice. So he enjoyed consolation from the brute beasts, some by the sounds they make, others by fawning. Of the many creatures providing him with consolation, then, the serpent was wilier than all the beasts of the earth, as Scripture says, *Now, the serpent was the wiliest of all the beasts that the Lord God had made.*[4] It was therefore better at mimicking than the mimics and better than those that fawned. Do not focus on its appearance today, the fact that we both shun and abhor it; it was not like that in the beginning: the serpent was friendly and better at fawning on people. So who made it hostile? God's sentence: *Accursed are you beyond all the wild animals. I shall put enmity between you and the woman.*[5] That enmity did away with friendship. By friendship I mean not the rational kind but an unreasoning acquaintance: just as today a dog gives evidence of an appearance of friendship, not in word but in its natural movements, so too the serpent fawned upon the human being. Because of its close familiarity, therefore, it struck the devil as an ideal instrument; on seeing Adam taking pleasure in the serpent, then, and the latter fawning on him and mimicking many human ways, the architect of evil was moved to pondering, like those who hatch plots and carry them out by foisting them on others. After all, no one prevails through someone else's efforts unless first through his own; as the Savior

---

[3]Severian is preparing to introduce the serpent, and so he exploits the mention of Adam's naming the animals (Gen 2:19-20) to suggest that some of them were his pets, against the evidence of the text. In so doing he develops this charming account of children beguiling their parents, a presentation so carefully crafted as to imply previous development by Severian or someone else. [4]Gen 3:1; the accent on mimicking prepares the congregation for a talking serpent. This homily, too, is moving beyond the six days of creation, proceeding to deal with the Fall. [5]Gen 3:14-15.

said, "One's enemies are those of one's own household."[6] Accordingly, he speaks through the serpent, with Adam as the object.

I beg your good selves not to take these words idly. It is not a pointless question; many people inquire how it was that the serpent spoke: was it by a human voice or a serpent's hissing, and Eve understood it? Before the Fall, Adam was filled with wisdom, understanding and divine inspiration. Consider the extent of his wisdom, the fact that a single human being was capable, without a teacher and instructed by no one, of giving names to all the birds, the animals, the wild serpents, and in short all of them. Imagine the species, the genera—in short, he gave as many names as today we with all our experience are unable to duplicate.[7] When God brought the animals to the human being, therefore, in his wisdom and possession of God's spirit he had regard to the specificity of each one. So he paid attention to the serpent as a wily animal, with senses, taking his movements as intentions. Since Adam was under this impression, the devil pondered both the serpent's wily nature and Adam's attitude to it in treating the serpent as intelligent. Accordingly, he spoke through it so that Adam might get the idea that it was the serpent in its wily ways that succeeded in imitating human speech.

So the serpent made its approach. Now, nowhere does Scripture say it was the devil speaking in the serpent; Moses passed by the incident without comment. Give careful attention, I beg you. Paul, who was the second person in paradise, did not personally explain the text, either, saying instead, "I promised you in marriage to one husband, to present you as a chaste virgin to Christ.

But I am afraid that as the serpent in its cunning deceived Eve,"[8] with no mention of the devil. He was a faithful custodian of the Scriptures, a minister of the Scriptures, a teacher of the Scriptures, an interpreter of the Scriptures; he declined to explain the text, his intention being not to explain the drift of the Scriptures; instead, he explained the obscurity by giving clarification. "But I am afraid that as the serpent in its cunning deceived Eve," he said, "so your thoughts will be led astray." "As": how? surely Paul was not afraid of the serpent's coming again and deceiving some people? Instead, I know (he means) that whereas that serpent does not make an appearance, the one working through him does. But while Paul, in being a faithful minister and custodian of the holy Scriptures, did not distort the text, clarifying its meaning instead, the one who is Lord of what is old, what is new and what is to come elucidated the obscurity in case anyone should attribute the sin to the serpent and not to the one activating it. To the Jews, therefore, when they said, "We are from God," Christ replied, "If you were from God, you would do God's works and will; but as it is, you are from your father the devil." He mentioned the devil and immediately introduced this incident, saying, "He was a murderer from the beginning."[9] Being a servant, the servant commented; as Lord the Lord elaborated, presenting the one who murdered Adam, saying not merely "killer" but "murderer"; it was not a single person he destroyed but in him the whole of humanity.

"He does not stand in the truth," he said, "because he is a liar." Notice how he explained what a devil is, what a liar is. How did it lie? *The serpent said to the woman, Why did God*

---

[6]Mt 10:36; Mic 7:6. Chrysostom depicts the devil's employment of the serpent in similar terms, the phrase "ideal instrument" occurring in his Homily Sixteen. [7]While Severian here, too, seems to resonate with a naive comment by Chrysostom, "The names Adam imposed on the animals remain up to the present time," the latter chose not to respond to the question that proves irresistible to Severian, how was it that the serpent spoke? [8]1 Cor 11:2-3, "second in paradise" (on the basis of 2 Cor 12:2?) after Luke's brigand, presumably. [9]Jn 8:41-42, 44. Instead of explaining the story of the Fall and its characters as figurative or representative, Severian is going to the trouble to say that, yes, there was a talking serpent, but the devil was using it for his purposes. Adam took it this way, as did Paul, as did Jesus.

tell you not to eat of any tree?[10] Do you see the liar? God had said, Eat of any tree, but do not eat of one tree, whereas the liar says, *Why did God say not to eat of any tree?* Christ's statement was not wrong, "He is a liar." He lied, and gravely, too. You see, when someone wants to commit a deed of malice, that person pleads necessity or ignorance so as to avoid suspicion of knavery, as if to say, I was not aware, there was no premeditation, I came unsuspecting, I know nothing. Have you not had experience of many such people? Are we not familiar with the forms of deception? Do they not commit such crimes and pretend ignorance? The devil was like that, too: *Why did God say?*—in other words, I overheard, or imperfectly heard, him tell you not to eat of any tree. Thinking it was ignorance, the woman corrected the statement: That was not what he said, she replies, God did not say not to eat of any tree; he gave permission for every tree, only forbidding us to eat of one particular tree. His words were, in fact, *Do not eat in case you die.*[11] He gave the impression of learning something he did not know; he was thus not suspected of premeditation and says to her, *You will not really die.*[12] Another lie, note: though God had said, *On the day you eat it, you will really die,* the devil says, *You will not die*—his second lie—*for he knows that on the day you eat it you will be like gods*—a third lie, note. See the devil's premeditated evil; he is already plotting to sow error in the world. And since he planned, as I said, to give rise to polytheism in the world, he began as if stating a fact by sowing in the woman's hearing the impression of there being many gods. While the architect of evil thus sowed the thought of gods, however, God in his foreknowledge took steps to ensure the future error not be uttered by a human mouth; his intention was that an utterance about gods not be the first rational statement but a serpent's opening remark, so

that every reference to idols be compared with the latter's.

I am aware that you both make allowances for the expression and grasp the holy meaning of the Scriptures. Let no one focus on the tone of the statement, therefore, but on the force of the sentiments. *God knows, in fact,* he went on, *that on the day you eat you will be like gods, knowing good and evil.*[13] It is the objection of many people, especially the followers of God's enemy Porphyry, who wrote diatribes against Christians and seduced many from the divine teaching—it is their objection, then, Why did God forbid the knowledge of good and evil?[14] Granted that he forbade evil; why also good? By saying, *Do not eat from the tree of the knowledge of good and evil,* they claim, he forbids the knowledge of evil; why also good? Evil is always scheming against itself and giving openings to its own disadvantage. God did not forbid the knowledge of good; Adam had it, even before eating. After all, if he did not have knowledge, how did he recognize the woman? Whence came his familiarity with natural science, *bone of my bones and flesh of my flesh?* How did he also prophesy the future, *She will be called woman, because she was taken from man. Hence a man will leave his father and mother* and so on? Did he know such things, and not know evil? He knew God, he kept what God wanted, he had knowledge, he gave all those names—so how could he have had no knowledge of good? What is the truth, then? Far from forbidding knowledge of good, God's wish is that along with good there be no knowledge of evil.

Now, from the Scriptures I shall unravel the tangled arguments of impiety. Paul says, "You cannot drink the cup of the Lord and the cup of demons." Far from forbidding both, he declares one holy and rejects the other as impure and profane. The Savior also says in similar

---

[10]Gen 3:1. [11]Gen 3:3. [12]Gen 3:4. [13]Gen 3:5. [14]Porphyry in the third century, raised a Christian in Tyre, turned neo-Platonist and attacked the Old Testament.

fashion, "You cannot serve God and wealth";[15] it is impossible to serve God and a demon at the same time. Likewise God forbade gaining a knowledge of evil in case the knowledge of evil be combined with good. Let us pay attention at this point. Why on earth was it called the tree of the knowledge of good and evil? That was not its nature; it only conveyed such a circumstance—it was Scripture's way of speaking, I mean. Let me quote an example: one spring of water in the desert was given the name water of contradiction, "I tested you at the water of contradiction." Surely the water did not have that nature, prompting the people to rebellion? So why in drinking did Moses not rebel? Because it was given the name water of contradiction, not through having that nature but on account of the incident that happened there; since it was there that the people rebelled, accordingly it was called water of contradiction.[16] Again, Jacob saw God (in so far as it is humanly possible to see him) and called the place Form of God; the place did not bear the form of God or shape of God—instead, since the vision happened to him there, he called the place after the incident.[17] Another place was called Peace of God; when an angel appeared to Gideon, he was afraid, and said, "Alas, alas, I am dying, I have seen God's angel. But the angel said, Peace be to you, do not fear. Gideon built an altar and called it Peace of God."[18]

So just as the altar itself did not possess peace but was a symbol of the peace that occurred and was bestowed, and just as the water did not contain contradiction but was given that name on account of the incident that happened there, so too the tree did not possess knowledge; rather, it was because every sinner comes to a knowledge of the sins he has committed.[19] To quote a further example: sometimes we travel through robber-infested places, and people are in the habit of saying, These places are really fearsome. Surely it is not the place that has fear? Do they not say that on account of the robbers loitering in that place? Likewise that tree was also not by nature responsible for death-dealing knowledge; instead, it got that name from the tragedy befalling Adam. Now, I am being brief in explicating the matter; the divine Scripture does not offer problems.[20] Today we have an altar, and the faithful participate in it. Surely the gift itself does not contain salvation of its nature, or on account of the invocation of the glory you do not have a guarantee from those present not to be uncertain about those who have gone before? In that case food proved death-dealing; here it is life-giving. If this food saves by its nature and not by grace, that one also destroys by its nature and not by transgression.[21] I shall bring to your notice another death-dealing food outside paradise, namely, idolatry. Why, in fact, did the martyrs refuse to eat meat? Why were they afraid to eat it? Surely they would not have died if they had eaten it? Not at all; instead, since the idols were invoked, they shunned it, not the food but the invocation of those vile things. That was the way the tree gave knowledge of evil and good, not by offering knowledge but by conveying it through the transgression; experience always teaches the foolish that transgression is evil.[22]

The problem will be resolved in another way as well, not because the former ones were

---

[15]1 Cor 10:21; Mt 6:24. [16]Ps 81:7, where the LXX correctly renders Meribah as water of contradiction. Is Severian familiar with the incident recorded in Ex 17:1-7 of the people's unrest leading to the name, and does he presume his congregation likewise knows it? [17]Gen 32:31, the LXX again correctly rendering Peniel. Severian seems to have taken this point of naming places after events and this particular biblical example from Chrysostom's seventh sermon. [18]Judg 6:22, 24. [19]Severian, who proceeds to claim he has been concise in his explanation of the tree's name, suggests here and confirms later what a modern commentator like von Rad reminds us of, that "the Hebrew yd' ('to know') never signifies purely intellectual knowing, but in a much wider sense an 'experiencing,' a 'becoming acquainted with,' even an 'ability'" GenComm, pp. 89. [20]At the beginning of this homily, Severian had said the opposite. But he is right to the extent that many problems, or at least challenges, are of his own making. [21]Severian is comparing eucharistic bread with the fruit on the tree and then with meat offered to idols. [22]Chrysostom had labored the same point in his seventh sermon, that we learn best from experience.

wide of the mark but because of the richness of God's grace; let no one think that the addition of many ideas is the result of limitations in the former ones: God's grace is rich and supplies us with much from its treasury, provided we are worthy. So pay attention. The martyrs declined food of idolaters, refusing to eat it, just as Adam would have been saved if he had refused fruit from the tree. Now, the fact that it was not the knowledge of good and evil that was hateful is made clear by reality. When God asks without taking action, does he know it or not? Who would presume to claim that he does not know it? It is not knowledge, in fact, but action. Surely Paul in saying, "Shun fornication," was not unaware what fornication is? Is the person who shuns adultery unaware of what adultery is? Yet knowledge of it does not condemn him. God knows all our actions, listing them in the words, "From the heart proceed evil intentions, murder, adultery, false witness, incontinence, envy, avarice. These are what defile a person."[23] Is it in ignorance or in awareness that God and the apostle say this? So knowledge was no liability to Adam; it was not ignorance that did the damage but transgression. Now, I would like to put this question to him: what sort of good did he learn from the tree, what sort of evil? After eating, did he know what murder is? There was no one yet to punish him; adultery was unknown, there being no marriage yet; there was no fornication, no robbery, since there were no rich and poor yet; there was no slander or perjury. So what sort of evil did he know, or was it only the fact that it was good to obey God and evil to disobey God? I cite a common and widespread expression in case you accuse me of audacity; we are in the habit of saying to sinners, threatening them with conversion: I am going

to make you learn conversion. Surely by *knowledge* he does not mean learning? So knowledge comes from experience of misfortunes. He taught him to know how much trouble he was involved in by transgressing.

Pay careful attention, therefore; even if we told you this the day before yesterday, the topic requires treatment.[24] God, who had given everything, was invisible; the one who received everything from God was visible. The human being was alone; the brute beasts were around him. He had no one to outrank him. God gave him a law, the tree being a public reminder of it, in case he should forget that he had been given lordship. For example, he would go about eating the fruit with his wife, come near the tree and say, Let us not touch this tree, since God gave instructions about it. The visible thing was a reminder of the invisible, as happens these days, too. Think of all the rulers there are throughout the land; and since an emperor is not present to everyone, there is need to set up an effigy of the emperor in courts, in public places, in meeting rooms, in theaters.[25] In every place where an official does business it needs to be present so as to confirm what is enacted. So, as the emperor cannot be present everywhere, being only human, so it is impossible in turn for God to be visible to human beings, being divine. He gave the tree as a symbol of imperial power, providing a reminder to Adam that he had received lordship of everything; it said, Know the one who has given authority. And for you to learn how the tree reminded them, when the serpent wanted to deceive the woman and said to her, *Why did God tell you not to eat of any tree?* the woman did not forget the law, instead correcting his ignorance by saying, That is not what God said; we may eat from all the trees, except

---

[23]1 Cor 6:18; Mt 15:19-20. The response to the objection by Porphyry's followers is proving very lengthy. Severian, despite his claims, does not exemplify the conciseness of, say, a Theodoret. [24]It seems clear that Severian refers to the subject matter of Homily Five, which he now speaks of as being delivered "the day before yesterday" or "the other day" (*proēn*; certainly not "yesterday"). So in this case, unless he is just being vague, a day or so seems to have elapsed between the two homilies. [25]If the tree as an imperial effigy is an effective image, it resembles Chrysostom's presentation in his eighth sermon of the tree as an imperial decree.

this tree, of which God said, Do not eat of it or touch it. Note the precision: God had not said, Do not touch it, nor was touching it risky; but they possessed the divine gift of prudence, and since they were free to access the others, they determined for themselves, Whereas God said, Do not taste of this tree, we shall not even touch it. This was the degree of concern the woman had to observe God's command.

So the tree stood in the middle of the garden, and it was by it that he deceived them. Listen to the extraordinary event: he used an instrument for the deceit, something implanted in the human being; in forming the human being God instilled in him desire for God along with knowledge as well. So when he saw desire aflame in them, he said, *You will be like gods*: as it is, being human, you cannot be with God all the time; but if you become godlike, you will be with him at all times. He did not say to them, note, If you eat, you will become enemies of God. So it is longing for equality with God that deceives the woman, and she did not so much deceive as convince her husband; Paul confirms this in saying, "Adam was not deceived."[26] Why was he condemned? Note the dreadful business: the woman was deceived and ate; after eating it, she convinces her husband as well, so as not to be the only one to go astray. She convinced him, she did not deceive him, as often happens today, too: a man comes to know the faith, loves the law, is enthusiastic about right teaching but is persuaded by his wife to give no evidence of his enthusiasm, not out of ignorance but under the influence of his partner. Many people, in fact, were under the impression that it was in ignorance that Adam took it from his wife, not knowing from where she had taken the fruit. But he had no excuse: God censures him in saying to him, *Because you listened to your wife's words;*[27] he did not say, Because you took it from your wife. He could not really claim, I was unaware, I did not know from where she got the fruit. The husband's fault lay not in being deceived but in being beguiled.

Let us now come to the sentencing. We see the primary evidence provided in that holy, impartial and loving court, written in everlasting script; even the passage of every age is incapable of expunging the glaring record and sight of it. Pay attention at this point. *Adam heard the sound of the Lord as he strolled in the garden in the evening.*[28] He noticed it from the sound and from the usual practice. Could God appear in a loud noise? He appeared, not as he was but as he wished. Blessed be the God of the saints for visiting Adam in the evening on that occasion and in our time at the crucifixion; the Savior endured the passion in those hours that Adam passed from the eating up to his going into hiding,[29] and the judgment, from the sixth to the ninth hour. He ate at the sixth hour—the norm of nature—he went into hiding after the sixth; in the evening God came to him. Adam longed to become God, he longed for the impossible; Christ fulfilled his longing. You longed to become what was impossible for you; I long to become man, which is possible for me. In fact, God compensated for his deception. You longed for what is above you, I receive what is beneath me; you longed for equality with God, I become equal with man—hence Paul's saying "found to have a likeness with man."[30] You longed to become God, and I am not angered by that—I want you to desire equality with God—but my anger is due to your wanting to wrest the dignity against the Lord's will. You longed to become God and failed; I have become man and have made possible what was impossible. The fact that it was through desire that he

---

[26]1 Tim 2:14—though as Severian will later show, this passage from the Pastorals lays the blame clearly at Eve's feet, despite his relative mitigation of it here. [27]Gen 3:17. Again we note the relative balance in apportioning blame by Severian; Chrysostom had railed against the woman, attributing only indifference (*rhathymia*) to Adam. [28]Gen 3:8. [29]The following sentence suggests to Montfaucon that the *parabasis* of the text ("up to the Fall") is unlikely. The balance of Old Testament and New Testament scenarios here is effective. [30]Phil 2:7.

came to this point he personally confirms in word; when the feeder ate the Passover meal with the fed, and the meal was prepared by the one who feeds the earth under heaven, he said to the apostles, "With desire I have desired to eat this Passover meal with you."[31] Surely I did not envy your equality with God? You wanted to wrest what was mine and failed; I succeeded in receiving what is yours.

Pay attention. He came down at evening and said, *Adam, where are you?* The former case and the latter are related, both former and latter coming from the one God: surely it is not one God who came to the passion and another coming down into the garden? He went into hiding; after eating he came to his senses. *Their eyes were opened,* the text goes on, *and they realized they were naked.* Since the devil had said, *On the day you eat, your eyes will be opened,* lo, it says, Satan told the truth. It behooved Paul to say, "For we are not ignorant of his designs";[32] the saints know the devil's wiles. Observe the malice: how did the devil know that their eyes would be opened after eating? Surely they were not blind? Scripture says, before they ate from the tree, *The woman saw the tree*—so she was not blind—*The woman saw that the tree was fair to behold.* She first saw and then ate; so how were their eyes opened?

Pay attention, I beg you; there is a problem here. The devil had experience of loss, that is, of transgression, and he knew what the transgressor suffered and what transgressors experience. The experience is common to all; even today when we sin, we are like blind people in sinning; and when we have sinned, we then see what we have done. For example, if someone complains, Why did you do that? we plead lack of choice: I really did not see what I was doing—not that I was blind but because in sinning my reason was dulled, totally involved

in the act, and was blinded by the act. Afterwards he sees in his conscience what he has done. Let me cite a case: someone gains entry to rob a house and enters as though blind, not thinking of whom he may meet, who may overpower him, fear of judges, the risk involved; he is blinded by the ailment. When he enters, when he takes, when he leaves after stealing, though no one is present he is filled with fear, senses what he has done and reasons that if he is sought, they will discover whose work it is; what he did not consider while doing it, he considers after doing it. For example, the adulterer exposes himself to someone else's fire; he gains entry and does not give thought to the fact that there are laws, courts, condemnations, sharpened swords; but when he has done the deed, he is terrified, suspecting children, maidservant, neighbor, relatives, and what he did not look to in committing the sin, he does after committing it. Again, you urge someone to abstain from evil; if people are unresponsive, they are normally told, I told him many times and he did not respond—not that he did not hear. Then, when you set about beating him, you say, I'll teach you to hear, not that you give him hearing but that the beating corrects his abstraction and brings him to his senses. The prophet also spoke in those terms, "The Lord's correction opens my ears."

When the devil fell, therefore (I have not forgotten the theme),[33] he realized the position he was in after falling and then came to a sense of what he had done. So he learned from his experience and said, *If you eat, your eyes will be opened*—that is, like mine: I realize what it is I fell from, what I experienced, I know what I suffered, I know what I lost. They then ate, *and their eyes were opened, and they realized they were naked.* In fact, they were naked before this without being ashamed. They had

---

[31]Lk 22:15. [32]Gen 3:7; 2 Cor 2:11. [33]Is 50:5. Severian does well to acknowledge implicitly that he is (not for the first time) guilty of straying from the text (let alone the six days—if that choice was his) and of overkill. He might well admit that, even in commenting on Gen 3 on the Fall, he has been moving backwards and forwards.

taken off immortality, the garment of glory was removed, and their body was stripped and was now mud. Immediately the inventiveness of the artisans comes to the fore. Adam's first skill was sewing; before exercising any other skill he took fig leaves and stitched them together.[34] Who was the teacher? Who was the instructor? He received it from God, he was an image of God, and do you have doubts about his knowledge? When you ponder how it was a human being made the first plow, who gave him the idea of fashioning wood, inserting iron, tightening it and yoking the oxen, how the woman discovered the art of weaving, getting the fleece, washing it, combing it, spinning it, making the weave fine and attaching it when broken—where did this come from? Who taught broiderers to embroider? Take the loom: one thread is inserted, but it is not the hand that does it but the brain, the brain produces the shapes; it is not the craftsman inserting his hand but the plan behind the craft that shapes the garment, and the craftsman's intentions are prompted by visible forms. Then it is not the broiderer who moves his hands and prompts the shapes. And if you hear that it is God who is responsible, do you think that he achieves it by moving his hands? And if you sought out every skill and every invention and asked, How did they think of this or this? remember the first words that said *Let us make a human being in our image*, and you would find the solution to the difficulty. An *image of God*, and he does not think? An *image of God*, and he does not imitate the master? *He stitched together fig leaves*.

Let the allegorists be confounded in their teaching that paradise is in heaven and is spiritual. What does a fig tree produce in heaven? But granting that paradise is in heaven: whence come the rivers—not from earth? If paradise is on high, it follows that the rivers also flow from on high; surely Scripture did not say as much, that a river flows down from Eden? That is only playing with words. The allegorists mock us with the taunt, *God clad them in garments of skin*: surely he did not slaughter oxen and sheep, open a tannery and perform the work of a tanner?[35] Our reply is that he produced the animal fully grown, without breeding, without copulation. He made what did not exist: surely he is not incapable of making part of what does exist? Conceding that for the time being, nevertheless God never makes part of an animal, God makes nothing incomplete. He hears the word *skin* and looks for the source; I hear of blood in Egypt and look for the way he turned the Nile into blood, the great number of animals he slaughtered. The river turned into blood, and no animal was slaughtered; there were two skins, and he wonders about the number of animals they came from—yet in that case as well there was skin without an animal.

Pay attention to the movement of thought, and see whether the text limps, and we with it. To avoid truncating the text, however, I shall terminate my treatment after making a few mild remarks. *He stitched fig leaves together*. If only the heretics had learned that skill! Adam did the stitching after transgressing, his intention being to cover his private parts; heretics in their unbelief do the rending, their intention being to uncover holy things. Often we hear the story of the crucifixion, wonder at the soldiers taking Christ's garments and dividing them, and immediately the thought comes to us, God's longsuffering is extreme in not sending a thunderbolt and dispatching a sword. Yet the Holy One is insulted, and does

---

[34]Gen 3:7. Severian reverts to his proclivity to ferret out, in his literalistic approach to the text, how skills and implements could have been available in the garden. [35]Gen 3:21. Commentators like Origen and Didymus, who took the creation story spiritually and placed paradise in heaven, found a literalistic approach like Severian's grist to their mill. In Homily Thirteen, Chrysostom briefly rebutted the allegorical view before invoking his principle of *synkatabasis*, the considerateness of biblical language, and passing on; Theodore in an extant fragment from a work on Galatians pilloried such spiritual interpretations. But Severian cannot leave well alone (had he been reading Didymus?).

not profane acclamation arise? Do you wonder at those soldiers daring to divide the garments? Wonder at these people's tearing the garment of the church. The soldiers saw Christ's seamless tunic, woven in one piece from the top,[36] and left the garment as one, whereas Christ's clothing, the vesture of the church, heretics have rent, divided, cut to pieces.

Let us, however, return to the text in hand. *He stitched together fig leaves. They heard God strolling* in so far as it was possible to hear him; *they heard and hid.* Nature is well-disposed; even if we sin countless times, our conscience is free. Sometimes the face is shameless, but conscience reproves; sometimes the tongue says, What sin have I committed? and conscience reproves from within. Adam's kind were most simple and guileless, making open confession. God said, *Where are you?* Many people have taken that in a pious manner, but we must give it careful attention;[37] I accept their interpretation since it is pious, and I state this one because it is true. *Adam, where are you?* Where have you been? Where have you come from? From what glory have you fallen? I really accept the interpretation as pious, it is proper and attractive; but I am looking for the movement of thought.[38] God asks, *Adam, where are you?* As his maker he knew the nature of what he had made, the fact that every sinner loses openness and that the mouths of sinners are stuck fast. He noticed that with the loss of openness he had fled. A slave suffers anxiety particularly when he senses that his master knows what has been done; but as long as the master is in ignorance, he consoles himself with the thought that he has managed to get away with it. Adam fled because he was discovered; God pretended ignorance

so as to allay his fear; as we say of a friend, I gave the impression of being unaware in case I distressed him. Such things happen frequently with us, in fact; but if such things happen with us, much more with God in his lovingkindness.

Adam, where are you? as if to say, I do not know. Then, with God pretending ignorance, the well-disposed and free spirit did not conceal the truth: *I heard your voice and was afraid, because I am naked, and I hid.*[39] Why were you afraid? Why did you hide? I was afraid because of the transgression; I hid because of the nakedness. The statement of the transgressor really moves one to tears: *I heard your voice,* the voice that is so desirable, that bestowed everything on me, that bestowed good things on me and was solicitous for me. *I heard your voice.* I considered whose voice it was that I had scorned, whose voice I had spurned, *and I was afraid,* having transgressed a commandment of such a Lord, *and I hid, because I am naked.* Then God persists with his admonition: *Who told you that you are naked—unless you have eaten from that one tree I told you not to eat from?*[40] In other words, unless you have done what I forbade. Note how he asks as though in ignorance, Unless you have eaten from that tree from which I ordered you not to eat. Observe God's lovingkindness: *Who told you?* He protracts the dialogue so as to dissipate the fear and promote frankness; Adam was wondering how it was that there was no harsh word, no abrupt remark, no abuse, no blows. You have what is customary as a model: when a slave offends and approaches his master, he acquires either confidence or dread from the first word spoken. If he begins by being angry, calling him a thief and a cheat and deserving of death times without number, his spirits fail;

---

[36]Jn 19:23-24. [37]Severian claims that piety is not a sufficient hermeneutical criterion: precision, *akribeia*, is more reliable, even if we have seen it being taken to extremes—ad nauseam, in Montfaucon's phrase. Chrysostom had labored the role of conscience, even at greater length, and had proceeded to the pious interpretation of the divine inquiry after Adam that Severian rejects (perhaps with his benefactor open before him), highlighting the losses Adam sustained. He is not above faulting his source. [38]Where the pious interpretation might properly have been faulted on the evidence of the text, Severian cites instead *akolouthia* as a criterion, as had often Diodore and Theodore in interpreting the Psalms. [39]Gen 3:10. [40]Gen 3:11.

if he hears him reproaching him, *Wretch, why have you done this? Why did you do wrong?* he immediately takes heart and grows in confidence for the time being, since he is not punishing as a master, only laying down the law as a teacher.

God was like that, too: *Who told you that you are naked—unless you have eaten from that tree I told you not to eat from?* Surely I did not forbid many? I forbade only one, and this not in hatred but in foresight. *Who told you that you are naked?* He said nothing shameless in reply, I did not know; instead, what? *The woman you gave me—she gave it to me, and I ate,*[41] that is, she who was given me as a helpmate; when I had been formed, but not she at that stage, I heard you say, *Let us make him a helpmate like himself.*[42] *The woman you gave me—she gave it to me.* He did not say, She deceived me, She lied; *she gave it to me, and I ate.* Then God said, Should you have believed a woman and not me? Is the woman more worthy of trust than me? I gave you good things, I honored you in deeds, she beguiled you with words. Note further: just as if a judge accepts the defendant's defense and questions him no further but moves to the other party, the defendant immediately gains confidence and says, I am no longer under examination, so too God moves from Adam so as to relieve his fear and says to the woman, *What is this you have done? The serpent deceived me, and I ate.*[43] Since she told the whole truth, he does not call in question the truthful defense, instead leaving her unexamined. He did not say, Was that creature, the serpent, believed in preference to me? He promised equality with God and brought you death.[44] Instead of condemning

her immediately, he preferred to show her pity as the weaker vessel and moves to the serpent so as to convince both the man and the woman that he was moving to the guilty party, saying, *Because you did this.*

Do you see an admirable judge? He questions the deceived, he does not question the deceiver; instead of saying to him, What have you done? he says, *Because you have done this.* In keeping with the same figure David says, "The impious will not stand in judgment," not that they do not rise but that they are not examined. *Because you have done this.* The sentence against the serpent lightened the punishment of the deceived; unless God had attributed everything to it, he means, he would not have condemned it without examination. *Because you have done this, accursed are you beyond all the wild animals of the earth. Upon your breast and your belly shall you travel.*[45] *Because you have done this,* because you deceived the heart and persuaded the belly to take the fruit, *upon your breast and your belly shall you travel.* Not that it used feet before; God is now decreeing movement on its belly because the serpent stood up to converse with the woman. It would not otherwise have been possible for it to conduct a dialogue with Eve; the very process of the dialogue by which it deceived Eve condemns it to moving on its breast and disqualifies it from regular walking. After all, even if its initial formation left it without feet, it still reared up with certain ugly contortions and advanced on its extended breast.[46] Hence even today when provoked the serpent often rears up and moves at speed with easy writhing; though advancing to a degree that provides a reminder of its former manner of

---

[41]Gen 3:12. [42]Gen 2:18. [43]Gen 3:13. [44]Severian, who likes to dramatize a scene, seems disappointed that there is no interplay between God and Eve, suggesting what might have been the makings of a dramatic exchange. However, as a preacher Severian is much less ready to moralize on the original sin (a term not found in these Eastern commentators) than Chrysostom. His accent is rather on chasing up in literalist fashion items in the text—what Theodore would dismiss as *akribologia.* [45]Ps 1:5; Gen 3:14. [46]Denial of a spiritual interpretation to the events and protagonists in paradise and the Fall scene commits a literalist to mount a case for a talking serpent that could lift itself up to converse with Eve and to face the possible objection of its being originally footed. Chrysostom, familiar with divine *synkatabasis,* never engages with the text at that level.

movement, it is still brought down to earth by dint of the sentence.

You shall eat dirt all the days of your life. I shall put enmity between you and the woman.[47] What is the meaning of *You shall eat dirt?* Eat what you were responsible for Adam's becoming; he is on the point of hearing, *Dirt you are, and unto dirt you shall return.*[48] *I shall put enmity between you and the woman*: since you deceived her as though a friend, she will drive you out as though an enemy. That statement passed into law, so pay attention. *You shall eat dirt all the days of your life.* Take note: he is not saying of the serpent, Dirt will be your food; dirt has never been what serpents eat— instead, they are nourished on flesh, are fond of fruit, chew seeds, lay hold of plants. Rather, by saying *You shall eat dirt* it means, You will consume dirt, you will crawl in it.

Some people say, If it was the devil that deceived, why did the serpent bear the curse? He chastises with an invisible curse the demon that is invisible; on the visible instrument he inflicts a visible punishment.[49] Why? Just as God, who is invisible, gave the tree as a visible reminder, so the devil, being invisible, speaks to human beings through the serpent. Accordingly, God imposes a curse on the serpent so that, if you suffered something at the hands of the devil, you would on seeing a serpent rearing up and constantly hissing be reminded that if the minister was punished for evildoing in that way, what must the responsible party be suffering? So pay attention.[50] You will find a related explanation in the Gospel: just as he condemned along with the visible one the one speaking in the serpent, so too in the Gospel, when the demons begged Christ not to be dispatched into the abyss, they said, "Let us go into the swine,"[51] he allowed them to go so that he might drown the invisible beings along with those bodily visible.

You shall eat dirt. I shall put enmity between you. He turned friendship into enmity, and the sentence became the norm; people are anxious to tame the other wild beasts as well. If you see a serpent, you are alarmed, for the decree is still in force: *I shall put enmity between you.* If it sees you at home, it wants to kill; if it sees you in the street, its frenzy is for killing, the ancient sentence goading it. Even if a bystander strikes the serpent countless times, if he sees its head intact, you immediately urge him, You have not struck the serpent's head, hit it in the head, because God said, *He will watch for your head, and you will watch for his heel.*[52] What does that mean? He does not mean, I shall cause the human being not to use violence against all the other members of its body and only punish its head. In fact, the human being directs blows on the serpent in all its members with the intention of punishing the whole wherever he strikes. And the saying of the Lord to the serpent, *You will watch for his heel,* does not imply that the serpent's attack is made on the heel; it attacks also when they are asleep, often biting the stomach, inserting venom, and directs bites at the hands and the other limbs. It never leaves any of people's limbs unharmed when it attacks. Yet the force of the sentence is this: Far from being emboldened any longer to scheme against the human being, you will remain under cover and have such fear of human beings as to hide yourself in holes, hardly peering out of crannies in fear and merely observing the passage of human beings with a view to a safe emergence. The human being, he says, will walk about fearlessly, even if your head is observed in holes, since you are hiding like an enemy, not speaking to him like a friend.

Since time presses, however, let us also

---

[47]Gen 3:14-15. [48]Gen 3:19. [49]The question and its answer occur also in Chrysostom, even if Severian elaborates it differently. [50]We have seen Severian countless times bidding the congregation to attend. Is it just a mannerism? Or does their attention to a less than engaging preacher show signs of flagging? [51]Lk 8:31. [52]Gen 3:15.

bring the sermon to a close. Having questioned the woman who was deceived, he turns to the deceiver; the sentence arises from its root, namely, the deceiver. He then moves to the woman who was deceived and delivers a threat. The first word, *accursed*, was to the serpent; and *God said to the woman, I shall greatly aggravate the pain of your labor.*[53] He does not deliver a curse, that she would not bear children, since previously he had blessed her; when he formed them, the text says, *God blessed them, saying, Increase and multiply, and fill the earth*; and Paul says, "God's gifts are irrevocable."[54] So he does not curse the ones he had blessed; instead, what? He applies to the injured a novel remedy, *pain* and *labor*. In appearance it is imposition of a sentence, but what is promised is recovery from the Fall. *I shall greatly aggravate the pain of your labor.* The remedy of repentance; pay attention: just as surgeons in the course of treatment both strike and soothe, and cure is the result of the actual incision, the knife and the pain that accompany the surgery, so God applies two means of repentance to the woman who has sinned, *pain* and *labor*. What is the good of pain? Listen to Paul's words: "Pain in God's plan produces a repentance that leads to salvation and brings no regret." And what is the effect of groaning? Listen to Isaiah: "When you turn back and groan, then you will be saved." *I shall greatly aggravate the pain of your labor.* Pain distorts the countenance and makes it sad: "When the heart is glad, the countenance beams, but when it is in pain, it is clouded."[55] Since her eye saw the tree and she pondered equality with God in her mind, God gave labor in the heart and pain in the face so that she might be punished in the way she had sinned, and the woman might be convinced by the punishment—or, rather, the salvation—of the fact that he had

not reneged on his original blessing.

After having told them, *Fill the earth*, he goes on to say, *In pain you will bear children.* I am not doing away with childbirth, having once blessed you; instead, you will suffer pain and anxiety. It is the most severe pain, as the Savior confirms: "When a woman gives birth, she suffers pain."[56] She is in pain when giving birth and is anxious when feeding; when the child grows up, she is anxious lest it be mentally impaired; if it leaves home, lest it die, get ill or be in distress. The husband does not experience this; if the father worries, it is not like the mother—rather, he consoles himself by saying, He is a man, he knows how to stand up for himself—and does not worry. Why? Because it was not he who was told, *In pain you will bear children.* A strange form of justice, as experience testifies. When pangs come upon a woman, she does not renounce her husband even in the very hardship; she does not say, Would there had been no marriage, would there were no childbirth! God does not allow her to hate her husband even after the experience; instead, she is aware of what she suffered and what she put up with and still loves her husband.

Hence, *In pain you will bear children, your yearning will be for your husband, and he will be in control*: since just now you exercised control badly and became a slave to your whims, I shall reverse the order; let the one who was not deceived be master. Hence Paul says, "I permit no woman to teach, or to have authority over a man"; initially in the garden her teaching was wrong. "Or to have authority over a man"; her exercise of authority was wrong. So it is assuredly on these grounds, what happened in the garden, that Paul gives instructions for a woman not to teach. Lest we quibble over this, listen to him: "I permit no woman to teach

---

[53]Gen 3:16. [54]Gen 1:28; Rom 11:29. [55]2 Cor 7:10; Is 30:15; Prov 15:30. The image of the surgeon who has to cause pain to effect cure is an effective, if traditional, one. [56]Jn 16:21, a text cited by Chrysostom, who also lists a mother's concerns for her offspring but not a father's relative lack of concern.

or to have authority over a man"; and to show that it was on account of the original events, he goes on, "For it was not Adam who was deceived; the woman was deceived and was guilty of transgression."[57]

So what? Has the female sex been subjected to condemnation and left to suffer pain, without the bondage being undone? Christ came, and he undid the bondage. The bearer of the Lord[58] appeared for the defense of her sex, the holy Virgin in place of the virgin, Eve also being a virgin when she sinned; she abolished the pain and the labor of the condemned one. In other words, just as if you were invited to the palace, you would be anxious to bring honor on your kith and kin, and if they were in trouble, resolve it, so the holy Virgin was invited to the palace to serve in the divine birth, entered into unaccountable birth pangs and begged this as a first favor—or, rather, received it. Since it was not becoming for the guilty woman to give birth to the innocent one, there came the one whose first task was to undo Eve's pain through rejoicing. The angel came, saying to the Virgin, "Rejoice, O graced one." Then through the word *rejoice* he undoes the bondage of pain. "Rejoice:" the one who is to undo the pain has come. "Rejoice, O graced one,"[59] since to that stage she had been an accursed one. At this point note God's grace: "Rejoice, O graced one, the Lord is with you": since the serpent was with the other woman in pain, "rejoice" because God is with you. And note the angel's statement, how he interprets completely the incarnation of Christ. "Rejoice, O graced one": since the other woman received a double curse, pain and labor in birth pangs, he introduces the birth that undoes that other birth. "Lo, you have conceived, will bear a son

and call him Jesus," "for he will save his people from their sins."[60] The fruit springing from you will undo the sins of your ancestors.

The situation is now reversed: up to that day those hearing the story bemoaned Eve, Alas for the wretch, from what glory she fell! Alas for the wretch, what she suffered! Mary daily hears blessings from everyone, filled as she is with the Holy Spirit. And hear what the Virgin now says in prophecy: "Blessed be the Lord the God of Israel, because he has looked with favor on the lowliness of his servant, for from now on all generations will call me blessed."[61] To bring out that she plays the role of Eve, she says, Though to this point I have been abused, from now on all generations will call me blessed. What good does it do, you ask, to the one who does not hear it? But she really does hear it, from a light-filled place, from being in the land of the living, the mother of salvation, the source of visible light—visible in the flesh, spiritual in the godhead—so she is thus totally blessed. Yet she was blessed even while still living in the flesh; she heard the blessing even while being in the flesh. One woman first saw and then tasted the tree; the other first spoke and then heard the blessing. When the Savior was teaching, "a woman in the crowd raised her voice" and said to him with everyone listening, "Blessed is the womb that bore you and the breasts that nursed you."[62]

To Adam, God delivered the sentence—or, rather, the cure by way of repentance—in the words, *Because you listened to the words of your wife, and ate of the tree from which I bade you not to eat, accursed will be the soil from your actions.*[63] Again it is not the one who was blessed who bore the curse, but the earth; one sinned, another was punished. As with Eve's curse—

---

[57]1 Tim 2:12, 14 (omitting 1 Tim 2:13, "For Adam was formed first, then Eve"). While Severian does not go to the lengths of Chrysostom in attributing Adam's fall to Eve, he had also previously said that Adam was not deceived, just beguiled. On the strength of the text in Genesis and of the verses from the Pastorals, he now declares the subjection of women—though admitting that not all his congregation may agree. [58]*Kyriotokos*, not *theotokos*. The following eulogy of Mary does not arise from the Fall scene in the true Antiochenes. (Eve's virginity is hardly a datum drawn from the text.) [59]Lk 1:28. Is it Mary who has thus far been "an accursed one"? [60]Lk 1:31; Mt 1:21. [61]Lk 1:68 (words of Zechariah); 1:48. [62]Lk 11:27. [63]Gen 3:17.

or, rather, chastisement: it was not so much curse as correction—as Eve's curse, *In pain you will bear children*, has continued to this day (every woman bears children in pain), so too Adam's, *Accursed will be the soil from your actions* (our actions were unlawful, and the earth was chastised). We sin, and the earth bears the curse; God spares what he formed as a noble child, and he punishes the earth as its tutor. *Accursed will be the soil from your actions.* Take note not of nature but of God's grace: he did not say, *Accursed be the earth,* since it remained cursed, not bearing fruit; just as he said to the fig tree, "May no fruit come from you, and it dried up,"[64] so was the case with the earth. Instead, he said, *from your actions*: when I sin, the earth is punished; when I keep to the straight and narrow, he blesses it.

Take note of something remarkable. When God created the earth, the sea, the birds, the reptiles, the wild beasts, the human being, he blessed them all; the crops he did not bless, since he knew that this punishment was being kept for the earth, to be stricken with infertility when human beings sin and to be granted fertility when they act righteously. He did not bless the crops; the gift was not to be the subject of second thoughts. *Thorns and thistles it will yield you:*[65] you showed scorn for the matters of moment; accept punishment in minor matters. Note how even the chastisement is commensurate: a thorn cannot kill, it can scratch. And he eats the crops of the earth in pain; she bears children in pain; for your part eat in pain. Be they rich or poor, ruler or magnate, examine whether you can find their life without pain,

without care. Why? *In the sweat of your brow you will eat your bread:*[66] you were unwilling to do so in peace, eat in sweat; instead of punishing him with starvation, he submits him to retribution and hardship. You now, person of faith, consider this: if Adam did not eat bread without sweat, how would we attain to the kingdom of heaven without sweat and tears? *Until you return to the earth whence you were taken,* the text goes on. What a sentence! What dread brimming with lovingkindness! What a sentence redolent of recall! He hardly banished before recalling, he hardly expelled before welcoming. *Until you return to the earth whence you were taken,* so that you may hold out to yourself the hope of resurrection.[67] I dispatch you to the place from where I took you; as I once took you, I can also take you again. *Because earth you are, and to earth you shall depart*—not "disappear" but *depart,* some commentators interpreting *depart* to mean come back.

To the best of our ability, therefore, with the grace of the Holy Spirit we have gone through paradise with you,[68] we have read aloud the royal records, we have seen the freeing of the guilty, the judge's lovingkindness. Thanks to it, may we also receive salvation from Christ and so enjoy those heavenly and eternal good things, in Christ Jesus our Lord, because in him is the glory and the power, now and forever, for ages of ages. Amen.

Homily Seven

How Adam was given his soul,
and on the passion of Christ[1]

---

[64]Mt 21:19. [65]Gen 3:18. [66]Gen 3:19. [67]In a manner typical of Eastern commentators, and almost against the evidence of the text, Severian ends his commentary on the Fall on an upbeat note. [68]Severian's intention at the outset of the six homilies was to treat the Gen 1 creation account day by day. When this proved insufficient material, he moved in the final homilies to life in the garden and the Fall in Gen 2 and Gen 3 (the seventh homily, as mentioned in the introduction, continuing commentary to the expulsion from the garden). Despite his early disclaimer, that the author (Moses, though his name has rarely been cited) is not a mere historian, Severian has used that term *historiographos* at times, and as here he has treated the text as "records" (*hypomnēmata*), not as *prophēteia*. **Homily Seven** [1]As noted in the introduction, this homily is not one of the group *In Cosmogoniam* contained in PG 56, occurring only in the earlier edition of Savile (still among Chrysostom's works). And while its current title would suggest it refers to the breath of life communicated to the man in Gen 2:7, it has been thought to follow ("immediately," in Zellinger's term) the sixth of the other homilies that brought the narrative of life in the garden down beyond the Fall to Gen 3:19.

The hardships of endurance are good, and best of all the fruit ensuing from the hardships; glorious is the fruit of meritorious hardships. Hardships generate virtues, the direction to fast involves hardship, the splendid option for martyrdom comes at the cost of hardship, the reward for hardship is the kingdom of heaven. The all-glorious week with these sacred hardships has come to an end for us, the initial exercise has run its course to the end, and the reward of piety gleams bright. Today is the day when Adam was formed, when he was made in the image of God;[2] and since the instrument of our voice did not obey us yesterday,[3] today there is need, on the very day when Adam was formed, to resume the text on his formation. God formed him on this day; likewise he reforms him on this day.

Why, then, are we to take up the promise before us? When God made the world, adorned heaven with sun and moon and stars, in similar fashion provided the earth with a variety of rivers and springs girding it and flowers and plants bedecking it, ringed it around with the sea and girded this world with total charm, as I often said, he created and formed the one appointed master of this world. He does not form him like the others, however, for the four-footed beasts, the wild animals and the cattle he simply gave the word and produced them from the earth: *Let the earth bring forth four-footed animals, reptiles and wild beasts.*[4] The slaves were summoned by a word, but the formation of the divine image was achieved by hand—not that God has a hand or any such member—instead, in its wish to highlight the dignity of what was formed it presents God's hand creating. While we perform more menial tasks by giving orders, in fact, the more congenial ones we put our own hands to. Hence Scripture says, God took *dust from the earth*: he took dust, not sod, not compact earth but the flimsiest dust.[5] Note how from the outset the hope of resurrection was set fast; since he was destined to dissolve into dust, according to the verse, "You brought me down to the dust of death,"[6] the intention was to prevent anyone's despairing of hope for human beings on seeing the dust of the grave, and so he set fast in creation itself the hope of resurrection. Hence he says God took "dust from the earth": in that place dust, in this place dust; that dust was remodeled by the power of the craftsman, this dust was transformed by the wisdom of the creator. He took dust and formed it; whence he took it and what he formed you were told, but how he remodeled it you were not given word; it mentioned the forming but concealed the manner, the purpose being for you to learn not to pry into God's creation. Now, if you were recommended not to pry into God's creation, much more should we refrain from busying ourselves with the origin of God.[7]

Next, whereas in making the four-footed animals he included the souls along with the bodies, in forming the human being he first prepared the instrument of the body and then created the soul and imparted it. Why? So as to show also from this the eminence of the human being. You see, when the other animals and cattle are dissolved in death, he does away with the soul along with the body and from that fact makes a statement about their origins, how eventually everything was destined to be done away with. Whereas God took the body from the earth in forming the human being, therefore, he breathed the soul into it.

---

[2]In other words, Friday, day six of the Hexameron. The week of Lent involved, in Carter's reasoning, is hardly Holy Week, when Good Friday was otherwise occupied; rather, it would have been the first week ("the initial exercise"), suggesting in Carter's chronology February 22 or March 1 of 401. [3]Severian has mentioned his voice problems in Homilies Four and Five—a hoarseness, in Carter's view, due to the strain of preaching. [4]Gen 1:24. [5]Gen 2:7. Severian had made this point about dust being employed rather than sod in Homily Five. He is rehearsing here what had been said there about the formation of the human being, when his voice was in poor shape. [6]Ps 22:15. [7]Earlier Severian had frequently warned against prying, especially concerning the generation of the Son.

Wait just a moment for me to present to you as far as possible the account of the breathing; from this as well he foreshadows the hope of resurrection from the outset.[8] First he forms the body: first the human being was given a dead image and then the soul's living activity; first he appeared as dead, then alive; first he formed a dead body in which the human being was destined to come to an end, then on completion of the dead body he gave a distinctive stamp. His reason for not making the soul first was to prevent its being a witness of what was made; his reason for not having the soul present at creation was to prevent its boasting that it was God's assistant—and not only to prevent its boasting but also to prevent its seeing the manner of what was being made. Even now God does this: he forms each of us in the womb; how he forms us he allowed no one to witness. The seed is sown, and we are formed, and nature takes its course; but no one grasps the manner of forming. What a marvelous thing! A ship is made within a ship, a house is built within a house, and from outside there is no impression of a house.

He makes the human being, then, as a dead image. Next he says, God "breathed" into the face of Adam "a breath of life, and the human being came alive." Many commentators had the idea that his "breathing" was the soul and that the soul was the body's share in the substance of God. The idea, however, is marked by deep folly, and not only folly but also absurdity; if the soul had come from God's substance, there should not be in one person a wise one and in another a dull and stupid one, nor in this person a righteous soul and in another an unrighteous one. God's substance, after all, is not subject to division or change, being unchangeable: "I am," he says, "and I do not change."[9] Further, brethren,[10] we not only find souls that are sinful and on that score open to censure, and hence not being of God's substance, but also we find them also subject to judgment; the Savior says, remember, "Do not fear those who kill the body but cannot kill the soul; rather, fear him who can destroy both soul and body in hell."[11] If the soul is part of him, then, God judges himself. So what is meant by "breathing" we need to see; just as the Savior breathed into the faces of the apostles and said, "Receive the Holy Spirit,"[12] so the "breathing," though from God, is taken in human fashion, whereas the "Spirit" is holy and to be adored. This Spirit preceded the soul and is not itself the soul—instead, it created the soul; it was not turned into a soul, instead creating the soul, for the Holy Spirit is creator, participating in the creation of the body and the creation of the soul.

Father, Son and Holy Spirit, in fact, are responsible for the formation by divine power. Do not get the idea that the Father contributed a part, the Son a part and the Holy Spirit a part. What I am saying instead is that even if the Father makes, the work is the Son's and the completion the Holy Spirit's; even if the Son creates, creation is the Father's and creation is the Holy Spirit's. If, however, someone does not believe that the Holy Spirit did not participate in our creation,[13] let that person be refuted by the sacraments: if we were not created by the Trinity, how is it that enrollment at initiation is done with mention of the Holy Spirit? How is it that creation is renewed in the name of Father, Son and Holy Spirit?

---

[8]The contrast between the order in creation of animals and human beings, where the latter receive "hope of resurrection," had been developed in Homily Five. One can understand how this seventh homily, reverting to a theme already developed, would be set apart from the series and given its own descriptive title, *Quomodo Animum Acceperit Adam.* [9]Ex 3:14; Mal 3:6. [10]R. E. Carter, "A Greek Homily on the Temptation (CPG 4906) by Severian of Gabala," 54, notes that "brethren" (in place of Chrysostom's preferred "dearly beloved") is typical of Severian. [11]Mt 10:28. [12]Jn 20:22. As often happens with Severian, the ensuing theological problem of the Spirit's role in creation is of his own making. [13]The double negative in our text may be a scribal error. The bishop's appeal to sacramental practice, if not as frequent as that of someone like Theodoret, is in this case telling.

When we were created (they object), there was no need of the Spirit; yet when we are renewed, the Spirit's assistance is invoked—so the Holy Spirit is creative, whether the foes like it or not. David also testifies to the creative power of the Spirit; in speaking of human creation he says, "All things look to you, Lord, to give them food in due season; when you give it, they gather it up, when you open your hand, they will be filled with goodness of all kinds," expressing the abundant supply. What does he say next? "But when you hide your face, they will be dismayed; you will take away their Spirit, and they will fail and return to their dust; you will send forth your Spirit, and they will be created."[14] So the Holy Spirit is maker and creator.

Note the precision of the words: when on the one hand he speaks of our soul, he says, "You will take away their Spirit, and they will fail and return to their dust," but when on the other hand he refers to the Spirit, "You will send forth your Spirit, and they will be created." If in response to this, however, the heretics presume to dispute the truth,[15] still other texts will refute them by proclaiming the creative power of the Holy Spirit; the role of the Holy Spirit is found to be greater than the whole creation of heaven and earth and sea. Christ's all-holy and adorable body, in fact, through which heaven and earth and the whole world are renewed and the universe saved, is a work of the Holy Spirit. When, for example, the holy virgin was at a loss in regard to an unexpected birth and asked, "How will this happen to me, since I am a virgin?" the angel said to her, "The Holy Spirit will come upon you, and the power of the Most High will overshadow you."[16] Some commentators thought that while "Holy Spirit" referred to the Spirit

itself, "power of the Most High" referred to the Son. We must acknowledge instead that by "Holy Spirit" and "power of the Most High" he referred to the same thing; just as the Son is called power of the Most High (Christ being God's power), so too the Holy Spirit is given the name "power." The Lord, for instance, says to the apostles, "Remain in Jerusalem until you have been clothed with power from on high." And in addition, the angel in speaking to Joseph says, "Joseph, son of David, do not be afraid to take Mary as your wife; what has been begotten in her (not "created," lest you think the divine and undefiled nature was created) is from the Holy Spirit."[17]

Accordingly, if the Holy Spirit created the body of Christ, show what difference there is between one creation and the other. Be careful not to be confounded, however, by attributing the earthly image to the Father and the heavenly to the Spirit; if by your reasoning, when Adam was created, the Spirit had no share in creating him, the Father and the Son will be found to be creating the earthly human being, and the Spirit the heavenly.

"He breathed into his face, and the human being became a living person." Pay careful attention. When Adam was formed, when he was created, when he received his particular imprint, the woman was not yet formed. What does God do? Just as it was not his will that Adam's soul be present at the creation of his body, so he allowed no mortal eye to be present at the creation of the woman. Hence when on the point of forming the woman, he sent sleep on Adam to avoid his being present and prying into God's creation. *He sent a spell* (that is, sleep) *upon him, and he slept; he took one of his ribs.*[18] The one who binds also looses; from what he produces he borrows; from what

---

[14]Ps 104:27-30. Severian had possibly not read Theodore's heated denial of a knowledge of the Holy Spirit to the Old Testament people in commenting on Joel 2:28 and Hag 2:5.   [15]We have seen Severian ready to use "heretic" of anyone who disagrees with him even on matters like flat-earth cosmology. His unquestioned *akribeia* in scrutinizing the text has in earlier homilies also led him to start hares, whereas in this case he has a valid point to make.   [16]Lk 1:34-35.   [17]Lk 24:49; Mt 1:20, Severian ensuring that his listeners distinguish between the two homophones, *gennēthen* and *genēthen*, respectively—another necessary instance of precision.   [18]Gen 2:21.

he makes he takes. *He took one of his ribs, and closed up the flesh in its place.* From where he took the filling the text leaves in doubt, but there is no doubt about the power. *He fashioned the rib he had taken into a woman.*[19] Again, how did he fashion it? How was a rib bone transformed into an eye? How was it shaped into hands? How was it twisted into nerves? How was it changed into a liver? How was a tongue inserted? How were lips rounded off? How were nostrils carved? How were ears attached? How did hair grow? Where did nails grow from? How does the blood course?[20] Explain your own creation, but if you are unable to say, put a stop to your slander of the Only-begotten.[21]

God put a spell on Adam, and he slept; he took a rib and created a woman. Note the utterly skillful wisdom: from one he fashions two, his purpose being that from the two he might in turn produce one through close relationship. From Adam he made the woman, from the one making two. In turn it was the same God who made the one from the two; what was born of woman and man becomes one body. The expression is human, the thought divine. Explain how she was fashioned, and you will not find how the rib was fashioned, how he "formed" the one but "fashioned" the other. Surely it is not the same thing to form from the earth and fashion a rib? God "formed" Adam from the earth, he "fashioned" Eve from the rib, he makes Cain and Abel and the other human beings from intercourse. Some are begetters, one is formed, another is fashioned. The terms are not identical. Was substance divided? Not at all.

Let this be a timely statement, I ask you, since the heretics claim that the begotten and the unbegotten are not alike; instead, to the extent that the terms differ, the realities also differ. Concede the difference, then, between Adam and his offspring, Adam being both made and unbegotten—made because he was created, unbegotten because he was not begotten; he was made and formed but not begotten, while Eve was neither made nor formed. Take up the statement again, and fasten on the term: Adam was formed and not begotten, the woman was fashioned and neither formed from the earth nor born from the womb like Cain, while the rest were not formed or fashioned but begotten. Since the ideas are considerably different, then—being formed one thing, fashioned another, being born still another—show me the difference in being between Adam and Eve and their offspring. Now, if there are distinctions in terms and no distinction in substance, why is that surprising? If you constantly twist the terms about, there is a discrepancy in sound but an accord in reality.[22] You denied the names of father and son; you proved wiser than the Holy Spirit in use of names. Was not God worthy of belief? Was he himself not able to find wisdom in this before your imaginings? He could not bring himself to say, Baptize them in the name of unbegotten and begotten.[23]

The battle, however, is with the heretics, and the contest over piety can keep till another occasion; let us instead return to our text. Since the occasion of the Fall was destined to emerge from this side (the woman bringing death on Adam, remember), in his wish to heal the blow the Savior sets side against side; on the cross he surrendered his side to the spear in order that salvation might blossom from where it inflicted the wound: "Out came

---

[19]Gen 2:22. [20]Severian had gone into similar anatomical detail in Homily Five (the day before?) in commenting on this incident of the creation of the woman. [21]In the previous homilies, Severian has been ever ready to enter polemic against Arian heretics impugning the status of the Son. Here he seems to forget that it is the Spirit's role that he has been upholding. He will proceed to deal with the former. [22]As suggested above, Severian has turned the occurrence of different terms in the accounts of creation of man and woman into a theological polemic against those who want to claim that the Son was made, not begotten. As in other homilies, he takes a detail in the text and turns it into a major theological issue. [23]Mt 28:19.

blood and water."[24] Ponder the mystery, show respect for the one who devises the plan and have regard to the marvel: since it was after falling asleep that Adam lost the rib (the rib was taken when he was not awake), the Savior was not awake when his side was pierced—instead, it was after his body's falling asleep that he surrendered his side to the soldier. Pay close attention. When the Savior on the cross fulfilled the inspired plan, some sufferings he endured while still in the body and visible, in keeping with his human condition. Suffering, in fact, does not affect God, suffering does God no injury, suffering does not degrade God, if he is not yet lower even than our souls. After all, if he also promises our souls, "Have no fear for those who kill the body but cannot kill the soul," how could he share in the sufferings of the body? A soul does not die, and does the one who created souls die? So, having endured everything in accord with the plan, humanly speaking, at the completion of the plan, to show the validity of the plan and his independent authority and its proof against the laws of nature, he says on the cross, "It is finished. Father, into your hands I commend my spirit."[25] With a cry he dissolved nature, with a word he adjusted what was fixed; he is the one who said, "I have power to lay down my life, and I have power to take it up."[26]

When he surrendered his side in human terms, then, when put to death—or, rather, when putting death to death through his dying—the soldiers were not convinced on account of the rapidity of his demise, and they thought that surrendering his soul with a mere word was beyond human nature. So they came forward to find out if he was alive. They found him truly dead in the body but alive in what he achieved; the one they killed as man they confessed to be Son of God after the crucifixion. When the soldier with a spear opened his side, in fact, out came blood and water, which is unusual in a corpse; blood never flows from a corpse.[27] Now, when the mystical blood flowed, then the side opened a fountain of salvation on account of the side that opened the transgression; then it was that the centurion standing by the cross said, "Truly this man was the son of God."[28] You denied him when he was alive: do you proclaim him now that he is dead? Pay close attention, then, to what was said: just as God put a spell on Adam and then cut open the side, so it was when the Savior experienced the falling asleep affecting everyone in the body that the side was pierced; in the former case after the sleep, and in this case after the falling asleep the soldiers saw the blood and proclaimed the Son of God. The heretics also behold the marvel but say, a creature.

Now, why was it that the side felt the impact of the spear? Everything that happened to Adam had to be undone by the scene of the crucifixion. In other words, God drove Adam out of the garden by setting the flaming sword to prevent his entering paradise;[29] the sword was flailing, and everything flailing does not stop until it collides with something it encounters. From experience we know the saying, that everything flailing, unless it collides with something, does not stop in its flight. So since no one was able to resist the fiery sword, in the divine plan he applied the sword to the side in the scene of the crucifixion in order that under the guise of the material spear the spiritual sword might strike the side and put an end to

---

[24]Jn 19:34. As occurred in Homily Five in connection with the creation of the woman, Severian exploits the two meanings of *pleura*, "rib" and "side." As noted there, some Johannine commentators think that the Evangelist in this pericope was also not unaware of the nominal connection with the Genesis narrative. [25]Jn 19:30; Lk 23:46. [26]Jn 10:18. [27]Having treated the Genesis account of Eve's "fashioning" as a surgical textbook in this homily and Homily Five, Severian is now doing likewise with the Gospel text. [28]Mt 27:54. [29]Gen 3:24. Only now, at the last gasp, does Severian move the narrative ahead from the point reached in Homily Six, Gen 3:19, without mentioning the bestowal of Eve's name or God's making garments of skin for them. The time has instead been spent reworking the material of Homily Five, and in particular the formation of the man, the fashioning of the woman from Adam's rib/side and the piercing of Jesus' side at the crucifixion.

the threat in the future, and no longer keep closed to human beings the entrance to paradise. The Lord accordingly was dealt a blow in the side with the sword, and immediately the door to paradise was opened. From the side there flowed out healing for the one struck in the side. Originally he took him out of paradise, and finally he admitted him into the kingdom. He chastised him but had mercy; he expelled him but did not do away with him; he turned him away but did not rebuff him.

I am aware, however, that it is time to make way for the liturgy.[30] Everything is possible to God, after all, and so what falls to us is to impart the thought of the remainder and present to the listeners the force of the entire passage by reference to a part; Scripture says, remember, "Give a wise man an opportunity, and he will be wiser."[31] Let us therefore give thanks to God that, while we lost one paradise, he planted countless paradises throughout the world; let us give thanks to God that though we lost paradise through the transgression, we were called into the kingdom of heaven, thanks to the grace of our Lord Jesus Christ, to whom be the glory for ages of ages. Amen.

---

[30]Is this a reference to a liturgy of the Eucharist, following upon the liturgy of the word that has been completed? In none of the other homilies is there reference to a liturgy of the Eucharist. [31]Prov 9:9.

Bede the Venerable

Commentary on Genesis: Book I

TRANSLATED WITH AN
INTRODUCTION AND NOTES BY

Carmen S. Hardin

TRANSLATOR'S INTRODUCTION

A Brief Introduction to Hexameral Literature

The following text is a translation of the first book of Bede's commentary on Genesis titled *Libri quatuor in principium Genesis usque ad nativitatem Isaac et eiectionem Ismahelis adnotationum* (hereafter *In Genesim*). Charles W. Jones has annotated and edited the critical edition that is published in Corpus Christianorum: Series Latina 118A. In its totality, this commentary on Genesis exists in four books covering the account of creation up to the birth of Isaac and the casting out of Ishmael by Abraham. The first book consists of a hexameron (lines 1-1092), or an explanation of the six days of creation, followed by an allegorical examination of the six ages of the world (lines 1093-1224) and concluding with the story of the transgression of Adam and Eve that resulted in them losing paradise (lines 1225-2332).

Since a great portion of book 1 of Bede's commentary is a hexameron, and since this portion had such an enduring and powerful influence on later commentators who wrote on the creation narrative, perhaps the best place to begin this discussion of the hexameron of Bede is to define what a hexameron is. In its most narrow sense the term *hexameron* (or *hexaemeron*), meaning "the work of six days," refers to that literary genre relating and limited to the creation account of Genesis 1:1 through Genesis 2:3. From about the fourth century onward the definition broadened to include treatises, sermons and other written materials that provided commentaries on the creation story.[1] Technically, exposition on the sin of Adam and Eve and the judgment of God on them is not part of a hexameron. A distinction soon was made between a general commentary on Genesis and a commentary devoted specifically to the six days of creation. The inclusion of a discussion of the six ages of the world immediately following the hexameron became the distinguishing feature of the genre. One source for this pairing of the hexameron and the allegory on the six ages was Augustine's *De Genesi contra Manichaeos*. Bede and Isidore of Seville popularized the practice, and the inclusion of material on the six ages of the world soon became a standard

---

[1]Gunar Freibergs, "The Medieval Latin Hexameron from Bede to Grosseteste" (Ph.D. diss., University of Southern California, 1981), 3.

addition to hexameral literature.[2]

Hexameral literature is conservative in its nature, and its structure is traditional in form. Authors followed a general outline, posing the same questions, often repeating the same answers, frequently quoting familiar proof texts and even restating the same popular allegorical interpretations. In this way, the traditional and orthodox teachings of the church were passed to the next generation by the patristic fathers, who carefully preserved the work of the men before them as they added their own insights. The value of the genre is that the diligent reader can detect shifts in thought as the collective learning was passed down, new teaching was introduced, fresh perspectives were given on older material, and ideas once held familiar and popular no longer appeared. Especially in the disciplines of science, philosophy and theology did these shifts become so evident.[3]

Gunar Freibergs, whose doctoral dissertation provides a history of hexameral literature up to the twelfth century, observes that most of the writers of hexamera appealed to local needs and regional audiences and exerted no lasting influence beyond their immediate age. Bede's exposition of the creation narrative, however, had profound influence beyond Anglo-Saxon England and became the authority of the works of subsequent authors treating the six days of creation.[4] His *Hexameron* provided more than biblical commentary. It reflected Bede's interests in science and chronology as well and became a carefully researched handbook for teaching his Anglo-Saxon audience about these matters. He discussed natural phenomena, the elements, the skies, the movements of the stars, sun and moon, the calendar, rocks and various plants, and rivers and their sources, among other topics. Bede's commentary on creation was the first medieval hexameron in Latin written outside the Mediterranean world, and the influence of his work can be traced throughout the hexameral literature of the Carolingian revival and beyond.[5]

The popularity of the hexameron declined as writers began to appropriate scientific principles from the works of Aristotle that had been recovered through Arabic translations and then translated into Latin in the twelfth century. There evolved a new method of inquiry that no longer analyzed the Scripture verse by verse but employed Aristotelian concepts of categories. The Aristotelian works, along with their new approach to investigation, made the hexameron obsolete, and those who did still write hexamera were no longer the leaders in the scientific arena. In the field of theological commentary, the new model became Peter Lombard's work *Sentences*, or the systematized compiling of opinions on varied theological topics.[6] Also contributing to this decline in hexameral literature were the invasions into western Europe by the Vikings, Magyars and Muslims. The cultural renaissance that Europe had experienced under Charles the Great halted as

---

[2]Ibid., 5.
[3]Ibid., 8-9.
[4]Ibid., 280-81.
[5]Ibid., 30, 281.
[6]Ibid., 283.

church leaders spent time and resources in military affairs to the neglect of education. Monasteries, the centers of learning, were abandoned, moved to safer locales, diminished or destroyed. The monasteries at Wearmouth and Jarrow, for example, where Bede had resided, were destroyed about 860 by the Danes. As a result, the literary activity, with the hexameral genre included, also diminished from the middle of the ninth century to the second half of the eleventh century, and there were produced no Latin hexamera or commentaries on Genesis of any significance. In the tenth century, Aelfric (955–1020) wrote the earliest non-Latin hexameron in the West, the *Old English Hexameron*, in his ongoing effort to educate the rural clergy in their own language. This work is the only representative of any hexameral literature written between the middle of the ninth to the late eleventh century.[7]

Bede's Life

Although his literary output was substantial, little is known about the life of Bede. He was born about 672 on the lands outside Wearmouth monastery, a descendent of Germanic barbarians. A son of a tenant farmer, Bede was sent by his family to the Northumbrian monastery of Saint Peter at Wearmouth when he was seven years old; there the abbots Benedict Biscop and Ceolfrith educated him. Wearmouth lay only about seven miles from the twin monastery at Jarrow in the northeastern corner of Britain. The two monasteries, so close they were considered as one, became the center of education and Christianity in a region that had pagan roots. Soon Bede was transferred to the newly opened companion monastery at Jarrow.[8] He was ordained deacon at age nineteen and was admitted to the priesthood at age thirty.[9] He made a single trip to Lindisfarne, one journey to York, and rare trips from Jarrow to visit friends, but he spent most of his days in his own community.[10] He died in 735, at age fifty-nine, after a lifetime of studying Scripture, teaching and inspiring others.

In the last chapter of *The Ecclesiastical History of the English People*, Bede provides some autobiographical details:

> I was born on the lands of this monastery, and on reaching seven years of age, I was entrusted by my family first to the most reverend Abbot Benedict and later to Abbot Ceolfrid for my education. . . . I have spent the remainder of my life in this monastery and devoted myself entirely to the study of the Scriptures. . . . [My] chief delight has always been in studying, teaching, and writing. . . . I have worked . . . to compile short extracts from the works of the Venerable Fathers on Holy Scripture

---

[7]Ibid., 91.
[8]Joseph F. Kelly, "1996 NAPS Presidential Address—On the Brink: Bede," *Journal of Early Christian Studies* 5 (1997): 90.
[9]Freibergs, "Medieval Latin Hexameron," 31.
[10]Kelly, "On the Brink: Bede," 92.

and to comment on their meaning and interpretation.[11]

He was declared a doctor of the church in 1899, and the title Venerabilis seems to have been associated with his name within two generations after his death. The Council of Aachen in 835 described Bede as *venerabilis et modernis temporibus doctor admirabilis Bede*. In 1859, Cardinal Wiseman and the English bishops asked that Bede be declared a doctor of the church. On November 13, 1899, Leo XIII decreed the feast of Venerable Bede would be celebrated on May 27 and the title Doctor Ecclesiae be granted to him.[12]

Bede's Writings

Studying the Scripture, teaching and writing were Bede's prime directives. His long teaching career commenced by educating young boys to count. On his deathbed, years later, he was translating John's Gospel into Old English for his students.[13] His literary corpus includes biblical exegesis, stories of the lives of the saints, biographies of the abbots of the twin monasteries, poetry on sacred topics, hymns, a martyrology, two texts on grammar and rhetoric, texts on orthography and tropes, major works of scientific import and numerous letters and essays. Every academic discipline for Bede provided an avenue for training the Christian teacher to discover that point at which sound biblical doctrine could meet and transform daily Christian life. History, for example, displayed leaders for Christians to imitate. The treatises on grammar, figures, tropes and music enabled the priests to better perform their liturgical duties. Presenting fundamental doctrinal and moral truths was the goal of the commentaries.[14]

Perhaps his best known work is *Historia ecclesiastica gentis Anglorum*, an account of Christianity in Britain from the time of Caesar until Bede's own generation which is foundational for understanding British history. The history includes a compilation of works of earlier writers, legends, traditions and Bede's own research, distinctive in terms of his critical consideration and careful citation of his sources.[15] Along with the *Historia abbatum* (of the twin monasteries), the *Epistola ad Egbertum* and an account of the life of Saint Cuthbert, the *Historia ecclesastica* sheds light on the state of Christianity in Northumbria in Bede's time.[16] Furthermore, in the *Historia* Bede popularized the idea of the *Anno Domini* era that had been created by Dionysius Exiguus in 525. Bede used *anno ab incarnatione Domine* or *anno incarnationis dominicae*, meaning "in the year of the incarnation of the Lord," referring not to time from the birth of Christ but explicitly to the time of Jesus' conception, traditionally dated March 25. Bede's use of

---

[11]Bede, *Ecclesiastical History of the English People* 5.24, trans. Leo Sherley-Price (London: Penguin, 1955).
[12]Herbert Thurston, "The Venerable Bede," in *The Catholic Encyclopedia* (New York: Robert Appleton Company, 1907).
[13]Kelly, "On the Brink: Bede," 95.
[14]Arthur G. Holder, "Introduction," in *Bede: On the Tabernacle* (Liverpool: University of Liverpool Press, 1994), xiv.
[15]Samuel Macauley, ed., *Schaff-Herzog Encyclopedia of Religious Knowledge* (Grand Rapids: Baker, 1949), s.v. "Bede."
[16]Thurston, "Venerable Bede," 2-3.

this dating system popularized its use in western Europe.[17]

Besides his historical pieces, Bede's corpus included various didactic works like *De arte metrica*, *De ortographia* and *De schematibus et tropis*. It was from pagan writers whom he had studied that the examples for these works were taken. Worried that using examples from such worldly sources would create a negative influence, he produced a grammar that drew only from Christian poetry and scriptural citations. In *De schematibus et tropis* Bede explains his concern:[18]

> Since Holy Scripture stands pre-eminent not only over all other writings in its au-thority, because it is divine, or in its benefit, because it leads one to eternal life, but also it excels in its ancient position of teaching, it pleased me to show from examples gathered from it because teachers of secular speech are able to offer nothing of this manner of schemes or tropes, because there is no precedence in it.[19]

Bede's *De temporibus liber*, *De temporum ratione* and *De natura rerum* primarily are trea-tises technical in nature and dealing especially with chronology and calculation. *De tempo-ribus liber* is an introduction to the principles of establishing the date of Easter, a topic of controversy and division in the churches at the time. *De temporum ratione* is a longer treatise that became "the cornerstone of clerical scientific education during the Carolingian renais-sance of the ninth century."[20] In this work, Bede defines the criteria for the date of Easter and treats how this date can be calculated. Although there is a long history of writings dealing with this calculation, many of which are fragmentary and are primarily charts and tables, *De temporum ratione* is the "earliest comprehensive treatment" of *computus*, or the construction of the Christian calendar.[21] His calculations related to the dating of Easter led him to offer a new *annus mundi* to overcome earlier problems of dating. This new *an-nus mundi* launched an unfair accusation of heresy that seems never to have been seriously considered by church leaders but very much upset Bede. Yet, he defended himself in the *Epistola ad Pleguinam* by appealing to the Old Testament chronology of Jerome's *Hebraica veritas*.[22] From this period also came *De natura rerum* and, according to Jones and in light of the similarity of topics, perhaps the first part of Bede's hexameron and the allegory of the six ages of the world, also written in support of his doctrinal views.[23]

In the autobiographical note at the close of *Historia ecceliastica*, Bede explained that he had worked "to compile short extracts from the works of the venerable Fathers on Holy Scripture" for the benefit of himself and his brethren. He then listed his commentaries

---

[17]"Bede," in *Schaff-Herzog*.
[18]Kelly, "On the Brink: Bede," 97.
[19]Bede *De schematibus et tropis* 2.1.13-19 (CCL 123A, 142-43; Hardin translation).
[20]"Bede," in *Schaff-Herzog*
[21]Faith Wallis, trans., *Bede: The Reckoning of Time*, Translated Texts for Historians 29 (Liverpool: Liverpool University Press, 1999), xvi-xvii.
[22]Ibid., xxx.
[23]Charles W. Jones, "Introduction," vii, in *Bedae Venerabilis opera, Part 2: Exegetical Works, 1-10*, CCL 118A.

on the New Testament, including the books of Mark, Luke, Acts, the seven canonical epistles and the Apocalypse of John. Bede's Old Testament commentaries include the beginning of Genesis, the first part of Samuel, Proverbs, Song of Songs, Isaiah, Daniel, the Twelve Prophets and part of Jeremiah, Ezra and Nehemiah, Habakkuk, Tobit, and chapters of readings on the Pentateuch, Joshua, and Judges; on Kings and Chronicles; on Job, Proverbs, Ecclesiastes and the Song of Songs; and on the prophets Isaiah, Ezra and Nehemiah, in addition to books on the tabernacle, on the building of the temple and thirty questions on the books of Kings.[24] His commentaries bring to his readers a collection of patristic writings at a time when books were very scarce. Bede lists the commentaries first in his autobiographical note, thus indicating their centrality to Bede's call to study and teach and a reflection of his love of God's Word.

While Bede did preach, it was not his sole responsibility at Jarrow. His homilies, collected in a two-volume set, were primarily commentaries on the Gospels and focused on major events in the church year. Included in these two volumes were homilies for the Christmas season, including the nativity, Advent, the presentation of Christ in the temple, the vigil, and masses on Christmas day, Epiphany and the five Sundays after it. There was a cycle for Easter, including homilies for Lent, Palm Sunday, Holy Week, Maundy Thursday, Holy Saturday, Eastertide, the ascension and Pentecost. In addition, he wrote homilies celebrating the feasts of the saints, of the holy innocents and of Peter, Paul and John the Evangelist. Some centered on events of local interest, such as the death of Biscop and the dedication the Church of St. Paul at Jarrow. The homilies are very similar to the commentaries and differ in terms of their intended audience only. While the commentaries provide other preachers material for their sermons, in his homilies Bede made the application of the biblical passage with the needs of his specific audience in view.[25]

Bede wrote on a variety of topics, all related to educating and equipping the Christian disciple. *Musica theoretica* and *De arte metrica*, some of the earliest witnesses to the Gregorian tradition, are studied in the current day by individuals interested in Gregorian chant. He wrote a martyrology of the feast days of the martyrs in which he states, "I have carefully tried to record everything I could learn not only on what date but also by what kind of combat and under what judge they overcame the world."[26] Through time this text has been so edited and interpolated that it is difficult to determine what part of the text is authentically Bede's. *De locis sanctis* is a topographical work describing holy sites and Jerusalem.[27]

Bede preferred the Vulgate to the *Vetus Latina*, and his use of it served to increase its

---

[24]Bede, *Ecclesiastical History* 5.24, a list of Bede's works in his own hand.
[25]Benedicta Ward, *The Venerable Bede* (London: Geoffrey Chapman, 1990), 62-64.
[26]Bede, *Ecclesiastical History* 5.24.
[27]Thurston, "Venerable Bede," 3.

popularity.[28] Bede used specifically the Codex Amiatinus, which had been copied from the Vulgate in Northumbria in the eighth century as the missionary effort had increased the need for Latin texts. Through using the Vulgate, Bede, who did not know Hebrew, had contact with the Hebrew text, which he called the Hebrew *veritas*. Psalm citations were from the Gallican Psalter, which had been taken from the Septuagint. Bede also cited biblical text from the *Vetus Latina*, which, although he may not have had a copy, he accessed through the writings of Augustine.[29] It was from the Bible that Bede developed his interests in science, history, grammar, the calendar, and all other matters he pursued.

In summary, Bede was a prolific writer and a dedicated scholar. Through his life-long literary activity he preserved the doctrines of the Fathers through the commentaries, enriched the liturgy through his sacred poetry and hymns, made accessible and advanced technical knowledge through various didactic treatises, and through every book sought to reveal the mysteries and beauty of the biblical text.

The Composition History of *In Genesim*

The following translation of book 1 of *In Genesim* is the combination of two texts produced at different times and under different circumstances. In his introduction to the text in *Corpus Christianorum*, Jones identifies these two individual texts as 1a and 1b. Jones believes the text of 1a may have been completed well before Acca had commissioned Bede to produce a commentary on Genesis. Bede's initial writing is didactic in intent, focusing on matters of the physical world and chronology. As stated above, Jones believes it comes from the period when Bede was writing *De temporibus* and *De natura rerum*, sometime between 703 and 709. Bede draws from one or more of his homilies that reflected his didactic interests and from patristic sources that he identifies in the dedicatory letter to Acca. At the end of the hexameral portion, he treats the theme of the relationship between the six days of creation and the six ages of the world.[30] This passage on the six ages is an original piece by Bede, although he had written on the topic in earlier writings. Some time later, around 725, Acca requested Bede to write a commentary on Genesis. Bede hurriedly constructed 1b after Acca's request because at the time he was composing the commentary on Ezra and Nehemiah. He promised in the dedicatory letter to Acca that he would return to treat further the history of Genesis, which he did in the form of books 2 through 4 that readers now have. The text of 1b is a *collectaneum*, a collection of quotations from various books of Augustine from which Bede copied passages, often in full. Then, between 725 and 731, Bede combined the two books into a single book now known as book 1. There followed three new books, books 2 through 4, concluding his

---

commentary with the separation of Ishmael from Isaac, the child of darkness from the child of the covenant.[31] The organization of *In Genesim*, in summary, is book 1, 1a being the story of the creation or the hexameron (ending at line 1224); 1b being the explanation of the fall; book 2, the narration of the end of the flood and the beginning of the second age; book 3, the account of Melchizedek and Abraham as prototypes of the church and state; and book 4, the presentation of Ishmael and Isaac as types of the old dispensation and the new.[32] The first part is didactic in focus and reflects Bede's scientific interests; the second half is different in tone and is a collection of quotes from Augustine with allegorical interpretation. The theme of this last section is judgment, a spiritual interpretation of the tree of life in the eternal garden and the redemptive work of Christ.

The Transmission History of *In Genesim*

M. L. W. Laistner had made the preliminary examination of the extant manuscripts of *In Genesim*, and Jones carried forward Laistner's work. In the introduction in *Corpus Christianorum*, Jones identifies eleven extant manuscripts representing three recensions of the work: L in the Bodleian Library at Oxford, C at the National Library in Paris and V at the National Library in Vienna. These are the only extant manuscripts of the first recension. Manuscripts of the second recension are housed in the libraries of Einsiedeln and St. Galls, and the remaining manuscripts of the third recension are in libraries in Cambridge, Dijon, Milan, Paris, Rheims and Troyes. Some of these manuscripts are damaged, have missing folios or are poorly copied and at times illegible; yet, Jones believes, they reflect sound tradition.[33] Jones also notes that the evidence of the extant manuscripts "confirms that Bede's *In Genesim* was . . . restricted in circulation to a belt across northern France and south through the territories of Lothaire to Bobbio."[34] There were more manuscripts of Bede on the Continent than in England. The three manuscripts C, L and V end at book 1, line 1224. L is entitled *Exameron Bedae*, and V is the *Expositio cuiusdam de operibus sex dierum*, limiting this text to Genesis 1:1 through Genesis 2:3. All extant manuscripts include the dedicatory letter sent to Acca.

Jones identifies five editions of *In Genesim*, including the editions of John Herwagen, Henry Wharton, Dom Edmond Martene, J. A. Giles and J.-P. Migne. John Herwagen published *Venerabilis Bedae opera omnia* in 1563. In this edition, Herwagen included some spurious writings as Bede's, including a text on the six days of creation and one on questions about Genesis. After he had finished his work and set it up in type, he then inserted into the front of his volume Bede's *Hexameron, sive De sex dierum creatione libellus*, which closely follows the text of the extant Vienna manuscript. Henry Wharton's edition

---

[31]Ibid., viii-x.
[32]Ibid., x.
[33]Ibid., i-iii.
[34]Ibid., iii.

appeared in 1692 or 1693. He copied the first part (1a) up to line 1224 and included the rest of the text of the present edition. He divided the whole work into three books, not four, by combining books 1 and 2. The edition of Dom Edmond Martene, appearing in 1717, was the first edition to organize the commentary into four books. Martene's work was copied without changes by J. A. Giles in 1844 and by J.-P. Migne in the Patrologia Latina cursus completus.[35] Jones states that the fact that there are so few extant manuscripts indicates that Bede's commentary on Genesis was "less influential" among his commentaries.[36]

Bede's Audience for *In Genesim*

Bede's primary audience would have been monks, but these men served outside the walls of their monasteries instructing people in the Christian faith and its practice. He was addressing both their lives as missionaries and pastors and their own need for spiritual nourishment.[37] For those who wished to preach or teach as missionaries, commentaries proved especially valuable. *In Genesim*, in particular, was so beneficial because it taught about creation, the origin of humankind, humanity's original transgression and ultimate punishment and God's plan for salvation and redemption.[38] Furthermore, Bede encouraged a reader who was eager to "engage himself in deeper and stronger learning of our predecessors"[39] to pursue a serious study of nature.[40] He stated that the faithful righteous are informed not through human reasoning but through attentive study and careful meditation on nature, to which end Genesis ably serves.

Bede, however, wrote for the less educated reader, too. In the prefatory letter to Acca, his patron, a missionary and bishop of Hexham from 709 until 731,[41] Bede lists the church fathers who had written previously on the creation account, but he observes that their works are too extensive to be accessible to the common audience and too intellectually difficult for readers not well acquainted with theological and philosophical debates. Bede wanted to make accessible to his audience the teachings of these great minds in terms they could grasp. He told Acca he would gather the teachings from these earlier patristic commentaries as "from the most delightful flowers in the fields of paradise"[42] and would create a text to meet the needs of the beginning, or *infirmis*, learner. For an easy, readable style he composed in transitional sentences, asked rhetorical questions, made clear references back and forth and emphasized key points with repetitions to enable the

---

[35]Ibid., v-vi.

[36]Charles W. Jones, "Some Introductory Remarks on Bede's Commentary on *Genesis*," *Sacris Erudiri* 19 (1969–1970): 118.

[37]Holder, "Introduction," xiv.

[38]Judith McClure, "Bede's *Notes on Genesis* and the Training of the Anglo-Saxon Clergy," in *The Bible in the Medieval World*, ed. Katherine Walsh and Diana Wood (New York: Basil Blackwell, 1985), 19.

[39]Dedicatory letter to Acca.

[40]Freibergs, "Medieval Latin Hexameron," 36-37.

[41]McClure, "Bede's *Notes on Genesis*," 17.

[42]Dedicatory letter to Acca.

reader to understand the text.[43]

Bede was able then to appeal to different audiences in *In Genesim*. He wrote with a clarity and simplicity to enable the less equipped reader to understand the fundamental teachings of the text, he empowered the clergy for their missionary work, and he inspired every reader to look to the created order and meditate on the mysteries it reveals about the nature of God.

Bede's Sources for *In Genesim*

The daily encounter with the liturgy, sacred hymns and Scripture readings all enriched Bede's understanding of biblical text. Bede also enjoyed well-stocked libraries in both monasteries at Wearmouth and Jarrow, and from these collections of manuscripts came Bede's inspiration and profound knowledge. The collection was partially the result of Benedict Biscop bringing back manuscripts from five trips to the Continent and Ceolfrid doubling the resources through his own trips abroad. In addition, friends loaned Bede books to study or to copy, and he borrowed from the libraries at Lindisfarne and Canterbury. He gained access to the writings of the church fathers, classical authors, Christian poets, scientific texts, histories, theological works, works of Greek authors and various versions of the biblical text, among other volumes.[44]

In the letter to Acca, Bede names the patristic sources of *In Genesim*. He states that the Fathers have "left behind many monuments of their own genius to future generations."[45] To Bede, these writers are important beyond their insights or sources of information; he views the values reflected in their works as the way to a better life.[46] Bede names Basil, whose nine sermons on creation had been translated from the Greek into Latin by Eustathius; Ambrose of Milan, whose commentary on creation existed in six books; and Augustine, from whom he quoted most frequently. Among Augustine's writings, Bede quoted from *De Genesi ad litteram* and *De Genesi contra Manichaeos*, as well as from *Confessionum*, *Contra adversarium legis et prophetarum* and *De civitate Dei*, with allusions to *De Trinitate*. In addition to these three Fathers, Bede draws from the writings of Clement, Filiastrius, Gregory, Jerome and Isidore. Jerome's *De situ et nominibus locorum Hebraicorum liber* became his main authority on Palestinian geography and the allegorical interpretation of proper names in the Scripture.[47]

Among the classical authors to whom Bede had access were writings by Virgil, Ovid, Seneca and Pliny. Specifically in the commentary on Genesis, he quotes briefly from Virgil's *Aeneid* and *Georgica* and from Ovid's *Metamorphoses* and extensively from Pliny's

---

[43]McClure, "Bede's *Notes on Genesis*," 25.
[44]M. L. W. Laistner, "The Library of the Venerable Bede," in *Bede: His Life, Times and Writings*, ed A. Hamilton Thompson (Oxford: Clarendon Press, 1935), 238-47.
[45]Dedicatory letter to Acca.
[46]Kelly, "On the Brink: Bede," 89.
[47]Laistner, "The Library of Venerable Bede," 249.

Historia naturalis on topics of chronology, scriptural geography and natural history.[48]

Additional resources for Bede's commentary on Genesis include Tertullian's *De resurrectione mortuorum*, Eugenius's *Dracontiana*, Avitus's *De originali peccato* and the *Acta concilii Caesareae* by Pseudo-Theophilus, although these cannot be determined with certainty. There are references from *De ratione paschali* by Pseudo-Anatolius and one reference from Athanasius.[49] Bede also used Josephus's *Antiquitates Judaicae*.

The research of such a wide scope of materials demonstrates just how vast Bede's learning was and the thoroughness of the text he has composed. *In Genesim* is the result of Bede's serious study, careful reflection and conscientious effort to preserve the learning of the past as he offered his own contributions to the future.

Bede's View of Scripture and Method of Interpretation

Bede in his commentary *On the Tabernacle* makes several statements that shed light on his exegetical theory. For example, in the prologue he appeals to 1 Corinthians 10:11, where Paul writes, "For all these things happened to them as an example, and so they were written for our instruction on whom the ends of the ages have come" (Vulgate). That is, while he assuredly holds to a literal interpretation, Bede understands that the words and actions of Scripture ultimately serve to teach about Christ and the church. While Bede was the first to give such a detailed account of the fourfold approach to scriptural interpretation that was popular with the Fathers (historical, allegorical, tropological, anagogical), Holder states that in practice Bede recognized only two senses, the literal or historical and one he calls at varying times spiritual, typic, sacramental, mystical, figurative or allegorical.[50] In his commentary on Genesis, Bede does deal at length with etymologies, history, geography and sciences like geology and astronomy, especially in the first part of the treatise, but all of this information is auxiliary and subordinate to the individual's search for the spiritual meaning, for discovering the presence of Christ in the text and for finding guidance for Christian living.

Bede's general style of commentary writing can be determined by observation. He followed verse-by-verse beginning with writing the biblical text itself, which is then followed by a paraphrase and an investigation of the literal sense. Being aware that problems in interpretation occur when there are differences between languages, he would note variant readings and examine the differences between the Hebrew and Greek. Viewing the whole of Scripture, Bede would then explore ways in which passages, and especially Old Testament passages, could apply to daily life or to teachings about Christ or the church. Figurative expressions were explained through a grammatical approach with a spiritual meaning allowed only after intentional study, and he drew similes from observations of

---

[48]McClure, "Bede's *Notes on Genesis*," 24.
[49]Freibergs, "Medieval Latin Hexameron," 34.
[50]Holder, "Introduction," xviii.

the natural order. The significance of numbers in the text required special attention.[51]

Bede, as Augustine and others before him, thought numbers had theological and mystical significance. Augustine had written:

> Yet when you see measures and numbers and order everywhere, seek out the artist and you will find no other than where the sum of measure and the sum of number and the sum of order is, that is God of whom it is truly said that he "ordered all things in measure and number and weight" (Wisdom 11:21).[52]

Isidore of Seville likewise had written, "The method of numbers is not to be neglected, for it elucidates many a passage of holy Scriptures otherwise mysterious."[53] One can see this interest in the mystical sense of numbers in lines 966-974 of book 1. Bede discusses the creation being completed in six days. Since God created all his works in six days, the number six is perfect. Bede explains that its perfection is revealed by the fact that it is an aliquot, that is, a number whose factors add up to the number itself. (6 = 1 + 2 + 3).[54] Bede, referring again to the passage from Wisdom, writes, "In six days, therefore, God completed all the adornment of heaven and earth so that he who 'orders all things in measure, number, and weight' also may teach that that number in which he made his own works is perfect."[55]

Some scholars have criticized Bede's writings for lacking originality because of his consistent and faithful borrowings from the church fathers. Yet, as he copied texts from the Fathers, he was not casual in his work. He made careful selections, emended and juxtaposed them and added personal comments. Bede viewed his work as part of the tradition of Bible commentary that had been handed to him and that he was then handing on to those who would follow.[56]

Bede's Theological Doctrines

In the commentary on Genesis, Bede discusses the nature of God, God's created order, the creation and destiny of humankind, and humanity's ultimate redemption through Christ. God is omnipotent and timeless, "pure intellect without noise and a diversity of tongues." The Trinity in its fullness created the world; God who created all things at one time out of nothing, Jesus who was present "in the beginning" and the Holy Spirit who hovered over the waters. Every created thing has been ordered in its "measure, number and weight" and is governed by laws that direct its movements and guard from breakdown

---

[51]Ward, *The Venerable Bede*, 46-47.

[52]Augustine *De musica* (PL 32), quoted by Jones, "Some Introductory Remarks," 167-68.

[53]Isidore of Seville *Etymologiarum* 3.4 (PL 82); see Augustine *De doctrina christiana* 2.16.25 (NPNF 1 2:543).

[54]See Augustine *Gen. litt.* 4 3.7.

[55]See Isidore of Seville *Eytmologiarum* 3.4: *Senarius namquam, qui partibus suis perfectus est, perfectum mundi quadam numeri sui significatione declarat.*

[56]Ward, *The Venerable Bede*, 49.

and return to chaos. Human beings were created in the image of God in the aspect of their rational being. In the beginning they were created immortal and incorruptible and granted dominion over the rest of the created order, a privilege they would have kept had they not transgressed God's mandates. God's original will was for them to live without pain and to bring forth many offspring like them. At the point determined by God, they would eat from the tree of life and be made immortal. All humans, however, have sinned in Adam, and the Garden of Eden has been shut off from them. Yet God has predestined for the believers in Christ to be saved through Christ's atoning sacrifice. In the last days after the universal judgment, the righteous ones will enter peace and rest in God. The antichrist will be killed, the righteous will resurrect body and soul to everlasting life, and those who have rejected Christ will enter eternal fire. In the last lines of the first book, Bede invites every reader to come to faith in Christ and be nourished with the souls of the blessed from the fruit of the tree of life in the spiritual paradise. To be with the tree is to be with Christ, he states, and the tree is for all who embrace it.

Conclusion

Bede's world, that small corner of northeastern Britain, is but a microcosm of our world. The need to penetrate our culture with the gospel is as urgent and compelling in our day as it was for Acca and Bede in theirs. Bede had inherited from the Fathers a Christian theology of history. Human history, he believed, is the working out of God's plan of salvation.[57] An understanding of the eternal truths about God, the world and the history of humanity's present failure and future deliverance derive from a serious study of Genesis. Bede made this knowledge accessible to all who will read and learn. The Christian's task is no less today.

Select Bibliography

Works Cited in Translator's Introduction

Augustine. *De doctrina christiana*. Edited by Philip Schaff et al. NPNF. 1st series. Vol. 2. Grand Rapids: Eerdmans, 1956.

————. *De musica*. Edited by J.-P. Migne. PL 32. Paris: J.-P. Migne and Garnier Freres, 1841–1880.

Bede. *De schematibus et tropis*. Edited by C.B. Kendall. CCL 123A. Turnhout: Brepols, 1975.

————. *Ecclesiastical History of the English People*. Translated by Leo Sherley-Price. London: Penguin, 1955.

Freibergs, Gunar. "The Medieval Latin Hexameron from Bede to Grosseteste." Ph.D.

---

[57]Holder, "Introduction," xx.

diss., University of Southern California, 1981.

Holder, Arthur G. "Introduction." In *Bede: On the Tabernacle*, xii-xxiv. Liverpool: Liverpool University Press, 1994.

Isidore of Seville. *Etymologiarum*. Edited by J.-P. Migne. PL 82. Paris: J.-P. Migne and Garnier Freres, 1841–1880.

Jones, Charles W. "Introduction." In *Bedae Venerabilis opera*, Part 2: *Exegetical Works*, 1-10. CCL 118A. Turnhout: Brepols, 1968.

———. "Some Introductory Remarks on Bede's Commentary on Genesis." *Sacris Erudiri* 19 (1969–1970): 115-98.

Kelly, Joseph F. "1996 NAPS Presidential Address—On the Brink: Bede." *Journal of Early Christian Studies* 5 (1997): 85-103.

Laistner, M. L. W. "The Library of the Venerable Bede." In *Bede: His Life, Times and Writings: Essays in Commemoration of the Twelfth Centenary of His Death*, 237-66. Edited by A. Hamilton Thompson. Oxford: Clarendon Press, 1935.

McClure, Judith. "Bede's *Notes on Genesis* and the Training of the Anglo-Saxon Clergy." In *The Bible in the Medieval World: Essays in Memory of Beryl Smalley*, 17-30. Edited by Katherine Walsh and Diana Wood. Oxford: Basil Blackwell, 1985.

Schaff, Philip, and Samuel Macauley Jackson, eds. *Schaff-Herzog Encyclopedia of Religious Knowledge*, s.v. "Bede." New York: Funk and Wagnells, 1887.

Thurston, Herbert. "The Venerable Bede." *The Catholic Encyclopedia*. New York: Robert Appleton Company, 1907.

Wallis, Faith, trans. *Bede: The Reckoning of Time*. Translated Texts for Historians 29. Liverpool: Liverpool University Press, 1999.

Ward, Benedicta. *The Venerable Bede*. London: Cassell, 1990.

Works Cited in Commentary

Ambrose of Milan. *The Six Days of Creation* and *Paradise*. In *Hexameron, Paradise and Cain and Abel*. Translated by John J. Savage. FC 42. New York: Fathers of the Church, 1961.

Augustine. *Against the Manichees* and *On the Literal Interpretation of Genesis: An Unfinished Book*. In *Saint Augustine on Genesis*. Translated by Roland J. Teske. FC 84. Washington, D.C.: Catholic University of America Press, 1991.

———. *Confessionum libri tredecim*. In *Aurelii Augustini opera*. Edited by Lucas Verjeyen. CCL 27. Turnhout: Brepols, 1981.

———. *Contra adversarium legis et prophetarum*. In *Aurelii Augustini opera*. Edited by Klaus-D. Daur. CCL 49. Turnhout: Brepols, 1985.

———. *The Literal Meaning of Genesis*. Translated by John Hammond Taylor. ACW 41, 42. New York: Newman Press, 1982.

Basil of Caesarea. *The Treatise De Spiritu Sancto*. In *The Nine Homilies of the Hexaemeron and the Letters of Saint Basil the Great.* Translated by Blomfield Jackson. NPNF. Second series. Vol. 8. Grand Rapids: Eerdmans, 1955.

Basil–Eusthatius. *Eusthatii in Hexaemeron S. Basilii Latina metaphrasis.* PL 53. Edited by J.-P. Migne. Paris: Migne, 1865.

Bede. *The Reckoning of Time.* In *Bede: The Reckoning of Time.* Translated by Faith Wallis. Translated Texts for Historians 29. Liverpool: Liverpool University Press, 1999.

Eusebius of Caeserea. *Onomasticon* (1971). Notes, 76-252. Edited by C. Umhau Wolf. <www.tertullian.org/fathers/eusebius_onomasticon_03_notes.htm>. Accessed June 16, 2006.

Isidore of Seville. *Etymologiarum.* PL 82. Edited by J.-P Migne. Paris: Migne, 1850.

Jerome. *Commentarii in Esaiam.* In *S. Hieronymi presbyteri opera.* CCL 73. Turnhout: Brepols, 1963.

————. *Epistle* 48. In *St. Jerome: Letters and Selected Works.* Translated by W. H. Fremantle. NPNF. Second series. Vol. 6. Grand Rapids: Eerdmans, 1952.

————. *Liber interpretationis Hebraicorum nominum.* In *St. Hieronymi presbyteri opera.* CCL 73. Turnhout: Brepols, 1959.

Josephus. *Jewish Antiquities.* Translated by H. St. J. Thackeray. LCL. London: William Heinemann, 1930.

Ovid. *Metamorphoses.* Translated by Frank Justus Miller. LCL. Cambridge: Harvard University Press, 1939.

Pliny. *Natural History.* Translated by H. Rackham. LCL. Cambridge: Harvard University Press, 1938.

Pseudo-Clement. *Recognitiones Rufino interpretante,* 1. PG 1. Edited by J.-P. Migne. Paris: Migne, 1860.

Vergil. *Aeneid* and *Georgics.* In *The Poems of Virgil.* Translated by James Rhoades. Chicago: Encyclopedia Britannica, 1952.

COMMENTARY ON GENESIS

Preface

A Letter to Acca, Bishop of the See of Hexham[1]

Bede, the most humble servant of Christ, sends greetings to the beloved and most reverend Bishop Acca.

Many writers have written a great number of things about the beginning of the book of Genesis, in which the creation of this world has been described. They have left behind to future generations many monuments to their own genius, especially, in as far as in my limited ability could learn, Basil of Caesarea, whom Eustathius translated from Greek into Latin, Ambrose of Milan, and Augustine, bishop of Hippo. The first (Basil) of these in nine books, the second (Ambrose) following in his footsteps in six books, the third (Augustine) in twelve books, and again in two others written especially against the Manicheans, poured out streams of the doctrine of salvation to readers. Through them the promise of truth was fulfilled in regard to which Christ said, "He who believes in me, as the Scripture has said, out of his heart shall flow rivers of living water."[2] With respect to these words, Augustine also made some mention of that primordial creation, with suitable explanation, in his *Confessions* and in his book that he wrote *Against the Adversary of the Law and Prophets* and even here and there in his other smaller works.

However, because they are so plentiful, these many volumes could be acquired only by the wealthy, and so profound that only the most learned could scarcely study them, it pleased your holiness to charge me to gather from all these sources, as if gathering far and wide from the most delightful flowers in the fields of paradise, those things that seemed to meet the needs of the weak. I was not slow in implementing the matters that you deemed worthy to command, but, rather, immediately I collected materials from these highly regarded volumes of the Fathers and divided them up in two little books, from which, besides being able to instruct the beginning learner, the more educated individual could engage himself in a deep and robust understanding of our predecessors. In this work I was eager to capture the meaning of the previously mentioned Fathers, and others equally catholic, at times in their very words, and at times, for the sake of brevity, in mine, omitting some of their words and recording others as fittingly as the subject matter dictated. And I have drawn the work up to the point when Adam, having been cast from the paradise of delight,[3] entered the exile of temporal life.

Also, I am going to write some things about the subsequent events of sacred history, God willing and with the help of your intercession, after first I have thoroughly examined the book of Ezra, the righteous prophet and priest, who as both a historian and a prophet wrote about the sacraments of the Christ and church through the allegorical figure of the release

---

Preface [1] Acca, bishop of Hexham (709–731), was Bede's patron who commissioned Bede to write many of his commentaries. [2] Jn 7:38. [3] "Delight" is the meaning of *Eden* in Hebrew.

from the long captivity,[4] the restoration of the temple,[5] the rebuilding of the city,[6] the returning of the sacred vessels to Jerusalem,[7] which had been carried away, the rewriting of the law of God that had been burned, the purification of the people from their foreign wives[8] and the people's return to one heart and spirit into the service of God; as the prophet who was a historian wrote and with God's help I will explain very clearly to the learned some of the sacraments that I have mentioned.

May you always be well, most beloved bishop, and remember me in the Lord.

Book I of *In Genesim*

[1]*In the beginning God created the heavens and the earth.*

From the first word, the holy Scripture teaches about the creation of the world and correctly shows the timelessness and omnipotence of God the Creator. It teaches that he, who created the world before the beginning of time, had himself existed eternally before time. Scripture relates that he created the heaven and earth at the very inception of time, and the swiftness of the outcome declares the omnipotence of the One who can will an act and it is done. This is not the case when in our human weakness we do something, as, for example, when we build a house. At the start of the work we gather the materials and then dig the foundation for support; next we lay down stones for the foundation; then with increasing layering of the stones we put up the walls. Little by little we come to the completion of the work according to the plan put forth. God, however, whose hand is all-powerful for completing his work, has no need for any passage of time, just as it is written, "He does whatever he pleases."[1] It is, therefore, well stated that "in the beginning God created the heavens and the earth," for clearly Scripture intends for us to understand that both were created by him simultaneously, although it could not be said for both to be created simultaneously by humans. Finally, the prophet writes, "In the beginning you founded the earth, Lord," but here it is recorded, "The Lord created heaven and earth in the beginning."[2] From this it can be deduced that the creation of both elements was simultaneous, and this with such swiftness of divine power that the first moment of the emerging world had not yet passed.

It is not unreasonable for one to understand "in the beginning God made the heavens and the earth" in terms of the only-begotten Son, who answered the Jews when they asked him why they should believe in him: "[I am] the beginning which I speak to you also."[3] "For in him," the apostle says, "all things were created in heaven and on earth."[4] But one must carefully contemplate lest he would so weigh down this study with the allegorical sense that he would then forsake the plainly faithful account of history by his allegorical approach. And, which and what sort of heaven it is that was made in the beginning with the earth may be made known in the following words when it is written:

[2]*The earth was without form and void, and darkness was upon the face of the deep.*

Indeed, since reference to heaven is omitted, what do these details about the earth mean except that the writer wants nothing of the same description to be applied to heaven? That is, the highest heaven which, having been distinguished from every condition of this changeable world, remains always undisturbed in the glory of the divine presence (for our heaven, in which lights have been placed that are necessary for this earthly life, in the following verses Scripture tells how and when it was made).

---

[4]Ezra 1:1. [5]Ezra 1:2-4. [6]Neh 3:1-16. [7]Neh 1:7-11. [8]Ezra 10. **Book I** [1]Ps 115:3 (113:11 Vg). [2]Ps 102:25. [3]Jn 8:25. [4]Col 1:16.

Therefore, the higher heaven that is inaccessible to the sight of all mortals has not been created without form and void as has the earth. In the very beginning, earth's creation brought forth no green plants and no living animals, but the higher heaven, having been created for its own inhabitants, was filled with the most blessed hosts of angels.

The Creator testifies that these angels were created in the beginning with the heaven and earth, and quickly they proclaimed their own creation and that of every primordial creature to the glory of the Creator. God declares to his righteous servant Job, "Where were you when I laid the foundation of the earth?"[5] Then, a little later God declares, and where were you "when the morning stars sang together, and all the sons of God shouted for joy?"[6] He calls "morning stars" those same angels he also calls "sons of God" to make a distinction from saints who after creation and just like evening stars were going to perish through the death of the flesh after the profession of divine praise. One of these morning stars because of his disrespect for this unified praise to God deserved to hear, "How you are fallen from heaven, O Day Star, son of Dawn! How you are cut down to the ground, you who laid the nations low! You said in your heart, 'I will ascend to heaven above the stars of God. I will set my throne on high.'"[7]

Saint Jerome, in his commentary on these verses, even mentions the higher heavens when he writes, "He [Lucifer] either said these things before he had fallen from heaven or after he had fallen from heaven. If he were still in heaven, how could he say, 'I will ascend into heaven'? But since we read, 'To the Lord belongs the heaven of heaven,' he [Lucifer] had been in heaven, that is, in the firmament, when he desired to ascend into heaven where the throne of the Lord was, not with humility but with pride. But, if he spoke these arrogant words after he fell from heaven, we ought to understand that he does not presently lie at rest, but still he makes grandiose promises for himself, not that he may be among the stars but that he may be above the stars of God."[8] Be that as it may, one should remember that the higher heaven had not been created without form and void, nor is it granted that any place in it or in the abyss has remained in the darkness because the Lord God illuminates it, and his lamp is the Lamb.

Indeed, "the earth was without form and void," since up to this point it had been wholly covered by the abyss, that is, an immense depth of water. Likewise, the "darkness was upon the face of the deep," since the light that would dispel the darkness had not yet been created. Do not listen to those who scorn God and say that he created darkness before light, because God did not make any darkness in the water or the air, but in a well-defined order of his providence he created the waters with the heaven and earth first, and when he wished, he beautified them with the gift of light. We recognize that he does this now both in the water and in the air through the daily rising and falling of the sun. Nor is it right to believe that waters were created other than by God; even though Scripture did not openly state it here, nevertheless it does clearly indicate it when it states that these things have been illumined by God and have been ordained according to his command; the psalm openly proclaims, "Let the waters which are above the heavens praise the name of the Lord, . . . for he commanded and they were created."[9]

In this same psalm it should be noted that the two elements of this world, namely, water and earth, are plainly recounted to have been made with heaven in the beginning. This knowledge establishes that from these two

---

[5]Job 38:4. [6]Job 38:7. [7]Is 14:12-13. [8]Jerome *Commentarii in Esaiam* 6.12.13-14 (CCL 73); also quoted in Bede *De temporum ratione* 5. [9]Ps 148:4-5.

elements the remaining ones emerge, being fire in the iron and stones that lie hidden, even now buried, in the innermost part of the earth, and air in the earth itself "which is recognized to be mixed with it, . . . from the fact that since the earth is moistened and heated by the sun, it soon exhales bountiful vapors."[10] Fiery fountains of waters spring forth the raging fire located in the innermost parts of the earth. They spill out onto the surface of the earth, not just hot but boiling, after "passing through some particular elements" in the depths of the waters.

Truly, these were not mingled together formlessly, as some argue, but the earth circumscribed on all sides by those same boundaries as it is now, was in the past completely submerged but now remains only partly under the deepest depths of the sea; moreover, the waters, which covered the whole surface to such a depth that they extended up to those places where, now resting partly over the firmament of heaven, they continuously praise the name of God the Creator with the highest of heaven. It is in this way that the material of the world has been made formless to which Scripture testifies and says in the praise of God, "You made the world from matter without form."[11] For all the things we typically see in the world made from earth and water had their beginning in them—or they take their form from nothing.[12]

Earth and water, moreover, share the name of unformed matter, because before they came into the light from which they held their beauty they did not exist. Why is it unreasonable to think that just as the mundane matter, which had existed in the primordial darkness, was rendered better by the approaching light, so also the condition of humankind progressing, as it were, as later would happen, is

signified in a similar manner,[13] as the apostle explains: "For it is God who said, 'Let the light shine out of the darkness,' who made it to shine in our hearts"?[14] Also, "For once you were darkness, but now you are light in the Lord,"[15] namely, in him who, when the "darkness was upon the face of the deep," said, "Let there be light, and there was light."[16]

[2]And the Spirit of God was moving over the waters.

One must not think in any childish way that the Creator Spirit, about whom it is written that "the Spirit of the Lord fills the whole earth,"[17] moved over those things that had to be created in spatial terms; but, rather, let one understand that the Spirit was preeminent over the creation by virtue of his divine being, possessing his own power: when he would bring light to the abyss of the waters, when he would separate them into one place so that the dry land could appear and when and how he would distribute particular creatures according to his own will, that is, in a way likened to a craftsman whose will is customarily transferred to the things which are to be crafted.

This verse also applies to that distinction of the highest heaven in which now the power of the Holy Spirit brings light fully to everything; yet the Spirit's intention from the very beginning of creation was to bring to perfection the primordial elements of the good creation in the inferior creations, that is, in the creatures of this world, in time. Moses only briefly commented on this upper realm, because he decided to speak about this world, in which humankind was made, for the instruction of the human race, believing it was sufficient if he included the general condition

---

[10]See Basil-Eusthatius *Hexameron* 1.7.9. [11]Wis 11:17. [12]Cf. Augustine *Gen. Man.* 1.5.9—1.6.10: "First there was made confused and formless matter so that out of it there might be made all the things that God distinguished and formed. . . . And, therefore, we correctly believe that God made all things from nothing. For, though all formed things were made from this matter, this matter itself was still made from absolutely nothing." See also Augustine *Gen. litt.* 1.4 for similar concepts. [13]Augustine *Contra adversarium legis et prophetarum* 1.8.11. [14]2 Cor 4:6. [15]Eph 5:8. [16]Gen 1:3. [17]Wis 1:7.

and adornment of the spiritual and invisible creation with the single term of heaven, which he said had been made in the beginning, believing it was necessary to describe the corporeal, visible and perishable creation in order more profoundly. Remaining silent about those things that are deeper and more profound that people search out by inquiry. He decided rather that those things that should be thought about were "commands from God" or promises to people.[18]

Wisely he remained completely silent about the fall of the lying angel and his allies, since this pertained to those invisible and spiritual creatures. Saint Basil, in the second book of the *Hexameron*, reminisces about this higher and invisible creation in this way: "We infer that if anything had existed before the formation of this visible and perishable world, certainly it would have existed in light. For neither the ranks of the angels nor all of the heavenly hosts, nor if there is any other named or unnamed rational power or other spirit,[19] would have been able to live in darkness but possessed a state fitting for it in light and in joy."[20] In sum, Scripture stated that "in the beginning God," that is, the Father in the Son, "made the heaven and earth." It even made mention of the Holy Spirit by adding, "And the Spirit of God moved over the waters," which signified that the concerted power of the Trinity had worked together in the creation of the world.

[3]And God said, "Let there be light"; and there was light.

It is fitting for the works of God that the adornment of the world would begin from light—since he is the true light and dwells in inapproachable light, whose most blessed sight the angels, who were created in the highest heaven, began to enjoy immediately after their creation. Aptly he also gave to this age the first gift of material light for its adornment so that there would be a way that the other things he would create could appear. What God is shown to have commanded, whether it is for light to be created or for any other thing, we must not believe that this actualized in a human mode as in our customary manner. Rather, we should understand more profoundly that God had commanded creation to be made, because everything was made through his own Word, that is, by his only-begotten Son.

The Gospel writer John speaks very clearly on this matter: "In the beginning was the Word, and Word was with God, and the Word was God. He was in the beginning with God. All things were made through him."[21] Therefore, what John said, namely, "all things were made through the Word of God," is what Moses said: "God spoke, 'Let there be light; let there be the firmament; let there be creatures,'" and other such statements. This is what is said in the psalm, with the person of the Holy Spirit added: "By the word of the Lord the heavens were established, and all the power of them by the breath of his mouth."[22]

If people should ask in what place this light was made when God commanded it, since the abyss still covered the fullest extent of the earth, let them remember that on the upper parts of the same earth, which even now the daily light of the sun illumines, the very first light shone forth. Nor must we marvel that by divine activity the light can shine through the water, since it is well known that frequently through the ordinary work of people these waters are illumined, as, for example, sailors, who render the waters more lucid and clearer for themselves when they are plunged into the depth of the sea and emit oil from their mouths.[23] If, indeed, a person is able to do such a thing through the oil of his own mouth, how much more must one believe that God can create through the breath of his own mouth—

---

[18]See Sir 3:22. [19]See Heb 1:14. [20]Basil-Eusthatius *Hexameron* 2.5.8. [21]Jn 1:1-3. [22]Ps 33:6. [23]Basil-Eusthatius *Hexameron* 2.7.6.

especially since the waters we are now accustomed to see are believed to have been created less dense in the beginning than now[24] before "they were gathered together in one place so that dry land could appear."[25]

[4]And God saw that the light was good.

When God declared the light good, he did not praise it as though he were suddenly discovering a light before unknown, but he praised it because it was good. Rather, he knew that he would make praiseworthy what was made, and he declared it to be worthy of praise and admiration by people. It is true that he did not dispel all the darkness of the world as the light increased—for it is appointed for the celestial world to enjoy thoroughly the eternal light— but illuminating it in one part, he left another dark, and directly it is added:

[4]And God separated the light from the darkness.

He separated them not only on the basis of their nature but also according to place, that is, by diffusing the light on regions in the upper part of the world where humans were going to live and by allowing the lower regions to remain in their former darkness.

[5]God called the light Day, and the darkness he called Night.

All of this is said for the sake of our understanding. For by what language had God called the light "day" and the darkness "night," be it in Hebrew or in Greek or in any other tongue? And, in the same way we can ask in regard to everything that he named, what language did he name them? For with God there is pure intellect without the noise and diversity of languages. Still, "he called" is spoken in the same sense as "he made them to be called," because he separated and ordered all things, so that the days were able to be both distinguished and receive names. Thus, as an example, we say that the father of the household "built" that home, meaning "he had it built." Many such expressions are found throughout all the books of divine Scripture.[26]

[5]And there was evening and and there was morning, one day.

Evening was made as the light gradually set after it had completed its daily course and entered the lower parts of the world, which now is done at night because of the customary circuit of the sun. Morning is made as the same light gradually returns over the lands and begins another day. At this point one day is completed, namely, twenty-four hours. By its careful choice of words the Scripture encourages us to understand that the light that has been created crossed the lower regions of the earth by its own setting, for if it did not do this, but rather, when the evening came, little by little it disappeared totally and little by little it reappeared again in the morning, Scripture no longer could say that one day had been completed in the morning of the following day, but rather it was completed in the evening of the first.

Hence, Scripture preferred to say there was evening and morning rather than night and day, in order to teach that what was done by the circuit of that first light is now agreed to be done by the circuit of the sun day and night—except that the night is also full of light after the stars were created (even if they are lesser lights than those of the day). During the period of those first three days night remained shrouded in darkness and imperceptible. It is right that the

---

[24]See Augustine *Gen. litt.* 1.12.26. [25]Gen 1:9. [26]See Augustine *Gen. Man.* 1.9.15. This is almost a direct quote from Augustine, and in the CCL text it appears entirely in italics, as do other direct quotes. Some of Augustine's sentences are not present, and Bede uses the word *dies* ("days") where Augustine's text is referring to "all things."

day beginning in light endured into the morning of the following day, because the work of the one who is true light and in whom there is no darkness was said to have begun and to have been completed in the light.

⁶And God said, "Let there be a firmament in the midst of the waters, and let it separate the waters from the waters." ⁷And God made the firmament and separated the waters which were under the firmament from the waters which were above the firmament. And it was so. ⁸And God called the firmament Heaven. And there was evening and there was morning, a second day.

Described in these verses is the creation of our heaven in which the stars are fixed. It is established that the firmament is in the midst of the waters, for we understand that waters were placed beneath the firmament and in the air and the land; and we are taught about the placement of these waters above it by the authority of this Scripture passage and by the words of the prophet who said, "Spreading out heaven like a tent, you cover your chamber with waters."²⁷ It is in agreement then that the starry heaven was firmly set in the midst of the waters, and this does not prevent the belief that it was made from these waters.

We know the great strength, purity and transparency of crystalline rock that was made by the congealing of the waters. What could keep us from believing the same arranger of things of nature solidified the waters into the firmament of heaven? But if it disturbs one how the waters, whose very nature is always to flow and to settle to the lowest point, can settle above heaven whose shape we know is round, let him remember the Scripture saying of God, "He binds up the waters in his cloud, and the cloud is not rent under it."²⁸

One may understand, furthermore, that the one who binds up the waters below heaven, when he wishes and occasion arises, supported it without a foundation of firm matter and sustained it only by the vapors of the clouds, so that the water does not fall, is also the one able to suspend the waters above the round sphere of heaven, not with some tenuous vapory mist but with the solidity of ice, so that they would never fall. Even if he willed these liquid waters to remain fixed, would this be any greater miracle than "he hangs the earth upon nothing," as Scripture states?²⁹

Indeed, do not the waves of the Red Sea and the flowing waters of the Jordan, when they are raised on high and fixed like walls so the people of Israel could cross over, give clear evidence that they could also remain fixed above the revolving dome of heaven? Of course, the Creator has known what type of waters they may be there and for what purposes they have been reserved; that these waters do exist there is no room for doubt because the holy Scripture says so. What there is to say of God declaring, "Let there be this or that creature thing," has already been said above. For he declared it to be when he made plans for everything to be created through his Word, that is, his only-begotten Son coeternal with him.

When, therefore, we hear, "Let there be a firmament in the midst of the waters, and let it divide the waters from the waters," let us understand that it was by the Word of God this was done; through whom God foresaw inwardly before all time whatever he did outwardly in time was to be done. When we hear "God made the firmament, and he separated the waters which were under the firmament from those which were above the firmament, and it was so," let us understand that the finished creation and arrangement of the heaven and waters did not overstep the limits set for them in the Word of God. For according to the word of the psalmist, "He fixed their bounds,

---

²⁷Ps 103:2-3 (Vg). ²⁸Job 26:8. ²⁹Job 26:7; see also Is 40:12 (Vg).

which cannot be passed."[30]

This fact should be understood as referring equally to the creation that was made in the following four days. When we hear it added, "And God saw that it was good," let us not understand that in the beneficence of his spirit that later, after it was made, it was pleasing, but rather it was pleasing for it to remain in that very goodness when it was pleasing that it was made.[31]

It should be noted that the addition of these words in this verse is not found in the original Hebrew. It is surprising that among all the things that we read God created, here alone, on the second day of his works, the approval from the divine perspective is not added. Yet these very works along with the others things that God made are shown to be seen as good by God, since in later verses it is written, "And God saw all that he had made, and behold, it was very good."[32] Perhaps, as one of the Fathers explained, the Scripture wishes us to understand that "there is something not good in the number two, separating as it does from unity and prefiguring the covenant of marriage. Just as in the ark of Noah all the animals that entered two by two are unclean, but those taken of odd number are clean."[33]

Concerning these things that have been explained carefully up to this point, namely, concerning the creation of the first and second day, it is reported that in the history of Saint Clement the apostle Peter had said, "In the beginning when God had created the heaven and earth as one house, the shadow that was cast by the material substances of the world upon those things that had been enclosed inside gave the darkness from itself. But when the will of God had introduced light, the darkness that had been made from the shadow of those substances was immediately devoured. The light was counted as day, the darkness as night.

Now the water that was within the world in that middle space between the first heaven and earth is expanded, congealed like ice and solidified like crystal. The space in the middle of the heaven and earth was enclosed as it were by a firmament of this sort, and the Creator called the firmament 'heaven,' so called from a name of that older one, and he divided the fabric of the whole world into two parts, although it was one house. The reason for this division, moreover, was so he could present the upper region as the habitation for angels, the lower one for people."[34] I choose to present these things in my work so that the reader might recognize how much this concurs with the general understanding of the Fathers.

[9]*And God said, "Let the waters under the heavens be gathered into one place and let the dry land appear." And it was so.*

The waters that had completely covered the heaven and earth are collected and gathered together into one place, so that the clear light, which illumined the waters the previous two days, beamed more brilliantly in the pure air; and so that the land that was hidden would appear, which earth having been covered by the waters and remaining a miry clay and unstable would be made dry and suitable for planting seeds with the receding of those waters. Should anyone ask where the waters, which had covered all the regions of the earth even up to heaven, have been gathered, let him know that it could have happened that at the command of the Creator, that same earth subsiding far and wide provided hollowed-out places into which the flowing waters could rush so that the dry land could appear in those areas where the moisture had withdrawn.

It is not unreasonable for us to believe, just as we indicated above, that these first waters

---

[30]Ps 148:6. [31]See Augustine *Gen. litt.* 2.6.14. [32]Gen 1:31. [33]Jerome *Epistle* 48.19. [34]Pseudo-Clement *Recognitiones Rufino interpretante* 1.37 (PG 1:1222).

that covered the earth like clouds were very thin; when they were gathered they became denser, and they were able to be contained in a designated place, and the dry area appeared in the rest. One will understand that although there are many seas, Scripture states that the waters are gathered into one place, namely, because all of the waters are tied together and are joined in an unending ocean and great sea. For even if the lakes seem self-contained, having made passage through certain hidden caves, they still follow their courses toward the sea. People who dig wells demonstrate this fact that the whole earth is filled with waters rushing through invisible veins that have their beginning from the sea.

¹⁰God called the dry land Earth, and the waters that were gathered together he called Seas.

From the first he called this whole more solid part of the world *earth* to its distinction from the waters, as when Scripture states, "In the beginning God created the heavens and the earth. The earth was without form and void." But now, after the world begins to be formed and the face of the earth appears as the waters recede into their own places, to make a distinction from that part that is still covered by the waters, that specific portion that becomes dry receives the name *earth*.

Earth is the word in Latin for that area that is worn away by the feet of animals. The waters that were gathered are called seas, namely, for the sake of the largest of them. For in the Hebrew all the collected waters, whether they are salty or fresh, are called seas. And, rightly, Scripture, which before, on account of the continuation of all the waters on the earth, said they were gathered into a single place, now names the gathering of those waters in the plural and says these are called seas in the plural, chiefly because of many outlets that are given different names in light of the language of the particular region.

¹⁰And God saw that it was good.

The earth had not yet sprouted vegetation, and the waters and the earth did not yet produce living creatures; yet, it is said that "God saw that it was good" that the dry land had appeared as the waters receded. The Judge of the water, of the whole universe, foreseeing what was going to be in the future, now praises things that are yet in the beginning of the initial work as if they were already perfected; nor should we marvel that in the one for whom the perfection of something is not in the completion of the work but lies in the predetermination of his own will.

¹¹And God said, "Let the earth put forth vegetation, plants yielding seed, and fruit trees bearing fruit in which is their seed, each according to its kind, upon the earth." And it was so. ¹²The earth brought forth vegetation, plants yielding seed according to their own kinds, and trees bearing fruit in which is their seed, each according to its kind. And God saw that it was good. ¹³And there was evening and there was morning, a third day.

It is evident from these words that the adornment of the world was completed in the springtime, for that is the season when living plants typically appear on the earth and trees are laden with fruit. Likewise, it must be noted that the first shoots of the trees and plants did not come from seed, but they sprang forth from the earth; for the earth, which appeared dry in accordance with the command of the Creator, suddenly was beautified with plants and arrayed with flowering groves, and fruits of every type continuously came forth from the seeds they bear. It was fitting that in the beginning whatever the form of each thing, it came forth according to the command of God as mature; in the same manner it must be believed that man, for whom all things on earth had been created, was fashioned in a mature form, that is, as a youthful man.

¹⁴*And God said, "Let there be lights in the firmament of the heavens."*

In fitting order the world advanced from unformed matter to its ordained shape. Even before any day whatsoever of this age, after God created heaven, earth and water, that is, the higher and spiritual world with its own inhabitants and the unformed matter of this world, as it is written, "He who lives forever created all things in general,"³⁵ on the first day of this age he created light, by which all the created things could be seen. On the second day, he solidified the firmament of heaven, namely, the upper part of this world, in the midst of the waters. On the third day, in the lower regions he separated the sea and the lands and the air within their own set boundaries, and as the water yielded, he diffused the air into its place. It was proper, therefore, that in the same order in which they were created the elements assume their fuller adornment; that is, on the fourth day, heaven should be adorned with lights; on the fifth day, the air and sea, and on the sixth day, the earth, are all filled with living things. For the fact that on the third day the earth is clothed with plants and trees, not for its adornment, as I have said, but for its own sake, applies to the surface of its form.

¹⁴*"To separate the day from the night."*

This division is clearly explained in the following verses: that the sun gives light to the day and stars and the moon to the night. After the stars were created to augment that primordial light, it happened that even the night passes with light, illumined either by the moon or by the stars or by both. Up to this point the night had known nothing except that ancient darkness. And even if in our thinking the night seems dark and black to us when the air that is next to it is darkened by the windblown clouds; nevertheless, the upper region that is called ether always is rendered bright on account of the revolving of the stars. With the addition of light the stars, after they appeared, offered through themselves, as a divine gift for the world, the ability to recognize the boundaries of the passing seasons. Hence, it follows:

¹⁴*"And let them be for signs and for seasons and for days and years."*

Before the stars were made, there really was no way for the order of the seasons to be determined by any indicators; there was no way the midday hour could be known before "the fiery sun had mounted to the midst of the orb of heaven."³⁶ Certain hours of the day and night could not be marked until the stars separated day and night by sharing among themselves equal parts of the heaven. They are, therefore, lights "for signs and for seasons and for days and years," not because the seasons, which one agrees had begun from the beginning when God made heaven and earth, or because the days and years had begun when God commanded, "Let there be light and it was so," began with their creation, but because the changing of the seasons and the days and the years is marked by the rising and crossing of these luminaries. For the whole three-day period before had passed with an unbreakable progress of their courses, having no internal marker for the hours, since, when that primal light still filled all things generally and had no beginning, which now it receives from the sun, the rays never shone so brightly, nor did any shade grow cold as if far under a tree or cliff. But not only for the marking of the times are the luminaries beneficial for this life. Sailors navigating the ships observe the stars, or all the travelers crossing the sandy deserts of Ethiopia, where

---

³⁵Sir 18:1. ³⁶Vergil *Aeneid* 8.97.

the slightest gust of wind erases previously discernable footprints, observe the stars. No less so for the ones traveling in those regions than the ones sailing on the sea is there the need for the signs of the stars for the day and night. They are thus "for a sign" because sometimes we can foretell even the nature of the weather about to come by our contemplation of them.

¹⁵"And let them be lights in the firmament of the heavens to give light upon the earth." And it was so.

The luminaries always shine in the heavenly firmament, as I have said, and they soak the places nearest to it with the brightest light, but they illumine the earth in favorable times. For sometimes a cloudy atmosphere thwarts them so that neither the light of the moon when it is young nor the stars are visible on the earth; but the sun, when it has arisen with its greater light, obstructs the moon and stars so that they cannot illumine the earth, whence it gets its name,[37] because the sun, the word *sol* in Latin, shines alone, *solus* in Latin, on the earth through the day when the light of the stars and moon are dim.

¹⁶And God made the two great lights.

We are able to understand the lights as great not only in comparison with other things but also in terms of their own function, like the great heaven and the great sea, for the sum is great which fills the whole earth with its heat, as is the moon with its own light. They illumine everything in whichever part of the heaven they are and they are viewed equally by all people. A clear proof of their magnitude is that their circle seems the same to all people. If it seemed smaller to people located further away and if it shone more brightly to people

positioned nearer, this would furnish evidence of its smallness.

¹⁶The greater light to rule the day, and the lesser light to rule the night; he made the stars also. ¹⁷And God set them in the firmament of the heavens.

The greater light is the sun, not only in the beauty of its body but also in the brilliance of its light by which it is believed to illumine the lesser light and the stars. It is also greater by virtue of its heat through which after its creation it warmed the earth, since the days previous to its creation had no experience of this heat at all. From the fact that the moon is perceived to be of equal and like magnitude to the sun they say that the sun moves much higher and further over the lands than the moon; and how great its magnitude is cannot be known by us who live on the earth. Typically we perceive things further away as smaller. Scripture states, "And the lesser light to rule the night and the stars. And he placed them in the firmament of heaven." Because even if it happens that the moon and at times the greater stars would be seen in the day, it is most certain that these never bring the same comfort of light to the day but only to the night.

¹⁷To give light upon the earth, ¹⁸to rule over the day and over the night, and to separate the light from the darkness.

These words are understood to concern the distinction between the large luminaries and the stars, as when it is written, "they rule over the day"; specifically, this phrase pertains to the sun; and when it is added, "over the night," this phrase pertains to the moon and stars; and when it adds, "and to separate the light from

---

[37] The Latin word for "sun" is *sol*; the Latin word for "alone" is *solus*. The sun gets its name *sol* from *solus* because it alone gives the earth light in the day. See Isidore of Seville *Etymologiarum* 3.71.1.

the darkness," this statement applies to all the luminaries equally. Wherever these luminaries go, they spread the light with them, and where they are absent everything remains in shadows.

If one should ask what kind of daily light existed before the creation of the heavenly lights, it would not be too far off to say it is similar to our experience when we see the light in the early morning, as the rising of the sun approaches but does not yet fully appear over the earth, when the day grows brighter as the rays of the stars grow dim, but the light continues shining just minimally until the sun has fully risen. Hence, then, there could be no distinction of the times except of the day and night only, and, therefore, when the stars were created it was rightly commanded, "And these were for signs and for seasons and for days and years." For the changes of the seasons began to be discerned when the sun, on the fourth day of the new world, proceeding from the midpoint of the east, inaugurated the vernal equinox by its own rising, and having set forth every day by mounting up to the highest point of the sky and once more descending from the highest point of the solstice to the lowest little by little, returning again from the lowest and wintry regions so that there was no lapse of the equinoctial cycles, fills the space of a year with its appointed days, with its four well-known and distinct seasons.

And the moon, appearing full in the evening, fixes by its first ascent the times for the celebration of Easter. Indeed, not only the ancient people of God but we also today keep as the first hour in observing Easter the time when the full moon in the evening, that is, the fourteenth day, appears on the face of the sky as the day of the equinox has passed. For presently after this, as the following Sunday comes, the time befitting the celebration of the resurrection of the Lord closely follows, as the word of the prophet is fulfilled to the letter,

who said, "Thou has made the moon to mark the seasons; the sun knows its time for setting."[38] The stars also, except for what we said above, show the nature of the coming weather by their appearance or by which watch of the night is their course; "they are for signs and for seasons," since those particular stars as they come into the sky indicate the summer season; these specific stars, the winter.

They are "for the days" since these stars accompany the sun in the spring days; those stars in the autumn days. They are "for the years" because the stars that at one time rise in the spring equinox in the morning, for example, appear in the sky at the same equinox every year, and those that appear in the sky in the solstice always rise in the same hours in the evening or in the morning. But there are certain stars that the astrologists call the planets, the "wandering ones," which require longer years by their circuits to return to the same place in the sky. For the planet that is called Saturn this circuit is thirty years, for Jupiter it is twelve years, the circuit of Mars is two solar years before the circuit of the heaven is completed and the stars return to the same places in which they had been before. The moon also when it travels through twelve periods of its course completes a common year, that is, 354 days, and so that it can harmonize its circuit with that of the sun it adds a thirteenth month to the following year or the year after, which those who calculate such matters call a embolismic year, and it becomes 384 days.[39]

[18] And God saw that it was good.

It is important that holy Scripture repeats many times that "God saw it was good" concerning what he had created, so that the devotion of the faithful could be informed not to judge the created things of the visible and invisible worlds in light of human understand-

---

[38]Ps 104:19. [39]Bede discusses this matter in 100.45 of *The Reckoning of Time*.

ing, which often is offended by even the good things whose causes and order in the visible and invisible creation people are ignorant to explain, but by yielding to and believing God approving it. In as much as an individual generally learns something more easily as he matures, by so much more the devoted one has trusted in God before he has learned something. Scripture says, therefore, God saw that what he had made it was good because the things made were pleasing to have been made; the things made were good as they were, in the fact that the standard of their existence and their duration had been constituted by such a great Creator beforehand.

19 *And there was evening and there was morning, a fourth day.*

These words refer to the memorable evening in Egypt in which the people of God offered the lamb for the Passover celebration. We understand this as the morning of their journey to freedom, after the arduous yoke of a long-borne slavery. It is written that the Lord said to Moses: "This month shall be for you the beginning of months; it shall be the first month of the year for you; on the tenth day of the month they shall take every man a lamb according to their father's houses, and you shall keep it until the fourteenth of this month, when the whole assembly of the congregation of Israel shall kill their lambs in the evening."[40] Likewise, besides establishing the sacrament of the Passover, on this evening after eating the lamb our Lord, in order to fulfill the sacrifices of the Law of the Passover, symbolically initiated for us the mystery of his body and blood that we celebrate; through which celebration, as the morning grew light, he freed us from the bondage of demonic power as he redeemed us by his own blood just like "an unblemished lamb."[41] The fourth day in the creation of the world, namely, the day of the full moon, passed, but in the time of the passion of the Lord, the gift of a deeper symbolic act fell on the fifth day of the week, namely, as the Lord having been crucified on the sixth day rested in the tomb on that very day; and he consecrated for us the first day of the week by his own resurrection on which the light of the resurrection of the dead was inaugurated, and he gave hope and faith to those entering the everlasting light.

20 *And God said, "Let the waters bring forth swarms of living creatures, and let birds fly above the earth across the firmament of the heavens."*

After the face of heaven was adorned with lights on the fourth day, on the following day, the fifth day, the parts of the lower world, that is, the water and air, were adorned with those creations that move with the breath of life, because both of these elements—water and air—are connected with heaven as if by a certain familial relationship. Indeed, the nature of the waters is very close to the properties of the air, from which it is shown that the "air grows dense from their vapors"[42] so that the cloudy sky thickens and is able to sustain the flight of birds, as Scripture attests: "suddenly the air is gathered into the clouds, and the wind passing will drive them off,"[43] and "on calm nights the air produces dew, and the drops of this dew are found on the grass in the morning on the plants."[44]

In this they are linked to the heavens; since that air is so similar to the heavens, it sometimes is called by name of "heaven," just as Scripture names the flying creatures of heaven, which means that they fly in the air; and the Lord answered the crowd, who had not

---

[40]Ex 12:2-3; 6:8. [41]1 Pet 1:19. [42]Augustine *Gen. litt.* 3.3.5. "Other water is in the rarefied form of a vapor distributed in the air." [43]Job 37:21. [44]See Augustine *Gen. Man.* 1.15.24.

recognized the time of his coming from the demonstration of his power, by saying, "When you see a cloud rising in the west, you say at once, 'A shower is coming,' and so it happens. And when you see the south wind blowing, you say, 'There will be a scorching heat,' and it happens. You hypocrites! You know how to interpret the appearance of the earth and the sky; but why do you not know how to interpret the present time?"[45] In this statement it is clear that he names the state of the air of heaven as "the face of heaven" for nothing other than variety.

Since there are creatures of the waters that do not move by swimming but by creeping or by walking on their feet,[46] and since there are among the birds those that have so many feathers yet are unable to fly, so that no one should think there is any type of winged or aquatic animal being overlooked in this word of the Lord, the following words are carefully chosen:

21So God created the great sea monsters and every living creature that moves, with which the waters swarm, according to their kinds, and every winged bird according to its kind.

There is, therefore, no species of creature left out, since every living creature that the waters produced in kind is created along with the great sea monsters, including ones that crawl, swim, fly and cling to the rocks, like mollusks, since they are not adapted to any manner of mobility. Moreover, although it is said, "flying above the earth along the firmament of heaven," there is nothing keeping us from the truth that as birds that fly above the earth fly under the starry heaven with a huge expanse of space lying between, in the same way we humans, having been placed here on the earth, are said correctly and truthfully to be living

under heaven and the sun, as Scripture attests: "Now there were dwelling in Jerusalem, Jews, devout men, from every nation which is under heaven."[47] And further, "And what does man gain by all his labor at which he toils under the sun?"[48]

Admittedly, it concerns some that another translation says, "And the birds flying next to the firmament, that is, near to the firmament." But one must understand that here it is said that the birds fly "under the firmament of heaven," since by this word *heaven* the upper air (ether) is indicated, that is, the upper region of air that extends from this blustery and foggy region in which the birds may fly even up to the stars, and it is believed not unjustly to be peaceful there and full of light. For Scripture says that the seven planets, which are shown to be following their courses in this area of the ether, are placed in the firmament of heaven. And so birds are rightly said to fly near to the firmament because this windy space of air that sustains the flight of birds is next to the ether, as I have said.

Nor must one wonder that the ether is called the firmament of heaven, since air is called "heaven," as we taught above. Nor must one overlook that when it is said that "God created every living creature," it added the words "and moving" to distinguish these living creatures from humankind whom God was going to make in his own image and likeness, so that if people would keep his laws, they would live blessed by an everlasting unchangeable state. For certain animals were made early in the creation then so that either they became food for others or perished through the weakness of their own natural decline.

21And God saw that it was good. 22And God blessed them saying, "Be fruitful and multiply

---

[45]Lk 12:54-56. [46]The Scripture text is quoted from the RSV. However, in the Latin text Bede used, the word *reptile* appears. RSV translates this as "swarms," but the word means "creeping." This allows for Bede's commentary for this verse; that is, creatures of the waters that do not move by creeping. [47]Acts 2:5. [48]Eccl 1:3.

and fill the waters in the seas, and let birds multiply on the earth." ²³And there was evening and there was morning, a fifth day.

Since it said, "Be fruitful and multiply and fill the waters in the seas," this verse applies to every type of animal created from the waters, including both the fish and the birds, because just as all fish are unable to live unless they are in the waters, so also there are many birds that, even if they sometimes lie at rest and birth their young on the earth, feed them not only on the earth but also on the sea, and they use the marine environment more willingly than the terrestrial. This addition, "let the birds multiply on the earth," refers to both types of birds, that is, those that feed on the waters and those that feed on the land, because even those birds that do not know how to live independently from the waters, in that often they lie under the depths of the waters like fish for a greater part of the year, yet sometimes they are accustomed to dwell on the earth, especially when they breed, birth and feed their young.

²⁴And God said, "Let the earth bring forth living creatures according to their kinds: cattle and creeping things and beasts of the earth according to their kinds." And it was so.

After the sky was illumined by the stars, after the air was filled with flying creatures (which because of its nearness to it warranted the name of heaven, as we said), after the waters, which themselves were closely related to the air in nature, became richly filled with their animals, from the waters then God brought forth living creatures, and from the air God brought forth rain, snow, hail, and various phenomena of this type; it was agreed that the earth would be replenished with its own animals, that is, animals reproduced from themselves. For the earth has a primary relationship with

the waters, in as much as without the waters' moisture and irrigation the land is unable to be fruitful or stable, as Peter attested who said, "That by the word of God the heavens existed long ago, and an earth formed out of water and by means of water."[49]

God commands the earth to bring forth cattle and creeping things and beasts of the earth. By the word *beasts* one understands every creature vicious in nature because of its bite or its claws, except snakes, for the serpents of the earth are included with the term "reptile." And by the name "cattle" those animals that are domesticated are designated. Here, therefore, the creation is described of certain four-footed creatures, for example, deer, roe, doe, oxen, goats, and others of this manner, unless by chance these animals are to be reckoned among the beasts because of the fierceness of their untamed spirit.

According to an older translation it is written, "Let the earth bring forth the living creature according to its kind: quadrupeds, and creeping things, and beasts of the earth."[50] There is no question that altogether by the word *quadruped* all animals are understood. The land brought forth these creatures, followed by the beasts and crawling creatures, both those under the care of humans and those creatures that are wild and undomesticated.

²⁵And God made the beasts of the earth according to their kinds and the cattle according to their kinds, and everything that creeps upon the ground according to its kind. And God saw that it was good.

A change in the words must be noted; where it is written above "God commanded the earth to bring forth cattle, and creeping things, and beasts of the earth," now it is expressed in a changed word order: "God created the beasts of the earth, the cattle, and everything that

---

[49]2 Pet 3:5. [50]See Augustine *Gen. litt.* 3.11.

creeps on the ground." It must be understood that by his command everything he willed swiftly came to be. It makes no difference that human speech names in some order the creatures that divine power created altogether at one time. Since it follows, "And God saw that it was good," one rightly asks why this statement is not also added: "And he blessed them saying, 'Be fruitful and multiply and fill the earth,'" since it is spoken about the animals that the waters bring forth. Or, by chance, does this suggest that what was said by God concerning the initial creation of living beings should also be understood as pertaining to the second day, especially since in the works of this day he was going to add many other things?

But concerning humans being created, by necessity Scripture takes care to repeat the statement: "And God blessed them and said, 'Be fruitful and multiply and fill the earth,'" lest any should think that sin had entered the honorable marriage and the bed of defilement and fornication is joined with it.[51] The earthly abode having been created and adorned, it remained that man, for whom all things were ordered, is created as its established occupant and master of everything.

[26]Then God said, "Let us make man in our image, after our likeness."

Now it appears more evident why it is commanded in respect to the created plants and trees, fish and flying creatures, and even the land animals, that they be created one by one according to their own species and kind. Truly, a future creation was foreseen that not only would be fitting in its likeness and kind but also would be made in the image and likeness of its Creator. That God did not say as with the rest of the creatures, "Let man be made,

and man was created," or "Let the earth bring forth man, and the earth brought forth man" is a testimony of the nobility of his creation. But before he was made, it is said, "Let us make man," so that a rational creature is fashioned and made with a design.[52]

Just as through diligent care he is created from the earth and by the breath of the Creator, he is raised up in the strength of the life-giving Spirit, so that he who is made in the image of his Creator would exist not through a word of command but through the dignity of his creation. When, moreover, it is written, "Let us make man in our image, after our likeness," the unity of the sacred Trinity is plainly mentioned. If, indeed, the same indivisible Trinity was implied in the preceding formation of things when it was written, "And God said, 'Let there be made'. . . 'And God made'. . . 'And God saw that it was good,'" now more clearly this very thing is known when it is said, "Let us make man in our image, after our likeness." And rightly, "because as long he who was to be taught did not exist, the revelation of the divine nature remains enveloped in shadow, but now the creation of man is expected, that faith unveils herself, and the dogma of truth appears in all its light."[53]

In that which is written there is shown the single work of three personalities; in the statement that follows, "in our image and likeness," a single and equal substance of the same holy Trinity is indicated. How is there one "image and likeness" if the Son is less than the Father, if the Holy Spirit is less than the Son, if the glory of the whole Trinity is not of the same consubstantial power? Or, how is it said "let us make" if there were no cooperating power of the three persons in one deity? Truly, this cannot be said by God about the angels, "Let us make man in our image after our likeness,"

---

[51]See Heb 13:4. [52]See Gregory *Moralia* 9.49.75. [53]Basil-Eusthasius *Hexameron* 9.6.13: "And rightly that up to the point that he who was to be instructed was not present the proclamation of deity was hidden in the depths, when the creation of man began to be awaited, faith was revealed and the teachings of the truth clearly multiplied" (Hardin translation).

since reason does not allow us to believe the image and likeness of God and the angels to be one and the same thing.

To which, moreover, the apostle testifies, "man is made in the image and likeness of God," when he skillfully reminds us that nature that we lost in the first parent we recover in us through the grace of that same Creator. He said, "Be renewed in the spirit of your minds, and put on the new nature created after the likeness of God in righteousness, holiness and truth."[54]

Adam, therefore, is created a new man from the earth according to God so that he may be made righteous, holy and true, submissive and humbly clinging to the grace of his Creator, who exists eternally and perfectly righteous, holy and true. Since he has corrupted this most unblemished purity of the image of God in himself by sinning and procreated a corrupt race of humankind from himself, the second Adam came, that is, the Lord and our Creator, born from a virgin, existing incorruptible and unchangeable according to the image of God, free from all fault and full of all grace and truth, so that he may restore his image and likeness in us by the example of his own character and gifts. He is the new man truly created according to God, as he took on the true substance of the flesh from Adam but to the extent that he brought nothing of defilement with it.

To follow his example to the best of our ability, to cling to his gifts, to obey his mandates, this is to recover in the new person the image of God that we lost in the old. Not, therefore, in respect to the body but in respect to the intellect of the mind is humankind created in the image of God. Yet, we have in that very body a distinct characteristic that indicates this, because Adam was created upright in stature, so that by this fact he is reminded that he does not take after the earthly crea-

tures, like the herds whose whole pleasure is from the earth. All of the other creatures go face down or crawl, as one of the poets most beautifully and truly said: "While other animals look face down at the earth, he gave to human beings an upturned face to see the lofty heaven; commanding them to look toward the skies and raise their faces to the stars."[55]

It makes sense, therefore, that the human body is suited to a rational soul, not in accordance with the shapes and features of its limbs but rather in that the body stands upright able to gaze on heavenly things in the corporeal world. In a like manner the rational soul ought to be lifted up toward spiritual things, which by nature excel, so that the soul may perceive heavenly things, not things that are on the earth. Well, moreover, it is added:

[26]And let them have dominion over the fish of the sea, and over the birds of the air, and over the cattle, and over all the earth, and over every creeping thing that creeps upon the earth.

Especially since man [i.e., humankind] is made in the image of God, he excels over the creatures that cannot reason. He was given the ability to reason, through which he is able to properly govern whatever was created in the earth and enjoy the knowledge of the one who created all things. Put in this place of honor, if he does not understand that he should live well, he will be put on the same level as senseless creatures over which he has been placed,[56] just as the psalmist testified.[57]

[27]So God created man in his own image, in the image of God he created him.

The phrase he had said before, "in his image," he repeats as a confirmation by adding, "he created him in the image of God," so that carefully the writer may impress on us in what

---

[54]Eph 4:23-24. [55]Ovid *Metamorphoses* 1.84-86. [56]Augustine *Gen. litt.* 6.12; see also *Confessions* 13.23.33. [57]Ps 48:12 (LXX).

condition we are made by God and skillfully fixes in our minds the hope of recovering the image of God. So, we who walk in the image of God are not foolishly troubled, storing up our treasures in insecure riches, but rather we wait on the Lord, thirsting as we come and appear before his face, certain that when he appears we will be like him, because we will see him as he is. Since it is now said, "He created him in the image of God," where above it states, "Let us make in our image," it indicates that the verse is not discussing that plurality of persons, to the effect that we believe many gods, but so that we may believe the Father and Son and Holy Spirit, in light of which Trinity it says "in our image" so that we may understand one God; it says accordingly, "in the image of God."

27Male and female created he them.

How God created the first created beings is explained more fully in the following text. But now, for the sake of brevity, the created beings are only referred to so that the work of the sixth day and the dedication of the seventh along with the other issues may be explained, and so for the sake of time, both this and other things worthy to relate but overlooked before are explained. From the first, God created one male and one female, not as with the other animals that in their own species he created not singularly but in multiple numbers, so that through this act he could bind more tightly the human race in a yoke of love because they would be mindful that they all had come from a single parent. Bearing in mind this union, sacred Scripture said, "And God created man in his own image, in the image of God he created him," and immediately added, "Male and female he created them"; it did not wish to add, "In the image of God he created them." For, indeed, the woman was created in the

image of God in that she had a rational mind, but Scripture did not think this needed to be added about her since it is left to be understood about her in light of the union. Indeed, it indicates that this should be understood about the whole human race that has born from them. Also, every man now, in so far as he uses reason, has the image of God in himself; thus John said, "The true light which enlightens every man was coming into the world."[58] This is the very light about which the psalmist glorified the Lord, saying, "Lift up the light of your countenance upon us, O Lord."[59] And appropriately so in this verse male and female are remembered to have been created, although the manner of that creation is not yet declared, so that the word of divine blessing may have its fitting place. Concerning the blessing that follows:

28And God blessed them and God said to them, "Be fruitful and multiply, and fill the earth and subdue it."

This multiplication of people and filling of the earth could not be completed except through the union of the woman and the man. If by the blessing of God the human race was fruitful and multiplied, how much are those people worthy of a curse who prohibit individuals from marrying and reproach the power of the heavenly decree as if it were invented by the devil. Marriage vows, therefore, which God instituted by the granting of his divine blessing for the propagation of the human race and for the filling of the earth, must not be cursed. But more to be honored, worthy of greater blessing is virginity, which, after the world is filled with people, desires to follow the Lamb with a chaste mind and body whithersoever he will go, that is, to follow the Lord Jesus in the heavens and to sing a new song, which no one else can do. Scripture teaches that God

---

[58]Jn 1:9. [59]Ps 4:6.

and our Lord, who made the woman from the side of the man in the primordial days of the world when it was created, in order to teach that the earth must be filled through their mutual union, at the end of the age became a man from the flesh of a virgin, free from moral defilement, perfected in the whole fullness of divinity, in order to show that he cherished the glory of virginity more than marriage.

²⁸*"And have dominion over the fish of the sea and over the birds of the air and over every living thing that moves upon the earth."*

Rightly one asks for what benefit did humankind receive dominion over the fish and birds and all animals of the earth or to what purposes or for which comforts would these creatures be to man if he never had sinned. To which questions the following Scriptures declare that it was granted to man at the beginning of creation that these were not for food, but only grass and trees and fruits were. Perhaps this was commanded because God foreknew that man, whom he had created immortal, was going to sin and was going to become mortal by sinning; and so he provided these solaces for him in the primordial days by which he, being mortal, would be able to care for his own frailty, in that he obtained food from them, or clothing, or help for his labor or journey. Nor is it worth asking why now man does not have dominion over all the animals. After he was unwilling to subject himself to his Creator, he lost the dominion over those creatures the Creator had subjected to him by right. And, finally, as proof of the first creation, we read that the birds offer services to the saints who humbly serve God, and the mouths of beasts close and the poison of serpents is unable to harm them.

²⁹*And God said, "Behold, I have given you*

every plant yielding seed which is upon the face of all the earth, and every tree with seed in its fruit; you shall have them for food. ³⁰*And to every beast of the earth, and to every bird of the air, and to everything that creeps on the earth, everything that has the breath of life, I have given every green plant for food."*

Now this shows that before the transgression of humankind the earth brought forth nothing harmful, no poisonous plant, no unfruitful tree. Since it clearly said that "every plant and every tree" were given to people and to birds of the air and to all the animals of the earth for food, it is clear that neither the birds were feeding themselves by pilfering the food of weaker animals, "neither was the wolf spying out ambushes around the little lamb,[60] nor was the bread of the serpent dust,"[61] but all were feeding together on the green plants and the fruits of the trees.

To be sure, among these verses a question arises that should not be ignored, as to how man is made immortal in contrast to other animals, and yet he has received earthly food in common with them. In light of this, we should observe that the immortality of the flesh that we received in the first creation in Adam is one nature, and the immortality we hope we are going to receive in the resurrection through Christ is another. Thus, without doubt man was made immortal in that he could not die if he did not sin; if, however, he sinned he would die. So truly immortal will be the children of the resurrection since they will be equal to the angels of God, in that they can neither sin nor die later. And so our flesh needs no refreshment from foods after the resurrection because it seeks for itself nothing out of hunger or weariness or any other weakness.

In this way the flesh of Adam was created immortal before his sin, so that, having been aided by the nourishment of temporal food, he

---

[60]Vergil *Georgica* 3.537. [61]Is 65:25.

existed free of pain and death, until through natural development he was brought to the age that was pleasing to the Creator. Then, after fathering many offspring, by God's bidding, he would eat from the tree of life. When he has been made completely immortal, he would require no further nourishment of food for the body. Thus, the flesh of the first humans is created immortal and incorruptible so that they would guard their own immortality and incorruptibility through observing the commands of God.

These commands included the one that they should eat from the lawful trees of paradise and should refrain from the food that was prohibited. Through eating the acceptable fruit they would safeguard the gifts of immortality given to them; in touching of the prohibitive fruit they found the ruin of death. Thus, our flesh will become immortal and incorruptible in the end, in order that it may remain in the same state of angelic sublimity forever, and so that it may not need material foods, which will not exist in the life of the spirit.

For the angels are said to have eaten with the patriarchs, not out of need but out of mercy. They were doing this so that in so doing they could relate more agreeably to the people to whom they appeared. The Lord also ate with the disciples after the resurrection, not as he needed refreshment but so that he could show that he had received the true flesh after death.

[30] And it was so.

That is, man had dominion over all things that were created on the earth or in the waters, in order that he received the ability and power of eating from the fruits of the earth along with the birds of the sky and animals of the earth.

[31] And God saw everything he had made, and behold, it was very good.

Because it was said about each one of the works of God one by one that "he saw that it was good," rightly this statement has been placed at the conclusion after everything was completed, with the addition that "he saw all he had made, and behold, it was very good." But one may rightly ask why this statement, "And God saw that it was good," was not added separately here concerning the creation of humans, instead of reserving their creation for universal praise along with the others? "Or since God knew that man was going to sin and was not going to remain in the perfection of his own image, did he not wish to say to him that he was good separately but along with the others corporately, thus hinting at what man would be? . . . Man, therefore, before the fall was good in his own created kind, but Scripture neglected to say this in order rather to say that which declared something other was going to be in the future. For God is the perfect Creator of beings of nature, he is the all-just ruler of sinners, so that men, even if individually they are disfigured by sinning, nevertheless the whole creation with them included always remains beautiful."[62]

[31] And there was evening and there was morning, a sixth day. [2:1] Thus the heavens and the earth were finished, and all the host of them.

It has been agreed that the number six is a perfect number because first it is the sum of its parts, namely, a sixth being one; a third, two; and a half, three. One plus two plus three adds up to six, which trait you will not find among the counting numbers except here, or in the tens except the number twenty-eight. In six days, therefore, God completed all the adornment of the heaven and earth, so that "he who ordered all things in measure and number and weight"[63] might teach us that his works are perfect even by

---

[62]Augustine *Gen. litt.* 3.24. [63]Wis 11:21 (Vg).

that very number in which he completed them.

2And on the seventh day God finished his work which he had done.

In another translation it is written that "God finished on the sixth day the works he had made."[64] There should be no confusion about this statement because the things that were created were described in clear detail so far. But rightly one may question how in our edition that comes from the original Hebrew[65] it says that "on the seventh day God finished the work he had done," on which day one remembers nothing new to have been created, unless on making the seventh day he fulfilled the measure and the number of the days in whose course all ages from then on have followed to the end. For in the reckoning of time the eighth is counted the same day as the first. "And on the seventh day God completed the work he had done," because on it he limited the sum of the days that he had made, the seventh day having been added that he willed to be created and to be called the sabbath, because he granted to that day a spiritual blessing and sanctification before all the others.

Hence, the day of judgment and the consummation of the age are going to come after the seventh day, which is called an octave because seven days had preceded it. It is written also in the title of Psalms, "For the end, a psalm of David among the hymns for the octave."[66] The entire text of the following psalm teaches what has been written about the day of judgment, on which the prophet, fearing the wrath of the day of judgment approaching, proclaims, "Lord, O Lord, rebuke me not in thy wrath, neither chasten me in your anger."[67] But, although the day of the resurrection of the Lord was going to come after thousands of days, nevertheless it was called the octave in

the title of another psalm.[68] The day of resurrection followed the seventh so that it would be the first day of the following week and the same day on which "in the beginning . . . God said, 'Let there be light, and light was made.'" The speaker of the psalm shows that indeed the psalm was written about the Lord's resurrection, saying, "Because of the misery of the poor, because the needy groan, I will now arise, says the Lord."[69]

One may understand this correctly as "on the seventh day God completed the work he had done," in the fact that he blessed and sanctified that very day. Indeed, it is not true that there is no work in the blessing and sanctification, just as it must not be said that Solomon did no work when he dedicated the temple. Yet indeed it was an exceptional work of God when he honored those things that he had made with an eternal blessing and sanctification. And, finally, concerning this work that he does on the eternal day of the week, he says in the parable of the faithful servants, "Truly, I say to you, he will gird himself and have them sit at table, and he will come and serve them."[70] He who girds himself, he who has them sit at table, he who comes, he who serves, he certainly works. But by all these words nothing less is suggested than that the Lord blesses and sanctifies his saints forever, that is, by the vision of his glory that he gave them after he rewards their good works.

2And he rested on the seventh day from all his work which he had done.

God did not rest after the creation of the world was completed, as if wearied from too much labor in the sense of human weakness, but it is said that he had rested from all his work because he stopped making any new creatures. For Scripture is often accustomed to indicate the cessation from work or speech with the word *rest*, as in the Apocalypse it said about

---

[64]Gen 2:2 (LXX). [65]Literally, "Hebrew truth." [66]Ps 6 (LXX). [67]Ps 6:2 (LXX). [68]Ps 11 (LXX). [69]Ps 12:5. [70]Lk 12:37.

the holy beings, "Day and night they never cease to sing, 'Holy, holy, holy is the Lord God Almighty.' "[71] Before him, as Scripture said, they did not cease to sing this at all times. Truly, the greatest and unparalleled rest in heaven for the saints is to sing with untiring voices the praise of the almighty Trinity, which is God.

In a more profound way one may understand that God had rested from all his works. Not that he had need for these works in which he rested, for in actuality his true rest is always in himself without beginning and end, but that he made the works that rested in him motivated only by his own goodness. This is more easily understood when we are reminded that human need draws one to labor so arduously that he understands rest in his works, as the Lord said to him, "In the sweat of your face you shall eat bread."[72] God, moreover, who possessed the perfect rest in himself eternally before creation, after the world was created rested not in the works that he made but from all the works he had made, in that he had no need in himself to rest in his creatures, but rather he offered rest to rational creatures, since he had perfectly rested always in himself, and he is blessed with that goodness that belongs to him.

³So God blessed the seventh day and hallowed it.

He did this chiefly by that blessing and sanctification that he made more fully known in the Law to his people, saying, "Remember the Sabbath day to keep it holy. Six days you shall labor and do all your work, but the seventh is a Sabbath to the Lord your God, and you shall not do any work."[73] And then a little later, "for in six days the Lord made the heaven, the earth, the sea, and all that is in them, and rested on the seventh day; therefore, the Lord blessed the Sabbath day and hallowed it."[74] Indeed, this blessing and sanctification of the seventh day were made as a type of a greater blessing and sanctification. For just as the blood of the Lord's suffering, which was poured out once and for all for the salvation of the world, is signified through the repeated daily offerings in accordance with the Law, so also through the rest of the seventh day, which was always celebrated after the works of the six days, prefigured that great day of sabbath on which the Lord was going to rest once in the tomb, after having completed and perfected all his works on the sixth day, through which he would restore the world now corrupted for ages that he had completed on the sixth day.

Also on that day, recalling the ancient works, he declared clearly that he had now completed the salvation of the world: "When Jesus had received the vinegar, he said, 'It is finished,' and he bowed his head and gave up his spirit."[75] But his sanctification and blessing of the seventh day and the rest of God on that day after his works indicated that they are very good, because we, one by one, after the good works that he "works in us to will and to do," strive for the rest of the heavenly life in which we enjoy his eternal sanctification and blessing. So fittingly it is written that the seventh day had no evening, because it indicates our everlasting rest in it.

³Because on it God rested from all his work which he had done in creation.

That is, after the completion of the adornment of the world, he had ceased from making any other new kinds of things. Nor ought this to be judged contrary to the opinion of the writer of the Gospel, "My Father is working still, and I am working,"[76] as he responded to those who, in light of the rest required by the authority of this Scripture in ancient times, questioned

---

[71]Rev 4:8. [72]Gen 3:19. [73]Ex 20:8-10. [74]Ex 20:11. [75]Jn 19:30. [76]Jn 5:17.

why the sabbath was not observed by him. He had ceased on the seventh day from creating different types of creatures because since then he does not create species. But even until now he has been engaged in the governing of these same species that were formed at that time; not that suddenly on the seventh day his power over all heaven, earth and all things that he had created had ceased from governing; otherwise the created order would fall into ruin.

Concerning the Six Ages of the World

Up to this point it has sufficed for me to speak literally about the beginning of the nascent world. It is now a good time to suggest a few things of how the order of those six or seven days in which it was made corresponds to the same number of its ages. The first day on which God said, "Let there be light, and it was done," corresponds to the first age in whose beginning the world was made and man was placed in the garden with the delights of enjoyments, where, grace being present, he enjoyed his Creator free and unaware of all evils. But this day began then to decline toward evening when the first created humans lost the happiness of the celestial home by sinning, and they were sent out into this "vale of tears"; the decline also signified the hour of that time when Adam, after his sin of transgression, "heard the voice of the Lord walking in the garden in the afternoon."[77] Certainly the Lord walked about so that he could signify that he had departed from mankind in whose heart he had remained quiet; and this phrase "toward the cool of the day" indicates that man knew the light of divine knowledge within him and the fervor of divine delight was diminishing. But the full evening of this day arrived with the increasing failures of humankind, and the "earth was corrupt in God's sight and filled with violence"[78] to the point that all flesh merited to be destroyed by a flood,

except the ones in the ark.

On the second day the firmament was created in the midst of the waters, and in the second age of the world the ark, in which the seed of the rest of humankind of the following ages was preserved, as I have said before, was placed in the midst of the waters, from which abundantly then "all the fountains of the great deep burst forth, and the windows of the heavens were opened."[79] But this day turned toward evening when the nations, forgetful of both of the recent wrath and mercy of God, conferred together to build a tower of pride; it became full evening when the social order broke down with the confusion of the languages of the human race.

On the third day, as the waters receded into their own places, the dry earth appeared and soon after was clothed with growing plants and leafy groves; and it was the beginning of the third age after the nations, whose wandering, unsure and tossed around as if by the winds of the empty doctrines of idols, were separated into their own territories, as indicated by the word *sea*. The seed of the patriarchs was separated from their fellowship and made fruitful with spiritual fruit, as the Lord said to Abraham: "Go from your country, and your kindred, and your father's house to the land that I will show you. And I will make of you a great nation, and I will bless you . . . and by you all the families of the earth shall bless themselves."[80] In this nation the separation of the faithful appeared just like the green plants and fruit-bearing trees were produced from one and the same earth, as they received the heavenly rain of divine blessings. This day also began to draw toward evening when the same Israelite nation cast aside the faith of the patriarchs and the religious duties of the Law given to them and were defiled by the wickedness of foreign nations and weighed down by slavery. Evening then came when that nation, along

---

[77]Gen 3:8 (LXX). [78]Gen 6:11. [79]Gen 7:11. [80]Gen 12:1-3.

with the king whom it had chosen in defiance of God, was for the most part destroyed by the sword of foreign nations.

On the fourth day the heaven received its luminaries, and in the fourth age the aforementioned people of God gained renown by the extraordinary reputation of David and Solomon and of the other kings ruling under the authority of God—by that very celebrated temple that Solomon built for God, by the prophecies of the prophets that did not cease flourishing in the times of the kings, and especially by the one the Lord swore to the first and most preeminent of the kings who was pleasing to him, saying, "From the fruit of your womb I will place upon my throne."[81] Truly, this day began to turn toward evening when later those kings and people alike, rejecting the temple and the laws of God, were laid waste and torn to pieces by their enemies. This was a most unpleasant evening for them, and by night, when the entire kingdom was overturned and the temple burned, all the people were led captive into Babylon.

On the fifth day the waters brought forth swarms of living creatures and birds flying over the earth under the firmament of the sky; and in the fifth age the children of the exile multiplied and grew in Babylon, which often is designated by the word *waters*. Many of them lived there like fish in the waters, yet there were some of them who, like the great sea monsters, strove to master the great waves of the times rather than to be subject to them; they were unable to be morally perverted by idolatry because of any fear. Others, freed from captivity, like those freed when given wings, returned to the land of Israel, and just like birds they were seeking the heavens with their whole being, so much that they even endeavored to rebuild the temple and city of God and to restore the Law to its highest prominence. But evening drew near when later, among other shadows

of wickedness, they became betrayers of their homeland to outsiders and even divided among themselves over domestic conflicts; this evening came when they were made to pay tribute and finally were subjected to the power of a foreign king.

On the sixth day the land brought forth cattle, wild beasts and crawling animals. On this day God created man, the first Adam, according to his image, and from man's side as he was sleeping God created woman, Eve. In the sixth age [the righteous lived] amid many wicked people who rightly could be compared with the serpents and wild beasts in light of their viciousness and since they clung to earthly concerns and enticements with their whole being. Also there were many righteous ones among the people of God who tried to ruminate on the Word of God in the likeness of clean animals who chew their cud to keep the cloven hoof of discretion on the narrow path, to bear the yoke of good works of the divine law and to keep the poor warm with the fleece of their own sheep. There is sufficient mention of both types of people in the Gospel and elsewhere. Among these people a second Adam, the mediator between God and humankind, in whom was the entire fullness of the image of God, appeared, and as he died on the cross, blood and water poured forth from his side, from which sacraments the church is born and nourished. This church is the mother of all the people living throughout the world, the true life, which the name Eve means. Concerning these same sacraments the Lord says, "He who eats my flesh and drinks my blood . . . will live forever."[82] We discern that even now the evening of this day draws near, "because [as] wickedness is multiplied men's love will grow cold."[83] Its arrival will be darker than the others, when, as the man of sin appears, the son of iniquity, who is raised up and placed over all because he is called God or because he is wor-

---

[81]Ps 131:11 (Vg). [82]Jn 6:56-58. [83]Mt 24:12.

shiped, there will be such tribulation that even the chosen ones may be led into error, if that is possible. Subsequently, immediately follows the hour of universal judgment, about which it is written, "Nevertheless, when the Son of man comes, will he find faith on earth?"[84]

"God rested from all his works on the seventh day and blessed it and hallowed it." And the seventh age is the age of everlasting rest in another life, in which God rested with his saints forever after the good works that he worked in them through the six ages of the world. Indeed, this is the age of greatest peace and rest in God, and it will be eternal; but it began then for people when the first martyr Abel entered into the tomb but his spirit entered the joy of eternal life. The rich man saw the poor man resting in that joy, while he himself was tortured in hades.[85] Moreover, this sabbath day of the righteous souls will persevere up to the end of the world, when in the final age its evening, about which we have spoken before, comes to the end after the antichrist is killed through the Lord Jesus. Then that very rest will be granted with a greater blessing and sanctification to the bodies rising to everlasting life. So, it is suitably written that evening did not follow on the seventh day, because there will be no sorrow by which this seventh age concludes; rather, it will be completed by the ample joy of the eighth age, as we said. Namely, beginning at that time in the glory of resurrection, when this entire life has passed and with no more change, it will be transformed by contemplation of the face of God with no end, with no concern for human affairs.

Here ends the explanation of the six days of creation.

⁴These are the generations of the heavens and the earth when they were created.

In this summary statement, holy Scripture strikes at those who assert that the world always existed without beginning or who think that it was created by God from matter that he did not create but that was coeternal from the beginning with the Creator. Indeed, it defines "the generation of the heavens and the earth" as that order of divine creation whose adornment of its natural phenomena is described above through the works of the six days up to the consummation. Accordingly, in the Decalogue of his Law the Creator said, "In six days the Lord made the heaven and earth, the sea and all that are in them."[86] And this is what follows:

⁴In the day that the LORD God made the earth and the heavens, ⁵when no plant of the field was yet in the earth and no herb of the field had yet sprung up.

This verse should not seem to contradict the previously mentioned word of God, but it ought to be clearly understood that this Scripture uses the word *day* to mean all that time when the primordial creation was formed. Nor indeed was the heaven created in any single one of the six days or the sky illumined by the stars or the earth separated from the waters and dry land established with trees and plants. But in its customary fashion Scripture used the word *day* for time, as the apostle did when he said, "Behold, now is the day of salvation"[87]—not one day specifically but signifying the entire time in which we labor in this present life for eternal salvation. And the prophet did not speak about one day specifically but about the very great season of divine grace: "In that day the deaf shall hear the words of this book."[88] Furthermore, it would be difficult to understand how in one day "God made the heaven and the earth and every plant of the field and every herb of the field," unless perhaps we

---

[84]Lk 18:8. [85]Lk 16:22-23. [86]Ex 20:11. [87]2 Cor 6:2. [88]Is 29:18.

could say that all creatures had been made in unformed matter at the same time, in accordance with what is written: "He that lives forever created all things together."[89]

At any rate, it was before any day of this age, since "in the beginning he created the heaven and the earth," when, although the "earth was without form and void and darkness was upon the face of the deep," yet in the nature of that earth and deep, that is, in the nature of the waters, lay hidden as a seed all those things that had to be brought forth from them individually by the hand of the Creator. Now if we say this, our previous question returns to the same conclusion, that we should understand "day" was used in the sense of "time," above all, that time in which the "LORD God created heaven and earth, and every plant of the field was yet in the earth and no herb of the field had yet sprung up." If we understand what he calls "day" as the "time" designated when, before any day of this age, all things were made together, it easily allows the meaning that every plant and every tree was intentionally made in the substance of that earth before they visibly appeared or sprang forth from the earth.

If, moreover, as we think more logically, we understand the word *day* is used in the sense of that time in which the world itself was made and adorned in six days, then we are able to understand now that Scripture wanted to explain how it said above that "the earth brought forth vegetation, plants yielding seed according to their own kind, and trees bearing fruit."[90] The earth did not bring forth these things in the beginning in the same way it does now.

When there is an irrigation of waters, the earth will spontaneously generate new growth, in accordance with God's will. Moreover, by an even more extraordinary work of the Creator at that time, before any plants appeared and sprouted from the earth, the mountains and

hills were suddenly covered with fields of grasses and trees having their suitable height, long branches, the shade of foliage, an abundance of fruit, which did not spring forth little by little or germinate through stages of natural growth but suddenly came into existence from it. For the next words seem to support this sense even more, which say:

[5]*For the LORD God had not caused it to rain upon the earth, and there was no man to till the ground;* [6]*but a mist*[91] *went up from the earth and watered the whole face of the ground.*

Who could not see that these words were not written about the initial creation of the earth when it was still "without form and void, and darkness was upon the face of the deep"?[92] Is it necessary to say anything about the rain not falling on the earth at that time when it still was not able to receive the rain, nor could the air give it since a totality of water filled both places? Nor was a spring able to come up from the earth to water it, as long as it was covered by an entire abyss. So, if I am not mistaken, it stands that what should be understood by the word *day* above, when it is said, "On the day when the Lord made heaven and earth," and the rest, is that time of the first six days in which every creature of the world is formed.

It is rightly remembered that God had not caused it to rain on the earth, and there was no man who worked the soil, so that we may realize how much the first appearance of vegetation on the earth differs from its current way of propagating. For now the earth flowers of its own accord because of the watering of the rains, and by the industrious tilling of people many things are sufficiently produced in gardens and groves; but far otherwise was the first creation of plants and trees completed, in which, through the renewing power of the al-

---

[89]Sir 18:1. [90]Gen 1:12. [91]LXX *pēgē* ("spring"); Vg *fons* ("spring," "fountain"); RSV "mist." [92]Gen 1:2.

mighty Creator, the earth, which had appeared dry, apart from the rain and human effort suddenly is filled far and wide with plants bearing much fruit for its peoples. But, Scripture said, "A spring went up and watered the whole face of the earth."

We are about to speak about this mist and its rising over the earth, but first let us see that the initial springing forth from the earth, of which the previous statement recalls, was created at God's command without any refreshing of the waters. Moreover, whatever type of mist this was, it came up after the earth was clothed with trees and grass. This fact is demonstrated by the grammatical construction of Scripture, which has the verb in the perfect tense stating that "God created the heaven and earth and all the plants of the field . . . all the herbs of the field"; it then added with the verb in the pluperfect tense, "God had not caused it to rain upon the earth, and there was no man who tilled the ground"—showing that before the creation of the plants and herbs God had not sent the rain; what was made later immediately is followed by a verb in the imperfect tense, saying that "a spring went up from the earth and watered the whole face of the ground." Through this inflection of the verb it is indicated not that something was done once and for all as a completed act but that it was often repeated; the phrase does not say "it goes up" but "it went up (again and again)."

Since, therefore, it is said that a "mist went up from the earth which watered the whole face of the ground," one might ask how it went up. It would not be wrong to think that through interchanges it arose for refreshing the earth and returned in a way similar to the Nile, which customarily rises annually for watering the flat ground of Egypt, like the Jordan at times waters the land of the Pentapolis, about which the Scripture says that the Jordan valley "was well watered everywhere just like

the garden of the Lord and just like the land of Egypt before God destroyed Sodom and Gomorrah."[93]

In the same way, as Augustine observes, "Concerning the variability of certain springs it is maintained that after a certain interval of years they so flood that they water that entire region, yet later the same springs supply sufficient water for drinking from the deep wells. Why is it therefore hard to believe," as he says again, "if out of a single source from an abyss the whole earth is watered by flooding and receding in alternate seasons?" But if, he said, Scripture called the magnitude of that abyss—except for that part that is called the sea and that surrounds the lands with deep and salty waves—in that part alone the earth holds in hidden cavities from where all the rivers and springs gather from diverse courses and cracks and burst forth each in its own place, a spring, not springs, because of its unity of nature and its ascending from the earth through innumerable paths of caves and fissures and everywhere watering the entire face of the earth like hair cascading down, not making a continuous appearance like in the sea or still water, but as we see the waters rushing through the beds of rivers and the bends of streams flooding the surrounding area—who cannot accept this fact unless he labors under a very contentious spirit?

Thus one can understand that the whole face of the earth is watered, in the same manner that it is said that a whole piece of material is colored, even if it is not colored fully but in spots; especially in the newness of the earth it is credible that although not all of the surfaces were flat, yet many were, on which surfaces the waters could be spread and dispersed farther by their spilling forth and flowing. Therefore concerning the size and measure of this spring, whether it had a single point for emergence from some source or other or whether through

---

[93]Gen 13:10.

a certain unity in the hidden caves of the earth from which all the waters of all springs great and small bubble out over the earth, it is called one spring, ascending through all its channels on the earth and watering the whole face of the land, or even, which is more believable since it did not say that one spring rose up from the earth, but it said, "a spring rose up from the earth," the writer is able to use the singular for the plural, although we may realize there are many springs watering localities and neighboring regions throughout the earth—as thus Scripture says "soldier" and many soldiers are to be understood, or as it says "locust" and "frog" in the plagues by which the Egyptians were crushed, when there were innumerable locusts and frogs.

Let us now not belabor this point further.[94] When it is said, therefore, that God created herbs and green plants, it was not yet raining, nor did humankind exist who tilled the land, and consequently the creation of man is now added, and it is written:

[7]Then the Lord God formed man of dust from the ground, and breathed into his nostrils[95] the breath of life; and man became a living being.

In this verse, the creation of man who was indeed made on the sixth day is more fully described. On the sixth day, man's creation is related briefly while here it is explained more fully that man clearly is made in the substance of a body and a spirit. Concerning these substances, the body was formed from the dust of the earth, and the soul was created out of nothing, being made complete by the in-breathing of God, but the woman was created from man's side as he slept. Plainly in this statement any carnal interpretation should be avoided, lest by chance we would think that God had formed the body of man from the dust of the earth with corporeal hands or

that he had breathed into his nostrils with his mouth or lips so that man could live and have the breath of life.

When the prophet said, "Thy hands have made and fashioned me,"[96] he used figurative speech more than presenting a literal picture; that is, the words reflect in familiar terms the way people usually speak. God is spirit, nor is it believed except by the uneducated that his pure substance is composed of the features of corporeal members. "God formed man from the dust," that is, he commanded him to be made from dust by his own word. "He breathed into his nostrils the breath of life, and man was made a living being" when God made the essence of his soul and spirit in which he lived. For the words "God breathed into the nostrils" by which he may live may be rightly understood that God created him, just as it is said above that "God called the light day" is used for what he made it to be called by people.

Moreover, it is properly said that God breathed into the nostrils of man so that he could become a living soul, because without a doubt the spirit within him considers carefully the things that are part of the outside world, in as much as "that anterior part of the brain whence all the feelings of the senses are diffused is located toward the forehead. In fact, the sense of touch, which is diffused throughout the entire body, also is shown to have its path from the anterior part of the brain, the path which is drawn back through the neck and the head to the bone marrow."[97]

This supports what was written above about man: "He created him in the image of God; male and female created he them." The phrase "in the image of God" is understood in respect to what man was made in his soul; "male and female" is added for the reader to understand it correctly in respect to what was made in his body. Those individuals, therefore, must not

---

[94]Cf. Augustine *Gen. litt.* 5.10.25-26. [95]Lxx "face." [96]Ps 119:73. [97]Augustine *Gen. litt.* 7.17.23.

be supported who think that the soul is a part of God, "because if the soul of man is a part of God, the soul could not be deceived by its own self or any other thing, nor could it have been compelled by any necessity to do anything evil or to suffer, nor could it have been changed for better or worse altogether.

"The breath of God that animated people was made by him, not from him, just as the breath of a person is not part of the person, nor did the person make it from himself but from the air taken in and pushed out by breathing. Truly, God was able to create breath from nothing, and he was able to create a living and rational being, which acts in ways humans are not able to, although some would think that it was not at that moment when 'God breathed into his nostrils and he became a living being' that the man had received life, but that at that moment he received the Holy Spirit. Whichever of these you find more believable . . . I am certain that the soul was not a part of God or generated by or produced from his essence and nature, but that it was created from nothing."[98]

[8]And the Lord God planted a garden in Eden, in the east; and there he put the man whom he had formed.[99]

From that beginning, at any rate, it must be believed that God planted a paradise, from which he commanded the whole earth to bring forth green plants and fruit-bearing trees after the waters that covered it had receded. In this paradise he placed the man on the sixth day, on the day he had formed him. We must not doubt at any point that it was a real paradise in which the first man was placed. Although it becomes a figure of the present church or of our future homeland, it still must be understood in a literal sense, namely, "a most pleas-ant place, shaded with large fruit-bearing trees, made fertile by a grand source of water."[100]

Where our text, which is translated from the original Hebrew, has "from the beginning"; an ancient translation uses the phrase "to the east." From this fact some wish it understood that the location of paradise was in the eastern part of the world, although being separated by a very long span of ocean and many lands from all the other regions where now the human race lives. Hence, the waters of the flood, which covered deeply the entire surface of our world, were not able to reach it. Whether it is true that paradise was there or somewhere else, God knows. We, nevertheless, should not doubt that this place is and was on the earth. Finally, Scripture explains in the following verses more fully how God planted it.

[9]And out of the ground the Lord God made to grow every tree that is pleasant to the sight and good for food, the tree of life also in the midst of the garden, and the tree of the knowledge of good and evil.

It is understood that paradise was made on this same day in which the earth brought forth the rest of the fruit-bearing trees, as God had commanded. But by necessity here it is repeated so that we can know what type of place paradise was, especially since there was reference to the tree of life and the tree of the knowledge of good and evil specifically; in one there is the sign of obedience for man that he owes to God, in the other the symbol of the eternal life that he merits through obedience itself. And, indeed, it is called the tree of life because, as we said, it received this quality through divine power so that the body of the one who ate from it "neither did he deteriorate through age or any weakness nor did he even slip into death itself."[101]

---

[98]Augustine *Contra adversarium de legis et prophetarum* 1.14.21-22. [99]"The Lord God had planted a paradise of delight in the beginning in which he put the man he had formed" (Vg). [100]Augustine *Gen. litt.* 8.1.4. [101]Augustine *Gen. litt.* 8.5.

But just as this is done as a corporeal reality, so also it is a figure of a spiritual mystery, that is, of God and our Lord Jesus Christ, about whom it is said in the praise of wisdom, "She is a tree of life to those who lay hold of her."[102] And in the Apocalypse, John wrote, "To him who overcomes I will grant to eat of the tree of life, which is in the paradise of God."[103] This is to say clearly, "To one who overcomes the temptation of the ancient serpent by which Adam was conquered, I will give that which I was going to give to Adam if he had overcome, so that he might be restored forever to the present vision of the glory of Christ." And there he is not troubled by the threat of death, because the Lord Christ, the virtue and wisdom of the Father God, is in the paradise of the heavenly kingdom, which Jesus considered worthy to promise to the thief on the cross who confessed him, along with other righteous people.

"The tree of the knowledge of good and evil"—Saint Augustine said about this tree: "It seemed good to me as I considered it over and over that the opinion cannot be embraced that the tree produced something harmful for food (nor indeed would he who had made all things very good in paradise create anything of evil), but the cause of evil for man was the transgression of the command. It is necessary that man, placed under the Lord God, should have been prohibited from something so that the virtue for him meriting his Lord would be that very obedience, which I am most truly able to say is the only virtue of every rational creature acting under the power of God; and it is the primary and greatest sin of pride, which is called disobedience, to wish to enjoy his own power.

"There is not, therefore, a way man could

feel and know God's governance unless something is commanded of him. And so that tree was not evil, but it is called the tree of 'distinguishing the knowledge of good and evil' because, if man ate from it after the prohibition, in that act was the transgression of the command, by which man learned through the experience of punishment the difference between the good of obedience and the evil of disobedience. Consequently, this tree is not spoken of figuratively, but it must be understood literally as a specific tree to which the name was given, not from the fruit or produce from which it comes forth, but the name is imposed on it from that very matter which was going to happen after it was touched in defiance of prohibition."[104]

[10]*A river flowed out of Eden to water the garden.*

That is, "those beautiful and fruit-bearing trees that shaded the whole earth of that region,"[105] where it must be believed to have happened repeatedly whereby in this earth we inhabit, the Nile floods on the plains of Egypt, which, as we stated above, is spoken about the land of Sodom, which "was watered everywhere like the garden of the Lord, and like the land of Egypt."[106] And, in light of his arrangement, the Lord and Creator of things in our world intended to keep some resemblance to that homeland, the possession of which land we were created in the first parent, so that he might encourage us by a familiar example about meriting its return—especially through that river that we agree flows from paradise. The Nile, which watered Egypt, is the Geon (Gihon),[107] which, one is reminded in the following verses, flows from paradise. In destroy-

---

[102]Prov 3:18.   [103]Rev 2:7.   [104]Augustine *Gen. litt.* 8.6.12.   [105]Augustine *Gen. litt.* 8.7.14.   [106]Gen 13:10.   [107]See Eusebius of Caesarea *Onomasticon* sect. G, Gen 2:13; K.60.3; L.251.24. The information depends on Scripture and Josephus *Antiquities* 1.1.3, which states, "Lastly Geon, which flows through Egypt, means 'that which wells up to us from the opposite world' and by the Greeks is called the Nile." This note derives from notes of C. Umhau Wolf, translator of the *Onomasticon*, available at <www.ccel.org/ccel/pearse/morefathers/files/eusebius_onomasticon_02_trans.htm>; see on K and L.

ing the city of Sodom that had been watered as the paradise of the Lord, God gave an example to those who were going to act unrighteously so that we, remembering the surest footprints of the destruction of the wicked, may more diligently flee their torments.

¹⁰And there it divided and became four rivers. ¹¹The name of the first is Pishon.

It is agreed by the most dependable scholars that the sources of all these rivers that are said to flow from paradise are known on our earth; the source of the Pishon[108] indeed, which they now call the Ganges, is located in the Caucasus Mountains; the source of the Nile, which Scripture calls the Geon (Gihon), as we said, is far from Mount Atlas, which is the highest border of Africa to the west; the source of Tigris and Euphrates is from Armenia.

"Since the very location of paradise is absolutely unknown to us, we must believe that the four divisions of waters are divided there but that these rivers, whose sources are well known, are said to flow somewhere under the earth and later to emerge after being drawn to various locations of far-flung regions where they are said to be known in their own sources. For who does not know that some waters do this frequently? But it is known there where it no longer runs under the earth."[109] And scholars say that these same rivers, the Tigris, Euphrates and Nile, dwindle in size in many places of the land and, after flowing for some distance, again merge to resume their customary courses. It is believed that the Lord does this as an indication of that course by which these waters go forth from paradise through

the more hidden cavities of the earth and its deeper veins from paradise to us. Pishon also is interpreted as "change of mouth,"[110] and rightly so because it shows a charm of its appearance in our land that is considerably different, one that is more ordinary than shown by the rivers of paradise.

¹¹It is the one which flows around the whole land of Havilah.[111]

This is the region of India having the name that it was given after the flood by Havilah, the son of Joktan, who was the son of Eber (Heber) of the Hebrew patriarchs. Josephus also states that Joktan with his brothers possessed the region from the river Cephene[112] and the territory of India as far as that place which is called Hieira.[113]

¹¹Where there is gold; ¹²and the gold of that land is good.

Pliny the Elder states that regions of India are richer than other lands in veins of gold. Their islands are called Chrysa and Argyra from their supply of gold or silver.

¹²Bdellium and onyx stone are there.

Bdellium is, as Pliny explains, an aromatic tree, black in color, the size of the olive tree, with a leaf like the oak, with fruit like the wild fig, which is by nature gum. Moreover, its gum is clear, whitish, light, rich and waxy throughout; it easily melts, is bitter to taste and of a good aroma, but once it is moist, more pleasant-smelling than wine. His writing re-

---

[108]See Eusebius *Onomasticon* sect. Ph, Gen 2:11; K.166.7; L.287.59. "One of these Phison, a name meaning 'multitude,' runs toward India and falls into the sea, being called by the Greeks Ganges." Josephus *Antiquities* 1.1.3: The name is also spelled Pheison and Fison. See also Jerome *Interpretation of Hebrew Names* 4, where Jerome identifies the Fison with the Ganges. [109]Augustine *Gen. litt.* 8.7.14. [110]Ambrose *Paradise* 3.15; also, Jerome *Interpretation of Hebrew Names* 66: "Pison, mouth of an orphan or change of mouth." [111]Eusebius *Onomasticon* Gen 2:11; K.80.22; L.259.95. Textual variants: Euelat (Gk); Cepene and Cephene (Lat); and Kophenos. [112]Josephus *Antiquities* 1.6.4: "These [the sons of Joktan] inhabited from Cophen, an Indian river, and in part of Asia, adjoining to it." [113]Eusebius *Onomasticon* Gen 10:30; K.150.14; L.282.69. Variants include Sefar, Sopheira and Sopheir. Josephus *Antiquities* 7.6.4: "These [ships] Solomon ordered to sail along with his own stewards to the land anciently called Sopheir but not the land of gold; it belongs to India."

minds one of Numbers when it says, "Now the manna was like coriander seed, and its appearance was like that of bdellium";[114] that is, clear and white in color. Onyx is a precious stone, so named because it has in itself thoroughly mixed the color like human fingernail. The Greeks call the fingernail onyx. Arabia produces this onyx, but Indian onyx is fiery, with white bands encircling it; the Arabian is also black with white bands.[115] An older translation has for these stones "carbunculus" and "prase." Carbunculus is, just as the name shows, a stone of fiery color, through which it is said to even enlighten the darkness of the evening. Prase is green in color, from which it gets the name from the Greek word *porro*, a leek that they call a *prason*.

13The name of the second river is Gihon; it is the one which flows around the whole land of Cush. 14And the name of the third river is Tigris, which flows east of Assyria. And the fourth river is the Euphrates.

Concerning the Euphrates, it does not say in which direction "it flows or which lands it encircles,"[116] because it was easily known by the people of Israel who were going to read these things and who lived in the same area, since it flowed in the vicinity of the promised land. Since there lies open to us a return to the heavenly kingdom through the waters of regeneration, it is sufficiently fitting in the sovereignty of the divine economy that that very element by which we are drawn back to the heavenly kingdom we hold in common with paradise, where man was first placed. And just as grace, renewing us unseen, prepares us to enter the heavenly kingdom, so also that very water that renews us springs up from paradise to our world through its courses in the earth. Just as, therefore, "the wind blows where it will, and you hear the sound of it, but you do not

know whence it comes or whither it goes,"[117] so also it is fitting that as the water that sanctifies those whom the Spirit wills comes to us through unknown paths from paradise, it returns to places unknown to us, because it is agreed that such was its origin in the paradise of delight.

15The LORD God took the man and put him in the garden of Eden to till it and keep it.

The words "he may till it and keep it" cause us to look back to the text where it is said, "And there was no man who tilled the ground." In the explanation of this verse let us discuss the words of Saint Augustine, who wrote, "Why did he 'till' it or why did he 'keep' it? Is it really possible that the Lord wanted the first man to till the ground? Or is it plausible that he condemned him to labor before sin? We would certainly think so unless we considered those who till the ground with so much delight that it is a great punishment for them to be called off to any other thing. Whatever joy working the soil has had, therefore, the delight was even greater when no disaster had happened, either in the earth or in the heaven. When these things, which God had created, turned out more joyfully and more fruitfully with the effort of human labor, there was not the stress of labor but the delight of will. The Creator himself should be praised more richly, who gave reason and the capability of working to the soul fashioned in a human body, as much as is enough for a willing mind, but not so much that the needs of the body would compel it to work unwillingly. . . .

"It says 'so that he might till it and keep it,' namely, to keep that same paradise for himself, in order that he not allow in anything whereby he would deserve to be cast out. And finally he receives the command, and it is through this command that he keeps paradise for himself,

---

[114]Num 11:7. [115]Pliny *Natural History* 37.34. [116]Augustine *Gen. Man.* 2.10.14. [117]Jn 3:8.

that is, by obedience he would not be cast out from it. It is correct to say that everyone who has not kept his own possession acts in such a way as to lose it, even if it is saved by someone else, who may have found it or deserved to receive it.

"There is another meaning in these words, which I believe worthy to propose, that God himself works man and keeps him. Just as man works the soil, not in that he can create it to be soil but in that he develops it and makes it fruit-bearing, thus God, even more so, works man, whom he has created, so that he may be righteous, if he does not turn away from God through pride."[118] God, therefore, placed man "in the paradise of delight so that he could work him and keep him." He works him so that he is blessed and good; he keeps him "so that he may be safe by humbly submitting to his rule and protection."[119]

16 And the LORD God commanded the man, saying, "You may freely eat of every tree in the garden; 17 but of the tree of the knowledge of good and evil you shall not eat."

It must not be believed that anything evil naturally grew on that tree, just as I stated above. But "from that tree, which was not evil, man was prohibited so that by keeping the command itself it would be a good for him and its transgression would be an evil. . . . Finally, nothing else was sought by the sinner except that he not be under the rule of God, when that act was committed by which the sole command of God that it not be committed should have been heeded. If this command alone had been followed, what other than the will of God would be chosen? What other than the will of God . . . would be preferred to human will?"[120] "Nor is it possible for man's will not to fall upon him with a great weight of destruction,

if he prefers it to the will of the Almighty by exalting it. Man experienced this by despising the law of God, and he learned from this experience the difference between good and evil, namely, the good of obedience, the evil of disobedience, that is, of pride, of obstinacy, perverse imitation of God, and of liberty expressed licentiously. Now this tree received its name from that very thing which happened to it, as was said above."[121]

17 For in the day you eat of it you shall die.

It does not say, "If you eat, you will be mortal," but it says, "For in the day you eat of it you will die." Indeed, man died in his soul when he sinned, because God, who is the life of the soul, withdrew from him. The death of the body rightly follows the death of the soul, when the soul, which is his life, departs from him. Death came, then, to that first man when he came to the end of the present life a long time after he ate that which was forbidden. It may be understood that the day on which they sinned enacted that death in them, "about which the apostle sighs, saying, 'For I delight in the law of God in my inner self, but I see in my members another law at war with the law of my mind and making me captive to the law of sin which dwells in my members. Wretched man that I am! Who will deliver me from this body of death?'[122] Indeed, it was not enough for him to say, 'Who will free me from this mortal body,' but rather he said 'from the body of this death.' Just as he said elsewhere that 'the body indeed is dead on account of sin,'[123] not saying there 'mortal' but 'dead,' although it is also mortal since it is going to die. So it must not be believed that those bodies though living, but not yet filled with the spirit, were not mortal, that is, that which was necessary in order that they might die—which happened on

---

[118]Augustine *Gen. litt.* 8.8, 10-11. [119]Augustine *Gen. litt.* 8.11. [120]Augustine *Gen. litt.* 8.13.28-29. [121]Augustine *Gen. litt.* 8.14.31. [122]Rom 7:22-24. [123]Rom 8:10.

that day they touched the tree in violation of the command."[124]

[18]Then the LORD God said, "It is not good that the man should be alone; I will make him a helper fit for him."

It must be believed that this word of God was not spoken in a human voice from outside into the air, but it was uttered ineffably, through the reasoning of the divine will by which all things on earth were created, in accordance with what we taught above, where it is written, "Let us make man in our image, after our likeness."[125] If, however, one should ask for what purpose this help would have been made, Saint Augustine, whom we quoted frequently above without attribution, would reply, "No other answer is more probable than for the sake of procreation, just as within the earth is the help for the seed, so that plant life may grow from the two (the earth and the seed). This purpose actually had been commanded in the original creation of things, male and female he created them and he blessed them saying, 'Be fruitful and multiply and fill the earth and have dominion over it.'

"The arrangement and blessing of the creation and the union of the male and the female did not fail after the sin and punishment of man; because of it, that blessing, the earth is now full of people who have dominion over it. Although they are said to have coupled and to have had children after they were cast out of paradise, I do not see what there was to keep them even in paradise from having an 'honorable marriage and an undefiled marriage bed.'[126] As God would have granted this to them as long as they lived faithfully and justly and served him obediently and purposely, so that without any emotional heat of passion, without any labor and grief of birth pangs, they would bring forth offspring from their

seed; not so that the children could take the place of the parents who died but so that those who had children would remain in some state of their youthful vitality and would maintain their bodily strength from the tree of life which had been planted there in paradise, and those who would be born would develop to the same state, until finally some definite number was reached. Then, if all lived justly and obediently, that transformation would be made, so that, without any death, their natural bodies would be transformed into another nature, so that they might devote themselves to every command of the spirit ruling them, and by drawing life from that spirit alone, without any sustaining from bodily nourishment, they would be called spiritual beings."[127]

"For if Enoch and Elijah, being dead in Adam, bearing in their flesh the seeds of death, which debt they owed, are believed to be going to return to this life again, and that which was so long delayed, to die, now nevertheless live in another life where, before the resurrection of the flesh, before the natural body is changed into a spiritual one, they are weakened by neither old age nor disease, then how much more justly and more likely would it be granted to those first men living without any of their own sin or without a parent, would fall into some better state after the birth of children, from which in the final age they would be transformed more happily with all the posterity of the saints into angelic form, not through the death of the flesh but more fortunately through the power of God?"[128]

[19]So out of the ground the LORD God formed every beast of the field and every bird of the air.

"If it disturbs someone that Scripture did not say, 'All the animals of the earth were formed from the earth and all the flying creatures,

---

[124]Augustine *Gen. litt.* 9.10.16.   [125]Gen 1:26.   [126]Heb 13:4.   [127]Augustine *Gen. litt.* 9.3.5-6.   [128]Augustine *Gen. litt.* 9.6.10-11.

birds of heaven from the waters,' but, as if God formed both kinds from the earth, it says, 'all the animals of the earth and all the birds of heaven were formed from the earth,' one sees that this can be understood in two ways: either now the writer is silent about that from which God formed the birds of heaven, because even in the silence we might understand that the Lord did not form both from the earth, but only the beasts of the earth, and so that we might understand, even with Scripture being silent, what it was from which then he formed the birds of heaven . . . or we understand that the earth, as a whole, including the waters, was so named, just as it is written in that psalm where, after the praise of the celestial beings is described, there is a change of emphasis to earth and it is written, 'Praise the Lord from the earth, you sea monsters and all you deeps.'[129] Nor does it afterwards say, 'Praise the Lord from the waters.' There in the deeps, indeed, are all the waters which praise the Lord from the earth; there also are the crawling and winged creatures, which no less praise God from the earth in accordance with that broader definition of 'earth,' which is also said about the whole world, 'God who made the heaven and the earth,' whether the dry ground or the waters and whatever else is created they are understood to be truly created from the 'earth.' "[130]

[19]*And brought them to the man to see what he would call them.*

It should not be understood in natural terms that God brought the animals of the earth or the birds to Adam, in the same way a shepherd is accustomed to herding his sheep from place to place; but it is better understood that just as he created these creatures from the waters by divine power when he willed it, so also in the same mysterious principle of his power, he brought them to man to be observed; in the same way, also, that beasts and birds of every species were called to the ark of Noah, not shepherded by the hand of people but by divine intervention, and they enter it. Indeed, those creatures, not knowing why they had come, but with the knowledge of the man, who took them as they came, by the command and leading of God, into the ark.

[19]*And whatever the man called every living creature, that was its name.* [20]*The man gave names to all cattle, and to the birds of the air, and to every beast of the field.*

It is agreed that Adam, as he gave the names to the creatures of the earth and the birds of the heavens, spoke in the language that the whole human race spoke up to the time of the tower [of Babel], at which point all languages became distinct. Certainly in the destruction of the tower, when God allotted different languages fitting for each people, then he must be believed to have assigned the names of the animals, as also of other things, to each people according to their own language—although it is not an unknown fact that people in their individual nations later would assign words to many things as they pleased, both for peculiar things that happened by chance or for defining the animals based on their individual types, as even now they are so accustomed to do. And, finally, Scripture says nothing about the fish being brought to Adam so that he might give names to them.

Nevertheless, it is credible that little by little, as they were recognized, a variety of names were given in respect to the diversity of peoples. It seems that the first language of the human race was Hebrew, for which reason it is agreed that all the names we read in Genesis up to the division of tongues are rooted in that language. The reason that all the animals of

---

[129]Ps 148:7. [130]Augustine *Gen. litt.* 9.1.1-2.

the earth and birds of the heaven were brought to Adam is for him to determine what to call each one, and he gave them names, that is, "so that God could show man how much better he is than all the animals who lacked reasoning. It appears from this that man is better than the animals because of this ability to reason, because only by reason is one able to distinguish and to discern things by name."[131]

20But for the man there was not found a helper fit for him. 21So the LORD God caused a deep sleep to fall upon the man, and while he slept took one of his ribs and closed up its place with flesh; 22and the rib which the LORD God had taken from the man he made into a woman and brought her to the man.

Since this woman was made from the side of the man, it must be believed that it was necessary that she be made this way to protect the strength of this union. The fact that this, moreover, was done while he was sleeping, that after the bone was removed from its place his flesh was filled up, was done as an example of a more profound mystery. It signified that through Christ's death the sacraments of salvation were about to pour forth from his side on the cross by the death of the sleeping one, namely, the blood and the water, from which his bride, the church, would be established. If there had not been prefigured so great a sacrament in the creation of woman, why was it necessary that Adam sleep, so that God could take his rib from which he made the woman, who could have done the same thing to him while being awake and not suffering? Why was it necessary that, when the bone taken from the side of the man was made into the woman, the wound in the bone was covered with flesh, not bone, unless it was a figure of Christ becoming weak for the sake of the church, but the church is shown strong by him?

Scripture has used a word as a type to express the same mystery, as it does not say "made" (*facio*) or "formed" (*formo*) or "created" (*creato*), as in the previous acts of creation, but it states, "The rib that God took from Adam he built (*aedificio*) into a woman," not as a human body but as a house, in "which house we are if we firmly maintain faith and the hope of glory up to the end."[132] Remarkably, indeed, it was fitting that the beginning of the human race, through God's creative activity, should proceed in such a way, since it gave a testimony in figurative language of that redemption that was going to come through that very Creator at the end of time.

23Then the man said,
  "This at last is bone of my bones
   and flesh of my flesh."

Since Adam had found none like him among the animals of the earth and all the flying creatures brought to him, now rightly, when he saw a help, created like himself, brought to him, he approved. And he rejoiced, saying, "This at last is bone of my bones"—at last, since after he had seen all the other animals, from the beginning he had not seen any like him. "Bone from my bones and flesh from my flesh," because the others he had seen having bone and flesh and had distinguished by names he knew were created not from his own substance but from the earth and the waters. Just as he had given names to them as they were led to him, so he waited to give a name to her who was like him.

23"She shall be called Woman,
  because she was taken out of Man."

In the same way, Latin etymology agrees with these words, since *virago* ("woman") is derived from *vir* ("man"), so also it happens in the Hebrew language "man" is called *his*, and

---

[131]Augustine *Gen. Man.* 2.11.16. [132]Heb 3:6.

derived from *his* is the word *hissa* ("woman"). So, the fact that "man" is called *his* in Hebrew is demonstrated by the word *Israel*, which is translated as "man seeing God." But the fact that Adam wished the woman, who had been created from his own flesh, to be made a partaker of his own name is most suggestive of the sacraments of Christ and the church, because our Lord Jesus Christ gave a share of his name to the church, which he redeemed at the price of his own body and blood and chose as his bride, such that from Christ she is called Christian, and from Jesus, or "salvation," she sought eternal deliverance.

"We should not overlook that sleep or the *ecstasies*, as an older translation has, that is, 'the trance-like state of the mind,'[133] 'which God cast upon Adam,' as Saint Augustine says, 'so that his mind through *ecstasis* might become a partaker, as it were, of the assembly of angels, "until I go into the sanctuary of God"[134] and understand the last things.' And finally, he awakened, as it were, full of prophecy; when he saw his wife brought before him, he immediately proclaimed that great mystery the apostle praised, 'This now is bone of my bones and flesh of my flesh; she will be called "woman" because she was taken from "man,"' and that which follows."[135]

[24]*Therefore a man leaves his father and his mother and cleaves to his wife, and they become one flesh.*

"While Scripture testifies what were the very first words of man, the Lord, in the Gospel, declared that God said them, 'Have you not read that he who made them from the beginning made them male and female,' and said, 'For this reason a man shall leave his father and mother and be joined to his wife, and the two shall become one flesh,'[136] in order that we

may realize that on account of *ecstasies*, which had come to Adam before, he was able to speak by divine inspiration like a prophet."[137] If, therefore, Christ cleaved to the church so that they would be two in one flesh, how did he leave his Father? How, his mother? He left his Father because, "though he was in the form of God, he did not count equality with God a thing to be grasped but emptied himself, taking a form of a servant."[138] This is the meaning of "he left his Father," not because he departed and withdrew from his Father but because he did not appear in that form to people that was equal to the Father. How did he leave his mother? By leaving the synagogue of the Jews, from which he was born according to the flesh, and by clinging to the church, which he gathered from all the nations, so that in the peace of the new covenant they could become two in one flesh; because he was God in the presence of the Father through whom we have been made. He has been made our participant through the flesh so that we are able to become the body under his headship.

[25]*And the man and his wife were both naked, and were not ashamed.*

And this is right, for why "would there have been shame when they knew no law 'in their members at war with the law of their mind'?[139] This punishment of sin pursued them after the action of their transgression, with disobedience violating the command and justice punishing the deed. Before this was done, they were naked, as Scripture said, and they were not ashamed. There was no behavior for which there ought to be any shame; they thought nothing ought to be hidden because they understood nothing should be restrained."[140]

[3:1]*Now the serpent was more subtle than any*

---

[133]Jerome *Hebrew Questions on the Book of Genesis* 5.21. [134]Ps 73:17. [135]Augustine *Gen. litt.* 9.19.36; Eph 5:32 is quoted. [136]Mt 19:4-5. [137]Augustine *Gen. litt.* 9.18.36. [138]Phil 2:7. [139]See Rom 7:23. [140]Augustine *Gen. litt.* 11.1.3.

other wild creature the LORD God had made.

"One can say that the serpent, since it is a being with no reasoning ability, is called 'more subtle than all the animals' in light of an alien spirit operating in it, that is, a demonic one. For however great was the fall of the rebellious angels, they were cast down rightly from their heavenly seats for their own wickedness and pride; yet they were more excellent in nature than all the animals of the earth on account of the preeminence of reason. Why, therefore, should one wonder if the devil on his own inspiration now filled the serpent, and mixing his spirit with it, in the same way in which the oracles of the demons are usually possessed, had turned him into the 'most subtle' of all the animals of the earth, or, as one text has it, he was the 'wisest' of the beasts living according to his living and irrational spirit."[141]

"If, therefore, one should ask why God allowed man to be tempted, whom he foreknew would yield to the temptation," a true reason appears;[142] "because man would not deserve great praise in the future if he were able to live well when no one had prompted him to live badly. For he has in his nature and in his power the will not to yield to such persuading, with the help of the One who 'resists the proud and gives grace to the humble.' "[143]

"Nor must one think that the tempter would not have cast down humankind unless a certain pride that should have been held in check had entered earlier into the soul of people so that through the humiliation of sin they could learn how much they had presumed about themselves was false. Most truly it is said, 'Before ruin the heart is lifted up, and before glory it is humbled.'[144] Indeed, some are disturbed that God permitted the temptation of the first man, as if they were now unaware that the whole human race is incessantly tempted by the snares of the devil. Why would God permit this? Because strength is shown and proven, and it is plainly more honorable not to have yielded to temptation than to not to be able to be tempted. . . ."[145]

"If, moreover, you ask why the devil was allowed to tempt through the serpent, in particular, this was done to express a sign. . . . Not that the devil wished to give a sign for our instruction, but, since he is unable to approach someone to tempt them unless he is allowed, so also he would not be able to approach through another creature, unless it was through one which had been allowed. Whatever, therefore, the serpent signifies, it must be granted by that providence under which the devil himself has his own desire of doing harm to others, but not unless such permission is given to him, either for subverting and destroying the vessels of wrath, or for humbling and proving the vessels of mercy."[146]

"And so the serpent did not understand the sounds of the words which were made from it to the woman. Nor must it be believed that its mind was transformed into a rational state, when not even humans themselves, whose nature is rational, know what they are saying when a demon is speaking through them in that emotional state for which the exorcist is required. How much less, then, does the serpent understand the sounds of the words, which the devil speaks through and by him? The serpent would not understand man talking, even if he heard him free from the diabolical frenzied state."[147]

[1]He said to the woman, "Did God say, 'You shall not eat of any tree of the garden'?" [2]And the woman said to the serpent, "We may eat of the fruit of the trees of the garden; [3]but God

---

[141]Augustine *Gen. litt.* 11.2.4. [142]Bede confidently recasts Augustine's tentative explanation as the "true reason." [143]Jas 4:6, quoted within Augustine *Gen. litt.* 11.4.6. [144]Prov 16:18, quoted in Augustine *Gen. litt.* 11.5.7. [145]Augustine *Gen. litt.* 11.6.8. [146]Augustine *Gen. litt.* 11.12.16. [147]Augustine *Gen. litt.* 11.28.35.

---

said, 'You shall not eat of the fruit of the tree which is in the midst of the garden, neither shall you touch it, lest you die.' "

"So in the beginning the serpent asked this question and the woman responded, so that the transgression would be inexcusable, and in no way could it be said that the woman had forgotten what God had commanded."[148]

⁴But the serpent said to the woman, "You will not die. ⁵For God knows that when you eat of it your eyes will be opened, and you will be like God, knowing good and evil."

"What does this mean unless that they were persuaded by him to refuse to be under the authority of God, but rather to live in their own power without God, and so they did not observe God's law, as if God were jealous that they might rule themselves—as ones not needing his interior light, but, lacking their own foresight to discern with their own eyes good and evil which he had forbidden?"[149] In these words it must be noted with what great skill the devil from the beginning tempted people to evil, the devil who not only taught people disobedience and contempt of their Creator, as if God were jealous of them, but also planted in their minds that they should believe in a multitude of gods, saying, "and you will be like gods," since even if he had been unable to compel people to disobedience, yet he would destroy the purity of the faithful, who worshiped one God. If in fact he could compel people into disobedience and destroy their purity, he would become the victor in both. "For how would the woman have believed the words that she and Adam had been forbidden good and beneficial things by the divine decree unless already that love for her own power had entered into her mind and there was a certain

haughty presumption from within her that had to be overcome and humbled through that temptation?"[150]

⁶So when the woman saw that the tree was good for food, and that it was a delight to the eyes, and that the tree was to be desired to make one wise, she took of its fruit and ate; and she also gave some to her husband, and he ate.

"And, finally, not content with the words of the serpent, she considered carefully the tree; and she saw, as Scripture says, 'that it was good to eat, and beautiful to the eyes, and a delight to behold,' and not believing that she then was going to die. (I think it is because she thought that God had said, 'If you eat, you will die a death' with some other meaning as a sign.) Therefore, 'she took from its fruit and ate; and she also gave some to her husband,' perhaps even with a persuasive word, which Scripture, now being silent, left to be understood. Or, perhaps, maybe it was unnecessary for the man to be persuaded when he observed that she had not died from eating the fruit?"[151] Therefore

⁷Then the eyes of both were opened.

"Opened to what, except to a mutual desire, and to the penalty of sin received by the death of the flesh, so that now the body was no longer only a living body, which would have been able to be changed into a better and spiritual dwelling without death if they had remained obedient, but it is a body of death in which 'the law in the members wars against the law of the mind'[152]—for, in reality, they had not been made with closed eyes, and they did not wander around the paradise of delights being blind and groping their way."[153] It is like what Luke writes in the Gospel "when he said about

[148]Augustine *Gen. litt.* 11.30.38. [149]Augustine *Gen. Man.* 2.15.22. [150]Augustine *Gen. litt.* 11.30.39. [151]Augustine *Gen. litt.* 11.30.39. [152]Rom 7:23. [153]Augustine *Gen. litt.* 11.31.40.

those two men, one of them was Cleopas, that when the Lord had broken bread with them, 'Their eyes are opened and they recognized him,'[154] whom they had not recognized on the road—of course they were not walking with closed eyes, but they were unable to recognize him. . . . In this way, therefore, the eyes of the first humans were opened to things to which previously they were closed, although they were opened to other things."[155]

7And they knew that they were naked; and they sewed fig leaves together and made themselves aprons.

"The rational soul blushed at the animal drives in its own flesh, and it experienced shame in it. This was not only because it felt something there it had never felt before, but also because that shame came from the transgression of God's law. There, indeed, the man realized by what grace he was clothed before when in his nakedness he had suffered nothing shameful. . . . And, finally, in that troubled state of mind they hurried to the fig leaves, which by chance in their upset state they found first,[156] and they stitched together 'aprons.' And when they had forsaken the things one should honor, they covered their loins. Nor do I think that they recognized anything special in these leaves that was particularly fitting for their now contemptible members to be covered by such as them, but in their confused state of mind they were compelled by a hidden instinct to this action, so that such an important sign of their own punishment is made by them without their knowledge, in order to convict the sinner when performed and to teach the reader when it is recorded."[157]

The mystery of this tree, moreover, under which the Lord also saw Nathaniel sitting,

Saint Ambrose has explained briefly but clearly, saying, "Blessed are the ones who bind their horses beneath the vine and olive tree,[158] dedicating the outcome of their labors to joy. The fig tree—low in height, too weak for work, insignificant for use and barren of fruit—that is, the alluring itch of the delights of the world still overshadows me."[159] And in another place it says, "This, therefore, is a serious matter that Adam girded himself in that exact place where he should have girded himself rather with the fruit of purity; seeds of the generations are said to be in the loins around which we are girded. And so Adam girded himself with useless leaves, which indicates that it was the fruit of certain sins, not the fruit of generations to come."[160]

8And they heard the sound of the LORD God walking in the garden in the cool of the day, and the man and his wife hid themselves from the presence of the LORD God among the trees of the garden.

So then, after noon had become the fitting time to visit those who had fallen from the "light of truth."[161] Hence, appropriately, the Lord hung on the cross at noon, and, after he made the promise of a dwelling place in paradise to the thief, after noon, that is, the ninth hour, he gave up his spirit; namely, at that same hour when the first man touched the tree of transgression, the second Man mounted the tree of redemption, and at that hour of the day when he had expelled the transgressors from paradise, on that day he led the one confessing him into paradise.

Scripture says that "Adam and his wife hid themselves from the face of the Lord God in the midst of the trees of paradise. When God turned his face away inwardly . . . we

---

[154]Lk 24:3. [155]Augustine *Gen. litt.* 11.31.41. [156]The clause "which by chance in their upset state they found first" is added by Bede. [157]Augustine *Gen. litt.* 11.32.42. [158]See Mic 4:4. [159]Ambrose *De virginibus* 1.1.3. [160]Ambrose *Paradise* 8.67. [161]Augustine *Gen. litt.* 11.33.43.

should not marvel that these things that are like madness are done from excessive fear and shame, nor also is that hidden instinct being quiet, so that they unwittingly do things which one day would have meaning for their descendents, on whose account these things have been written down."[162] Those who commit sin hide themselves from the face of God, because they render themselves unworthy of the sight of divine kindness. They hide themselves from the face of God, not in a way that an inward judge does not see of their conscience but because they could never catch sight of the glory of his countenance unless they repented.

9But the Lord God called to the man, and said to him, "Where are you?"

Not that God asked out of ignorance, but by rebuking him God warned him that he in whom God was not should attend to where he was. Now for certain, because he had eaten from the forbidden tree, he would die the death of his soul, since his life is said to have departed from it. "And truly this applies with certain significance, because just as the command was given to the man through whom it was passed on to the woman, thus the man was first questioned. Indeed, the command came from the Lord through the man and then to the woman, but sin came from the devil through the woman then to the man. These words are full of important mysteries, not by the action of those in whom these things were done but by the most powerful wisdom of God doing it about them. But I am not here explaining the significance, but I am defending what was done."[163]

10And he said, "I heard the sound of thee in the garden, and I was afraid, because I was naked; and I hid myself."

"It is very likely that God was accustomed to appear to those first humans in human form by means of a creation appropriate to such action. He never allowed them to perceive their nakedness, and he raised their attention to heavenly matters, until after their sin they realized the shameful movement in their members according to a law that brought punishment to their members. Thus they felt as men and women are accustomed to feel before the eyes of men or women, and such was the effect of the punishment from sin that they wished that which nothing could hide. . . . Because now they felt shame in each other's presence, for which reason they made aprons for themselves, even thus girded they were more anxiously afraid by far to be seen by him, who brought with an amiable demeanor, as it were, human eyes for the purpose of seeing them through as a creature that had sight. . . ."

"The Lord, therefore, after questioning the transgressors in the way customarily used in the courts, wished to punish the transgressors with a greater punishment than the punishment about which they were compelled to feel shame."[164] God then said,

11"Who told you that you were naked? Have you eaten of the tree of which I commanded you not to eat?"

"Hence, indeed, death, which was acquired in accordance with the judgment of God, who had thus threatened it, caused their members to be perceived with lust. When their eyes were opened, that which brought shame followed."[165]

12The man said, "The woman whom thou gavest to be with me, she gave me fruit of the tree, and I ate."

Was it pride that he never said, "I have

---

[162]Augustine Gen. litt. 11.33.44. [163]Augustine Gen. litt. 11.34.45. [164]Augustine Gen. litt. 11.34.45-46. [165]Augustine Gen. litt. 11.35.47.

sinned"? He had the burden of embarrassment but not the humility for confession. These words were written because those questions, of course, were asked for this purpose: so that they may be written for our benefit so that we may perceive how pride oppresses people today, that is, trying to assign blame to the Creator if they do anything bad and then wishing to assign approval to themselves if they do anything good. He said, "The woman whom you gave to me, gave me fruit from the tree, and I ate," as if she were given for this purpose, that she would not obey her husband and neither of them obey God.

13Then the Lord God said to the woman, "What is this that you have done?" The woman said, "The serpent beguiled me, and I ate."

"Nor did she confess the sin, but she blames another—different in her type, alike in her arrogance. She said, 'The serpent deceived me, and I ate,' as if his persuasion ought to be put ahead of the command of God."[166] And she, moreover, blames, as the cause for the sin, the Creator, who created the serpent in the garden by whom she was deceived.

14The Lord God said to the serpent, "Because you have done this, cursed are you above all cattle, and above all wild animals."

"Since the serpent was not asked why he had done this, it seems that he himself had not altogether done this by his own nature and volition, but the devil, who had already been destined to the fire on account of his own impiety and disobedience, had worked from him and through him. So now then what is said of the serpent is assuredly applied to him who had worked through the serpent—and

without doubt it was spoken figuratively. For in these words the tempter is described as what he was going to become to the human race."[167]

14"Upon your belly you shall go, and dust you shall eat all the days of your life."

Truly the serpent crawls on his belly because all the steps of the devil are fraudulent and evil-bearing; for "upon your belly" indicates the cleverness and cunning skill of his thinking, by which he crawls to those he wishes to deceive, for which idea an old translation has, "You creep on your belly and on your breast." He creeps on his belly when he brings up to people whom he wishes to make his own members carnal thought. He crawls on his belly when he arouses them, overcome by gluttony, to the heat of passion. For everything that crawls drags the body on the ground. The body of the devil is every wicked person. He crawls on his breast and belly when he presses them down to hell with perverted thoughts and alluring revelries. He eats the dust when he feeds on and delights in the error of sinners, and seducing them he snatches them to destruction. Just as the saints often are called by the name of heaven, so also these who are wise in earthly matters are indicated by the name of earth. In the same way it is written in the following verses about Adam, "You are earth, and into the earth you will go," which our translation has, "You are dust, and to dust you shall return." This is a symbol of spiritual nourishment that even the serpent, unable to reason, whom the devil used for deceiving people as through its own mouth, now is commanded to eat the dust of the earth, who before was permitted to eat along with the other animals the grasses of the earth and the fruit of the trees.

---

[166]Augustine *Gen. litt.* 11.35.48. [167]Augustine *Gen. litt.* 11.36.49.

¹⁵*"I will put enmity between you and the woman,*
  and between your seed and her seed."

The seed of the woman is the seed of the whole human race; seed of the devil is the rebellious angels, who are corrupted by the example of his pride and wicked rebellion. This seed signifies perverse suggestion, and "the seed of the woman the fruit of the good word by which one resists such perverse suggestion."[168] How much the human race has borne the enmity in their memory of this serpent and his seed, and how great the enmity against him all the elect can exercise by living rightly is understood more profoundly than the sun by all the faithful. The sign of this enmity of the irrational serpent appears even in its nature, in that it is the common enemy of all the animals and beasts of the earth by virtue of the curse of the poison within it; surely it must be believed that venom was set permanently in it from the time of the curse, and not before.

¹⁵*"He shall bruise your head,*
  and you shall bruise his heel."

The woman will bruise the head of the serpent when the holy church drives away the snares of the devil and the poisonous persuasions that were discovered from the beginning, and just as if treading them under foot, the church reduces them to nothing. She will bruise the head of the serpent when she resists the pride through which Eve was deceived, having being humbled under the mighty hand of God, for "the beginning of all sin is pride."[169] And the serpent lies in ambush for the heel of the woman, because the devil encircles the church as a "roaring lion seeking someone to devour,"[170] in the way the steps of our good deeds can ruin him. He lies in ambush for the heel when he busies himself to snatch us at the end of this present life. For "heel," which is at the end of the body, fairly designates the end of our life, because the state of the serpent, who is bruised by all who can and who never stops lying in ambush to viciously attack the feet of people, allows both interpretations figuratively.

¹⁶*To the woman he said,*
  "I will greatly multiply your pain in childbearing;
  in pain you shall bring forth children,
  yet your desire shall be for your husband,
  and he shall rule over you."

"These words of God about the woman also are understood more appropriately figuratively and prophetically. Really, because the woman had not yet given birth to children, and there is neither grief nor pain from birth except from the body of death, which was conceived in the transgression of the command. . . . This punishment, then, is related literally, for following it says, 'And you will be subject to your husband, and he will rule over you,' when before sin it is not right to believe that the woman was not created otherwise than for the husband to rule over her and for her to live under his authority; rightly one is able to understand this servitude as significant, as the state of a certain condition rather than a state of love, so that this servitude, by which later men began to be slaves to men, is found to have arisen from the punishment of sin. Indeed, the apostle said, 'Through love be servants to one another,'[171] but he never said, 'Rule one another.' And so married people are able to 'through love be servants to one another,' but the apostle does not allow the woman to rule over the husband. This ruling rather hands over the power to man, and man deserves to have this power of the woman, not because of his nature but because of fault, because unless she is so ruled, she will become more fully

---

[168]Augustine *Gen. Man.* 2.18.28. [169]Sir 10:15 (Vg). [170]1 Pet 5:8. [171]Gal 5:13.

depraved and her fault will increase."[172]

These words apply appropriately in a figurative sense to the church as the bride of Christ, whose afflictions in this life after the sin of the first transgression were multiplied, so that she, having been corrected, could gain eternal life. Her children are multiplied when she busies herself to give birth to spiritual children to God by living rightly and praising. Hence she speaks to these children through the words of the preeminent preacher, "My little children, with whom I am again in travail until Christ be formed in you!"[173] She gives birth to children in suffering when she, becoming anxious, fears lest the senses of her offspring would be corrupted, just as when the serpent seduced Eve with its cleverness, and they would drift from the innocence that is in Christ. She lives submissive to her husband because she is submissive to the Lord in fear, and she exalts him not from a peaceful spirit but with fear, to whom, if she had never sinned, she would be united together only by the embrace of love that is trouble-free. And he would have dominion over her, restraining his fleshly drives, and he would rule over her, and directing her to an understanding of the celestial life with the constant experience of a heavenly instruction from which if she had never withdrawn, she would have ruled with him always in freedom.

[17]*And to Adam he said,*
"Because you have listened to the voice
of your wife,
and have eaten of the tree
of which I commanded you,
'You shall not eat of it,'
cursed is the ground because of you;
in toil you shall eat of it all the days of
your life;
[18]*thorns and thistles it shall bring forth to*
you;
and you shall eat the plants of the field."

"Who does not understand that these are the labors of the human race on earth, and that they would not have existed if the happiness that was in paradise had been maintained?"[174] On account of the sin of man the earth has been cursed, so that it produces thorns, not in order that the earth, which is without feeling, may feel the punishments but so that it could always put the fault of human sin before people's eyes, by which we are admonished to turn back from sin and to turn toward the commands of God. Indeed, poisonous plants have been created for punishment or for the instruction of our mortal selves. And this fact must be noted in regard to sin, because after sin we became mortals. Also, by the sign of unfruitful trees, people are mocked so that they may realize how shameful it is to be without the fruit of good works in the field of God, that is, in the church, and so that they may fear lest God abandon them, because they left unfruitful trees in their own fields and they did not take care of them.

Before the sin of man, therefore, it was not written that the earth brought forth anything except fruit-bearing trees and plants for nourishment; after sin we see frightful and unfruitful things being born, for that reason that I addressed. In a mystical sense the earth, which is said to be cursed in the act of the transgression of Adam, is understood not otherwise better than as the flesh. It sprouts thorns and thistles in us, since we, having been born through the lust of the flesh, suffer the wounds and enticements of the faults from that very flesh.

[19]*"In the sweat of your face*
you shall eat bread
till you return to the ground,
for out of it you were taken;
you are dust,
and to dust you shall return."

---

[172]Augustine *Gen. litt.* 11.37.50. [173]Gal 4:19. [174]Augustine *Gen. litt.* 11.38.51.

Here understand him who is that bread who said, "I am the bread of life. . . . I have come down from heaven."[175] On this earth we eat by the sweat of our face because we rise up to the view of divine heights only through the trial of inevitable affliction.

20*The man called his wife's name Eve, because she was the mother of all living.*

It is agreed that Adam gave this name to his wife through divine inspiration. It also applies fittingly to the holy church, in whose unity only, called catholic, lies the door of life.

21*And the LORD God made for Adam and for his wife garments of skins, and clothed them.*

"This was done for the sake of an allegory; but it was absolutely done."[176] By clothing of this type the Lord demonstrates that they had been made mortal. Actually, skins, which would not be sewn together until after the death of the animal, suggest an allegorical figure of death. So, "when man against the command sought to be God, not through lawful imitation but through unlawful pride, he was cast down to the mortal nature of the animals."[177] And they made aprons for themselves from the fig leaves, by which they could clothe their loins, but God made garments from skins by which they could cover their whole bodies. Because, after they had lost the glory of their innocence through transgression, they wove for themselves a skin of excuse, by which they transferred their own fault on the Creator; and the Creator through the sentence of righteous judgment, chastised them when, having taken away the state of eternal life, he punished them with the penalty of mortality in body and soul.

The parable in the Gospel states that the affectionate father received his son who returned to him with contrition in a lavish way

by offering, among other gifts, the finest robe to clothe him, suggesting in a mystical way that the elect are going to receive the garment of immortality in Christ at the end of the age, which they had lost in Adam in the beginning of the age, and indeed with grace more fully. For Adam thus was made immortal, in that he could not to die, if he had kept the command; the children of the resurrection also will be immortal so that they cannot ever die, nor are they able to be affected by the fear of death. Concerning their receiving of the robe the apostle says, "For this perishable nature must put on the imperishable, and the mortal puts on immortality."[178] When it says "to put on" it means even the nakedness was removed that made Adam and Eve blush at themselves after the recognition of it.

22*Then the LORD God said, "Behold, the man has become like one of us, knowing good and evil."*

Concerning this verse Saint Augustine said, "Through whatever means or whatever manner it was said, nevertheless since God said it, and because he said 'one of us' it must be understood in no other way except plural in number on account of the Trinity, as when it had said, 'Let us make man,' just as also the Lord spoke of himself and his Father, 'We will come to him and make our home with him.'[179] The proud one reflected in his mind how much he desired what the serpent had offered to him, 'You will be like gods.' He said, 'Behold, Adam is made like one of us.'

"These are truly the words of God, not only for scoffing at Adam, but for discouraging others lest they likewise fall into pride. For the sake of those individuals these things are written down. He said, 'He is made one of us knowing good and evil.' What else can we understand except that this is offered as an

---

[175]Jn 6:35-38. [176]Augustine *Gen. litt.* 11.39.52. [177]Augustine *Gen. Man.* 2.21.32. [178]1 Cor 15:53. [179]Jn 14:23.

example to strike fear in us? For not only did Adam not become what he wished to become; he also did not keep that condition in which he had been created."[180] In another place Augustine comments, "Nor are these the words, 'Behold, Adam has been made just like one of us,' words of a yielding God but of a reproaching God, just as the apostle when he said, 'Forgive me this wrong!'[181] He certainly wished it to be understood in an ironic manner."[182]

22"And now lest he put forth his hand and take also of the tree of life, and eat, and live for ever"—23therefore the LORD God sent him forth from the garden of Eden, to till the ground from which he was taken.

"These are the words of God in the text above, and this deed follows on account of these words. For he was denied the life not only which he would have received with the angels, if he had kept the command, but he was also denied the life which he was living in paradise with a certain blessed state of the body. He had to be separated from the tree of life, whether because from it that blessed state of body was sustained for him by an invisible power from a visible thing, or because there was in the tree a visible sacrament of an invisible wisdom. He had to be separated from the tree now since he either was going to die or to be excommunicated, as in this paradise so also in the church individuals are customarily denied the visible sacraments of the altar through ecclesial discipline."[183]

24He drove out the man; and at the east of the garden of Eden he placed the cherubim, and a flaming sword which turned every way, to guard the way to the tree of life.

An older translation has here, "And he cast Adam out and placed him over against the paradise of pleasure, and he appointed cherubim and a flaming sword," and the rest. Now, if we follow this, "we ought to believe that this was done as to signify something, but yet it was actually done, and it shows that a sinner would live altogether in misery opposite to paradise in which the blessed life is mystically indicated."[184] Since it is said that God placed cherubim and a flaming sword in front of the garden of desire, "it must be believed that this was done by heavenly powers in a visible paradise so that through ministering angels there would be a certain fiery guard there, yet it was not done without purpose; since it signifies something also of the spiritual paradise which ought not to be doubted."[185]

This guard is asserted to be turning around so that whenever the time comes it can also be removed. It was removed when Enoch was translated from sinners; it was removed when Elijah was whisked up in a fiery chariot; it was removed for all the elect when the heavens opened as the Lord was baptized; it is removed again when one by one the elect are washed in the baptismal font; it is removed more completely for them when, as their chains are loosened, they ascend each in his own time to the glory of the heavenly paradise.

Since the word *cherubim* means "the multitude of knowledge" or "knowledge multiplied," it is well expressed that the "cherubim and a flaming sword" are placed for guarding the way of the tree of life because through the discipline of heavenly knowledge and through the trial of temporary afflictions lies open for us the return to the heavenly homeland, from which through the foolishness of transgression and through the lust of carnal desires we have departed. But well it says the "flaming sword," not simply a "flame," was placed before paradise, so that the allurement of the temporal

---

[180]Augustine *Gen. litt.* 11.39.53. [181]2 Cor 12:13. [182]Augustine *Contra adversarium legis et prophetarum* 1.15. [183]Augustine *Gen. litt.* 11.40.54. [184]Augustine *Gen. litt.* 11.40.55. [185]Augustine *Gen. litt.* 11.40.55.

desires within us are struck down by the sword of the spirit, which is the Word of God, if we eagerly desire to make our way to the tree of life, who is Christ the Lord.

Well it states that the same sword is "turning every way" so that it may show symbolically that this sword is not always inevitable for us, but as it is written, "there is a time for war, a time for peace"[186]—of war, namely, when in the course of this life we struggle against powers of the air and even the failures of our own minds or bodies; of peace when we are crowned with the completed victory and are filled without being proud with the fruit of the tree of life forever.

The adversary of the law and prophets, moreover, seeks "Whom does that tree benefit that bears the fruit of life in paradise?" To this question Saint Augustine replies, "To whom unless to the first humans placed in paradise from the beginning? Then, when they were cast out from paradise, rightly so because of their own iniquities, the tree remained to signify the spiritual tree of life, that is, the wisdom of the blessed, the immortal food of souls. But whether anyone now enjoys that food, unless perhaps Elijah and Enoch, I think ought not to be taken lightly. Unless the souls of the blessed were nourished on that tree, which is in the spiritual paradise, we would not read that paradise was granted on the same day to the soul of the thief who trusted in Christ as a reward of his piety and his very faithful confession. He said, 'Amen, I say to you, today you will be with me in paradise.' To be with Christ there, that is, to be with the tree of life. He himself is truly wisdom, about which it is written, 'She [Wisdom] is the tree of life for all embracing her.' Amen."[187]

---

[186]Eccl 3:18. [187]Augustine *Contra adversarium legis et prophetarum* 1.15.

Scripture Index